íreLanᴅ, my íreLanᴅ

memoríes from the heartlanᴅ

arnolᴅ j. meagher

PublishAmerica

Baltimore

First printing

ISBN: 1-59129-267-0
PUBLISHED BY PUBLISHAMERICA BOOK PUBLISHERS
www.publishamerica.com
Baltimore

Printed in the United States of America

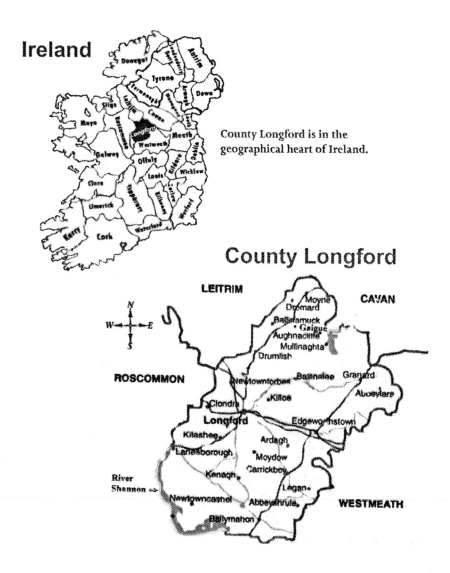

Ireland

County Longford is in the
geographical heart of Ireland.

County Longford

acknowledgments

The author is particularly indebted to:

Jackie Devlin, my wife, who for 30-plus years listened to stories of my boyhood, and urged me, "Write them down, write them down." Her constant encouragement and advice helped get these stories down on paper.

Several friends who were gracious and generous with their time read drafts of the manuscript, including Dr. Eileen Meagher, Dr. Philip Brady, Richard Purdue, Robert Jagoda, Pam Kingsbury, Anne Donnelly, Brig O'Halloran and Una Dempsey. Their constructive criticisms, suggestions, and encouragement were invaluable. I am especially indebted to Robert Jagoda whose insightful comments and persistent promptings challenged me to dig deeper and flesh out my memories of people and events.

Luke Baxter, the County Longford Historical Society, the Ballinamuck Centennial Committee, and Ann Reynolds for permission to use the photographs that help to give the stories a sense of place; and to Carl Selfe and Dan Schumaker for their help in scanning and formatting the photographs and maps for publication.

Members of the Eufaula Writers Group, particularly Dr. Frank Propst, Margaret Garrison, Marian Dolwich and Donna Booth, and also Jeanne Dykes and Fonnie Strang, who served as sounding boards, listening to or reading rough drafts of the stories and providing feedback.

Several members of my immediate family, including Eamonn Meagher, Frank Meagher, Niall Meagher, Mary O'Keefe, Colm Meagher, Seamus Meagher, Teresa Meagher Sullivan and my son, Brian, who read some of the drafts, corrected errors of fact, and gave me much appreciated moral support.

Arnold J. Meagher
ajmcaghcr@aol.com

Dedication

To my parents, May and Arnold, in love and gratitude;

To my grandmother, uncle Michael and the people of my village, who made me feel important each day that I woke up;

To the corncrake, who traveled over 4,000 miles to sing me asleep on summer nights; and

To Shep, who licked his way deep into my boyhood heart.

table of contents

prologue

Ireland, My Ireland captures a country boy's joys and fears in Ireland's heartland in the 1940s as he romps through dew-covered pastures, newly cut meadows and whispering bogs at a time and place where he could still hear the corncrake and the curlew and where his ears and eyes were constantly on alert for the activities of nesting birds, changes in mood of The Master and the subtle sounds and elusive signs of the Little People.

In my village and on my grandmother's farm I had a deep feeling of being wanted and being important each day that I woke up. I had an in-born sense of belonging to village, to the farm, to the animals, to the birds, to the wildflowers, to the fields and hedges, to the trees and tall grasses. I had bonded with the natural world around me, and felt somehow interconnected with and supported by everything that was within my experience. I was an integral part of a corner of rural Ireland, and was very much at home in it.

My most vivid memories revolve around village, farm, family, church and school—the five pillars of my youth with associated milestones, joys and fears. The joys were many: going barefoot in the summer months, Gaelic football (Ireland's premier sport), my first kiss, the corncrake's nightly summer lullaby, special feast days on my grandmother's farm, afternoon tea in the meadow, listening to the storytellers around my grandmother's hearth on long winter nights, fishing for trout and eel, threshing day, the singing of the lark on the bog, drinking the last drops from the wine cruets as an altar boy, my first Holy Communion and winning the Leinster final as captain of the St. Mel's football team.

The fears were also many and at the time loomed large and menacing: the graveyard and the ghosts of the dead, The Master's excessive use of the cane in primary school, the fairy forts, Mr. McCabe (the village chemist), the Little People, the banshee, shopping with my grandmother, the dentist, the silent tormentors of the bog—swarms of blood-sucking female midges—my first confession, finding worthwhile sins for subsequent confessions, getting caught smoking and abuse of the cane by priests in boarding school.

On balance, the joys of growing up in Ireland's heartland far outweighed the fears. Some fears I grew out of, such as the fear of falling through the hole of the outhouse at the bottom of our garden into the ditch beneath, but others, like my fear of The Master, ghosts and the Little People, were a daily constant in my youth. Yet, despite these fears, mine was a joyful boyhood, joyous in its living, and a deeper joy in its telling.

Like many before me, the fears and joys of my youth somehow coalesced to prepare me to leave Ireland and follow a steady stream of aunts, uncles and cousins in emigrating to the U.S. But content as I have been over the past 46 years living in such diverse places as the Sacramento Valley, California; Houston, Texas; Chicago, Illinois; Jupiter, Florida and currently Eufaula, Alabama, my boyhood experiences kept surfacing in conversations with family and friends. Like my Irish brogue, my boyhood experiences have clung to me over the long haul of half a century like barnacles to a rock. And now I am giving these experiences the attention they have long sought, or perhaps deserve, by committing them to writing to share with a broader audience of those who love Ireland and welcome storytelling as a means of renewing or energizing that love, and with those who wish to visit Ireland and travel through its heartland experiencing personally Irish hospitality and the warmth of people like my mother and grandmother found in every village and on every farm.

The stories I tell in and around the five pillars of my boyhood are true, and the names of the people in the stories are real. Some have gone to their eternal reward, but others are still adding to the stories of their lives. They may recall the events I tell here from a different perspective, but that does not invalidate either their memories or mine. It only demonstrates the richness of the fabric of our shared experience, and the limitations of one person's memory.

So boil the kettle, wet a pot of tea, throw your feet up on a stool and share in a boy's joys and fears growing up in a rural village in Ireland's heartland.

part í

víllage

chapter 1

the village at the back of the fort

She is a rich and rare land;
Oh! She's a fresh and fair land;
She is a dear and rare land—
This native land of mine.

—Thomas Davis (1814-1845)
Irish Poet and a Founder of The Nation

The only places in my village that I feared were the graveyard, the fairy forts, and the dark spaces of night. And the only people I feared were The Master, the Little People, the dentist, and the dead.

I had plenty of friends among the living in my village, but I was not so sure where I stood with the unnumbered ghosts of the dead: the dead of centuries, who were stacked and packed on top of each other, held down with great flags of stone in a maze of monuments, tall grasses, inscriptions and epitaphs. I had no close friends in the graveyard. To me the graveyard was full of strangers, dead strangers, many of whom came alive at night and crept out from under the great flagstones, which is why some flagstones tilted up.

I did not know how old the graveyard was, but one leaning gravestone that I could read had the inscription: "Bernard Corrigan, Melkagh, Died 14th November, 1838, Aged 65 years." To me, that gravestone was beyond old. It was ancient. Many older looking gravestones were so covered with moss and lichen that I could not make out what they said.

From the many ghost stories I had heard since I was a toddler, I had a compulsion to give these dead strangers and their "resting place" a wide berth, which I did scrupulously, except when I served as an altar boy at funerals, but then I was in the protective company of a priest and a small bucket of holy water. I was not sure which of the two gave me the best protection, the priest or the holy water, but there was no better protection in my mind against evil and the ghosts of the other world than a combination of the two—a priest wielding a sprinkler of holy water.

With the priest and the holy water by my side, I was able to control my fears of the dead and perform my duties as an altar boy as I stood beside the open grave with the row of skulls and bones the gravediggers had unearthed perched on a mound of dirt nearby. The dead peered at me through eyeless sockets as they patiently waited to be reburied. If these skulls and bones were representative of how the dead looked, and I had no reason to believe otherwise, for the graveyard was where the dead hung out. Then, the dead were indeed a very scary lot.

When it came to warding off evil, holy water was bigger than a big brother. A sprinkle of holy water not only served as a shield that protected the recipient from evil. It caused good things to happen. My house, Annie Catherine Kane's house next door, the Parish Priest's house, my grandmother's house and every house that I knew had holy water in a little font hanging on the wall by the front door or, in Annie Catherine Kane's case, by the kitchen door which opened onto her shop. The fancier holy water fonts had a small sponge in the font to conserve the contents. I had learned in catechism class in school that holy water was a sacramental with special powers of blessing and protection assigned to it by the Church. I believed that during storms and other threatening events these powers offered protection from evil and evil spirits.

Holy water was free and was obtained from the large holy water font at the entrance to the church. The water in that font was blessed by the priest, giving it a power to protect and bless everything that it was sprinkled upon. Why we felt we had to bless God's creatures, people, animals, crops and events was a question I did not ask, but bless them we did, over and over. The priest used holy water to bless people in church, couples at weddings, mothers at churchings, the dead at removals and coffins lowered into their final resting place. My family used it to bless ourselves on leaving the house, to protect the house in thunderstorms, to bless the fields and the sowing of crops and to bless people and animals. We used holy water before setting out on a trip, dipping the forefinger into the holy water font on the wall by the front door and crossing ourselves. We sprinkled holy water on mothers about to give birth and after giving birth, babies at their baptism, cows about to calf, sows about to pig, mares about to foal and people about to die. My grandmother also sprinkled holy water on pigs about to be slaughtered and on clucking hens when she first put them on settings of eggs.

The village graveyard. (Photograph taken by the author in the summer of 2000. In outward appearances the graveyard had changed little since the 1930s and 1940s. But the inhabitants were now not all strangers. I recognized some of the names on the newer gravestones, and said a quiet prayer for their eternal rest.)

My world of people, animals, fields, crops, graveyards and clucking hens was blessed with holy water many times. These blessings reinforced the belief that the objects blessed were all in some way sacred, requiring my special care and respect. Even the graveyard was sacred. It was the most blessed acre of land in the parish with each plot sprinkled with holy water on each successive burial. The graveyard was a very scary place, but I would have to admit that it was also a very sacred place. Holy water had the effect of giving me a reverence for my village and everything in it, including a fearful reverence for the graveyard and its inhabitants no matter how macabre they looked with skulls and bones picked clean of all skin and flesh.

My much-blessed village of Drumlish nestles at the foot of Corn Hill (known to geographers as Cairn Hill), which rises 916 feet to the highest point in County Longford, a small county almost smack in the geographical center of Ireland. The name Drumlish is Gaelic and translates as "the back of the fort." I was not aware of a fort in the area when I was growing up. But

15

then, my historical interests were as yet dormant, and forts, the hideouts of the mysterious Little People, were, to my limited understanding, merely clumps of bushes here and there not to be messed with.

The village of Drumlish long ago (sometime before Columbus sailed for the New World in the last decade of the 15th century) developed well beyond a clump or two of bushes. The village can be found on the better maps of Ireland, seven miles north of Longford town, the county seat, on the road between the towns of Longford and Cavan. Welcome to my beloved village at the back of the fort, at the foot of Corn Hill.

My family moved to the village in 1937 when I was four years old. The villagers watched me grow up. It was home for me through secondary school. The villagers knew me, and I knew most of them by name. I knew all their dogs' names. I was welcomed into their houses. The dogs wagged their tails as I approached, unmistakable evidence that all things were right with my world.

The village, the parish and the church of Drumlish were almost synonymous in my mind and were the center of my universe. My identity was tied to the parish of Drumlish, a distinct geographical, ecclesiastical and cultural entity. I cheered and rooted for its football team. And later I played for the team against other parishes. My brothers and I represented the parish of Drumlish on the Longford County football team. We felt very honored to be counted among those representing our village and parish on the football field.

When I told strangers that I was from Drumlish, that was all most people wanted to know about me. My reputation had gone before me, which was largely the reputation of the parish's football team, its prowess and sportsmanship, or lack of it, on the playing field. Drumlish football players were known to be rough and tough both on and off the field and, although I had no input to that characterization, it described who I was in others' eyes. My village and parish gave me an identity above and beyond my family and extended family of grandmother, uncles, aunts and cousins. And that identity had its advantages. It carried the kind of grudging respect that said, "you don't mess with Drumlishes."

Drumlish was a village of two churches, one Catholic and functioning and the other Protestant and boarded up, with separate graveyards across the road from each other. The village had twenty-four small shops, four large hardware and grocery shops, and seven pubs with family dwellings sprinkled among them that were at one time or another shops. Most village shops were two-story structures with slate roofs with the owner and family living on the second story or in add-on rooms at the back of the shop. Annie Catherine Kane's sweet shop next door to us was a one-story thatched cottage, the way all shops once were, with the shop at one end and living quarters at the other.

Each shop in the village had the owner's name over the shop door or over the large or small shop window. On slow days, which were most days other than fair and market days, the owner stood in the shop doorway greeting passers-by. The owners were at their doors to communicate with the outside world, for nothing much was going on inside their shops. They had no telephones, no computers, no e-mail and no television to keep them inside. Some held brooms in their hands to sweep the entrance to their shops, sweeping the same small area over and over, day after day. Others simply stood and gazed at the unfolding of a new day, hoping it would bring a little business. Both the sweepers and the non-sweepers appreciated the attention, even of a schoolboy like myself, which assured them that it was worthwhile to have gotten up that day. As I passed by, I lingered and chatted with each sweeper and non-sweeper. After the initial, "How are ya?" we talked about the last time I went fishing, or about walking Dad's greyhounds, or about our pony, Dick, the animal that replaced the Baby Ford and took our family to school and back during World War II.

All village residents, but shopkeepers in particular, loved to chat. Mom often wondered why it took me so long to go to Ned Cleary's shop for a pound of sugar or a pound of tea, but even a short trip of one hundred and fifty yards usually meant chats with several shopkeepers along the way. People not only greeted each other on the street, they stopped and chatted. Even Dick, our pony, knew the village etiquette. If people greeted us, Dick stopped dead in his tracks to listen to the chat. It would be un-neighborly not to stop and chat. Even the shopkeepers' dogs enjoyed the chat and wagged their tails in appreciation when I spoke their name, had them lick my hand, and gave them a pat on the head.

Dick Reilly and Mr. McCabe were the only owners I never saw at the doors of their shops. Dick always had a backlog of bicycles to fix, particularly during the war years, when bicycles were one of the principal modes of getting from place to place. I never missed an opportunity to step inside his corner shop to watch him ply his trade and to admire the row upon row of new bicycles. Bicycles were everywhere, some even hung from the ceiling. Dick was an entrepreneur and was always tinkering with some new contraption or other. When the war ended he opened a garage on the Mill

Road across from Roger's Mill to get the mothballed cars back in service, including ours. Within a year, he had a thriving auto repair business and in the early 1950s was one of the first in the county to have the dealership for the new German Volkswagen Beetle. Dick built a new garage and showroom at the edge of town out the Longford Road that was the pride of the community.

My village had two wide paved streets with wide gravel sidewalks that later became cement sidewalks. Only the police and the priests walked down the center of the street, as if to assert their authority, keeping a distance from the people and their shops. During the war years, with no cars around, as only the priests and doctors got petrol for their cars, the police and the priests had the middle of the street all to themselves. The rest of us used the gravel sidewalks. The only time we walked down the middle of the street was after Sunday Mass and before and after football matches when, because of the crowds, everybody walked in the middle of the road. Otherwise the middle of the road was reserved for people of status. My dad walked down the middle of the road, but he could do it, for he was a policeman. None of us kids walked the middle of the street with him, because, in a sense, he was on parade. Walking the middle of the road was to me a declaration of importance and status in the village.

St Mary's Street Drumlish in the 1930s with a Baby Ford, model Y Ford 8, parked on the left. (Photograph courtesy of the Co. Longford Historical Society.)

One day a tall stranger came to town. The left side of his face was clean-shaven while a thick beard covered the other side. He impressed me and my friends, for not only was he quite different but he walked the middle of the street with his open topcoat swaying in the breeze and carrying himself as if a telephone pole ran down the middle of his back. We were in awe of him and followed him, albeit at a safe distance. He talked to nobody. He walked out of town the way he walked in, his six-foot-six figure splitting the middle of the road. The shopkeepers in their doorways whispered that he was a little strange and beckoned us to stay away from him. To our disappointment, he did not return. He was so different that we thought he might be with a circus, but we learned later that there was no circus anywhere near. Our elders had little to say but to repeat that he was a "little strange," and that if he returned, we must stay away from him. We never saw him again.

Some villagers left lasting impressions on me. Mr. McCabe, the village chemist, was a bit of a mystery to me, and like the dead, I feared him as an unknown. His only visible activity was a daily evening walk out the Longford road. I never heard anybody use his first name. I still don't know if he had one. I envisioned him as a baby being baptized as Mr. McCabe. As the priest poured cold water on his bald head, he was crying, and his mother was saying, "Mr. McCabe, shush, shush."

Mr. McCabe was not a registered pharmacist but nonetheless dispensed over-the-counter type medicines for people and animals. I was only in his shop a couple of times. On the first occasion, Dad sent me to get medicine for Lily, his favorite greyhound. The tiny shop had shelving but the shelves were bare. It was a little eerie, a shop with no goods on the shelves. I was about to run out of there when a soft pleasant voice said, "What can I do for you, young man?"

Mr. McCabe appeared in a three-quarter length white coat. His big eyes peered out from under large bushy eyebrows and over wire-rimmed glasses perching on the end of his nose. A wisp of hair stood almost erect on top his bald head. He smiled a broad smile, showing very white teeth and repeated, "What can I do for you, young man?"

I could not run away now, so trying as best I could to hide my fear, I told him that my dad wanted a physic (a powder to stop diarrhea) for Lily. Mr. McCabe simply nodded and disappeared behind the empty shelving. I did not want to admit it, but I was shaking with fear. His smiling and pleasant voice made me feel better and helped me suppress the urge to run. But what really kept me there was the knowledge that Dad would send me right back, and then I would be in a worse pickle. It seemed like forever before Mr. McCabe reappeared with a small package and said, "Your dad will know what to do."

Forgetting my manners, I hightailed it out of there, without as much as a "thank you."

But Dad wanted to know what were Mr. McCabe's instructions. When I told him what he said, Dad ran me out of the house, saying that I was useless. I thought that in the circumstances, I had overcome my fears and done quite well. But I could not tell Dad that. I had met and spoken to the village's most reclusive inhabitant and was none the worse for it. Mr. McCabe was no longer a mystery man to me and I was no longer terrified of him.

Mr. McCabe was a bachelor, but, unlike other bachelors in the village, he kept very much to himself. It was said that he washed his clothes by putting them out on the clothesline in the rain, which saved him the effort of carrying water from the pump or from the wells. Today we would call him a conservationist. At that time, I thought of him as just a bit odd.

A few doors down the street from the chemist was Phil O'Reilly, the shoemaker. Phil helped us patch our pigskin footballs, as well as mend the soles of our boots and shoes. Phil seldom stood in the doorway of his shop. He sat at his cobbler's bench, just inside his small shop window, which enabled him to see and greet everybody who went by. Phil always seemed to have a half-smoked cigarette tucked in behind his left ear. He was a bachelor and hadn't gotten married by the time I left the village, but that was not unusual. Irish men traditionally got married in their late forties or early fifties, when, as my grandmother said, they were more settled.

It seemed like Phil always had a pair of boots or shoes from someone in my family waiting to get a pair of half-soles, so I always had an excuse to go into his shop, chat a while, and look over his assemblage of footwear. His small shop had shoes and boots everywhere. A motley gathering of all sizes and shapes of footwear filled his makeshift shelving and spilled onto the floor. Some boots and shoes had their leather tongues hanging limp, almost touching the shelf or floor. They looked forlorn as if they had been abandoned by their owners and were resigned to their fate of sitting idle on a shelf among hundreds of other idle sitters. Others had their tongues standing upright, presenting as it were a stiff upper lip of aggressive confidence in their future. Sooner or later, they would be where they belonged—on their owner's feet. While still others kept their tongues tucked inside, either unable or unwilling to express how they felt.

A small group of boots and shoes newly polished with new leather half-soles and rubber heels looked like they were ready to jump off the shelf, eager to be taken home or at least to be handled and admired. I could never resist lifting them pair by pair and admiring the workmanship of their new half-soles, new heels, sometimes new laces and always their new shine. I knew that each pair wanted to be taken home and to be proudly worn to church, to school, to town, to Sunday night dances, or to work. I would have loved to wear them all, to show off their new makeovers. Phil appreciated my admiration, and I liked to think the newly mended, newly shined shoes and boots did, too. I always left Phil's shop with lingering looks of longing at the newly mended shoes and boots.

Two doors from Phil Reilly's shop was the village's only butcher shop, where Mom got the lamb and beef for Sunday dinner and special occasions. Lamb chops and lamb kidneys spiced with a little Coleman's mustard were Dad's favorite dishes, and Mom had an understanding with Phil Davis, the butcher, to set some aside for her when he slaughtered a lamb. Dad had his own special way of eating lamb chops and would use his knife to pick every scrap of meat off the lamb chop bones. He relished every morsel. I inherited Dad's appreciation of lamb chops and lamb kidneys, including Coleman's mustard.

I was curious about how Phil Davis slaughtered the animals that he had in his butcher's shop. So on one occasion, I watched Phil and his oldest son, John, a few years older than myself, kill a bullock in the slaughterhouse at the back of their house, and hang the animal up for skinning and dressing. Phil used a pick-ax, hitting the bullock in the forehead several times. The experience left me trembling inside, though I did my best to hide how I felt and bragged of the experience to my classmates at school. I never returned for a second viewing. Once was enough. I often watched my Grandmother as she rung the neck of a chicken for Sunday dinner, and that did not bother me. And I even helped my uncle Michael kill a pig. But the bullock was a large animal that struggled terribly and did not want to die. I made up my mind that butchering was something I did not want to do when I grew up.

Beyond the crossroads and out the Longford road a bit was Lennon's Tailor Shop with three tailors, all men with spectacles balancing precariously on the tips of their noses. Spectacles balancing on tips of noses was a trait among professionals or near- professionals. Eugene Lennon, chief tailor and owner, worked just inside his shop window with a wide lens view of people going by. He cut the first suits for me and my brother, Eamonn, and suited out most of the men in the village and the surrounding area. I felt important being measured and outfitted for my confirmation by Eugene Lennon himself with a navy blue suit with short pants. I had two fittings right in front of the window with the sun shining through, one fitting for the jacket without sleeves and a second fitting with the sleeves sewn on loosely with white thread. Confirmation made me a full member of the church like the adults, and I felt very grown up with a tailor-made suit, even though it had short pants. Mr. Lennon sensed my pride, and smiled broadly with the smile of a man proud of the product of his hands.

No village worth its salt would be without a seamstress. Mrs. Brigid Heslin lived across the street from us one door down from the post office. She made dresses and coats for women and special female outfits for first communions, confirmations and weddings. But my interest was not in Mrs. Heslin. She had a granddaughter staying with her, Esther Devine, who was a few years older than I, but I enjoyed seeing her whenever she stepped out of the house and particularly when she wore her tight-fitting slacks. Esther's parents had emigrated to the U.S. with the intention of bringing Esther over after they had settled in. In the meantime, Esther had bonded with her grandmother and decided to stay in Drumlish.

Esther was the first and only woman in the village of my youth to wear trousers. It was considered a little shocking for a woman to wear slacks and certainly did not pass the unspoken dress code of the village. My brother Eamonn, Vincent Reilly and I would fight with one another to peek through the hole in our galvanized iron-gate to see Esther show off her figure. An older man with a blond head, Mr. Louis Goebels, rode his bicycle the seven miles from Longford town a couple of times a week to visit Esther and her grandmother. We felt it was well worth the trip, especially when she wore the slacks. To our disappointment, Mr. Goebels married Esther and we never saw her again.

Like every Irish village, the village at the back of the fort had a chief mourner, the undertaker, to bury the dead. As he sat atop a black hearse drawn by two black horses, Tommy Whitney wore a black top hat and a white armband on his black cape while he led the death parade from the church to the cemetery. It was a sobering, solemn spectacle. Tommy's outfit gave him much status in my eyes, second only to the priest, and he could have walked the middle of the street, but he didn't. Perhaps, he did not see himself as I saw him—a man with status in the village.

I often watched Tommy, out of uniform, build coffins in the shed alongside his home, and I played funerals with other kids among the finished and half-built coffins. On one such occasion, Bessie Dooris from the ice cream shop across the street came looking for her daughter, Ursula. We said that we were preparing to bury her and that she was in the birch coffin in the hearse at the front of the shed.

"Oh, God bless us and save us," screamed Bessie, "wait till I tell the priest what you were up to!" Ursula went home with her mother. We heard nothing more about it.

My village had but one active church, Roman Catholic, where people worshipped, were baptized, received First Holy Communion and Confirmation, got married and were sent to a final resting place in the village graveyard. I blessed myself going by the graveyard as well as going by the church, in the one case out of respect and fear of God and in the other out of respect and fear of the dead.

When I blessed myself going by the graveyard I was really asking God to keep those inside in their proper place. I knew about the teaching of the resurrection but I wanted the dead to stay in their graves and not be having any fancy ideas of getting up and about. It never entered my young mind that I might be in the same place one day. I never thought of death as something that might happen, let alone happen to me. Death happened only to old people. Sometimes the priest in church talked of death and the need to prepare for it, but that made as much sense to me as preparing to go to the moon.

Our village had a *Garda* (Gaelic for police) station with a sergeant and three *Garda Siochana* (policemen), who kept what little law and order there was to keep. The *Garda Siochana na h-Eireann* (Guardians of the Peace of Ireland) were established in 1922 shortly after the Irish Government won its independence from England and replaced the Royal Irish Constabulary, a police force established by the British a hundred years earlier in 1822. The Royal Irish Constabulary was an armed police force and was the principal instrument of British political control of the people of Ireland. In the war for Irish independence, from 1919 to 1922, the Royal Irish Constabulary was targeted by those fighting for independence, and about 400 police were killed.

The new police of independent Ireland, the *Garda Siochana*, were a uniformed but unarmed national police force that was equipped only with truncheons. Only detectives carried guns. The village *Garda* or police were responsible for law and order, census taking, licensing and administration of government programs such as the distribution of bounty for fox tongues.

The Drumlish *Garda* station policed a wide area that included the entire parish of Drumlish. Since the government did not provide the police with cars, they attended to their duties on their bicycles.

The one place in the *Garda* station I wanted to see was the jail. We often played putting one another in jail, and I wanted to see a real jail. Dad let me take a look inside the jail when it was unoccupied. Without saying a word, he led me to the jail cell. It was a tiny little room with a small opening high up in the wall that let in some light. All it contained was a bench that could be used both to sit on and sleep on.

Was Dad thinking the way I was thinking? I was comparing the jail to my bedroom at home with its two beds and four people, my three brothers and myself. I would not want to exchange what I had for the jail cell, even though it was only for one person.

I asked Dad, "Does the prisoner get out of the jail during the day?"

"Only to go to the bathroom," he said.

So the prisoner's only choice was between the jail cell and the outhouse, which was about half the size of the jail. I made up my mind, then and there, never to go to a real jail. The *Gardai* (plural of *Garda*) referred to the jail cell as the "guest room." But the guests were few and far between. I can only recall it being occupied on a couple of occasions when Mom made a sandwich for the prisoner, but that was only for a day or two.

Our village had a post office, which was directly across the street from our house. Two sisters and the husband of one of them who was retired from the Royal Irish Constabulary ran the post office. All three attended Mass and went to communion daily. Villagers could set their clocks when the three left the post office each morning for daily Mass. Besides the mail and stamps, the post office provided the village with daily and weekly national newspapers. Mr. Flanagan, the retired policeman, was a fly fisherman who made his own flies. He was one of the first in the village to own a car and before World War II he often drove to the river Shannon about twenty-five miles away to fly fish. He had no children of his own. I knew where to get the best worms, should he invite me along. It would have been a dream come true to fish in the Shannon, Ireland's largest river, and maybe catch a pike, which was a much larger fish than I was used to catching in the small local rivers: the mill river, Bandra and the river at the foot of my grandmother's farm. But I was never invited. Mom said that perhaps I was the wrong kind of fisherman, a worm fisherman instead of a fly fisherman.

My village had no electricity, no indoor plumbing, no solicitor, no accountant, no dentist, no bank, no restaurant, and no lodging house or place to stay overnight except the tiny jail cell in the *Garda* barracks. We seemed to get along very well without these services. Banks from Longford town set up temporary operations once a month on fair days, when local farmers brought their cattle, pigs, and chickens to market. Bessie Dooris and the large hardware and grocery shops made sandwiches on these days. But to get the services of a solicitor, accountant, dentist, or hotel we had to go to Longford town, seven miles away, which was an hour and half ride in a horse and cart or pony and trap. But being that far away from the dentist was not a bad idea. My first encounter with a dentist was by far the most terrifying experience of my boyhood.

I had to get a tooth pulled, one that had been a source of pain day and night for over a week. Mom led me up narrow stairs to the second floor over Cullen's shoe store on Main Street in Longford to a small room where I felt any cries for help could not be heard down on the street. There was a small elderly man there dressed in a long white coat. He had to be the dentist. He did not smile or say a word to me. With his back turned to me, he said something to Mom in a low voice that I could not make out. He was up to no good. He sat me in a strange looking chair, not unlike a barber's chair, but much more threatening. He leaned me way back in a very vulnerable position, and at his bidding, I slowly opened my mouth. Mom pointed out the tooth that was giving me so much trouble. The white-coated old man simply grunted and without asking my permission stuck a long needle in my gums, causing a quick dart of pain much more intense than the aching tooth. Then he left the room.

I looked at Mom with terror in my eyes. My whole body trembled with fear. She tried to calm me down, saying, "You are going to be all right," but her voice lacked conviction. Perhaps she, too, was a little fearful of this old man in the white coat, who was so menacingly quiet.

The white-coated figure returned and commanded, "Open your mouth wide." In my prone position, I felt I had no option but to obey. He leaned over me. I felt like he had his knee on my chest as he grabbed hold of my aching tooth with some kind of instrument that he kept hidden from me. He pushed the tooth down into my gums with all his strength, and then gave the tooth a couple of great big pulls that seemed to yank tooth, gum, and bone out of my jaw. I wanted to fight back, but he was already out of the room.

I was bleeding profusely. Mom gave me some warm salty water to rinse my mouth. There was a deep empty pain where the tooth once was. I could feel the big hole with my tongue.

The dentist returned, said something to Mom, and money exchanged hands. We left the way we came in. I felt terrible not only because of the pain and the blood that continued to flow from my violated jaw, but because Mom had to pay for this butchery. This experience convinced me that my village and all villages were much better off without a dentist.

My village had four pumps supplying its inhabitants with drinking water. In our family, the big cement tank at our back door caught rainwater from the roof of the house that we used for washing clothes, Saturday night baths for all of us kids, and for washing and boiling potatoes. That cut down on hauling water from the pump. The water pump was a lifeline that we appreciated, most villagers remembering when drinking water could only be had from nearby spring wells, which we still had to fall back on when the pump failed. The water pump also served as a meeting place where mothers chatted and children played.

Placed at the top of a hill, the pump was an easy source of water for slides down the middle of the road during the winter months. The iced road was a hazard to animals and people who attempted to walk on it. But what little traffic there was could easily move a little to the left or right, as the road was plenty wide to accommodate a three to four foot width of ice down the middle. We started at the top of the hill with a run, hit the ice and sat down on our hunkers, gliding to where the road leveled off right in front of our house. We competed to see who would slide the farthest. Phil Reilly put bands of steel on the heels and soles of our wooden clogs and boots to increase our sliding power, and we formed trains taking off one after another, sliding down the hill as a unit, linking our forward thrust for greater speed and longer slides. Sometimes the train busted apart and we all fell, but the next attempt would be better. The smaller ones went first and the "power houses" came behind. The train grew and traveled faster and longer.

A call to dinner, to do homework, or to do a chore always seemed to come too soon. But there were other days for sliding, as from late November to late February frost was a regular visitor.

Besides monthly fairs, Sunday night dances, and occasional plays and movies, the other big events that the village hosted were the annual visits of the circus, much anticipated and appreciated by the young and the young of heart; the annual church mission that reestablished the fear of God in people's hearts; and an occasional Sunday football match where most of the inhabitants of the village and the surrounding countryside gave a good airing to their lungs cheering on the home team.

The village went to church and rested on Sundays. The entrances to the shops went unswept. Shopkeepers stayed inside and shop doors remained closed. On Sunday evenings, the unattached young men of the village gathered at the village crossroads where the village's two streets intersected to chat, play pitch and toss and to plan the dance they would attend later in the evening. The young unattached women, behind curtained windows, readied themselves to accompany the young men to the dance. They dipped their right index fingers in the holy water fonts by their front doors and crossed themselves as they set out for an evening of music and dancing.

chapter 2

irish families were like that

What they undertook to do
They brought to pass;
All things hang like a drop of dew
Upon a blade of grass.

—William Butler Yeats (1865-1939)
Irish Poet, Dramatist, Nobel Prize Winner
in 1923 and Senator in the Irish
Government, 1922-1928

My parents broke with an established Irish pattern of family planning through late marriages and married in their twenties. There is almost always a price to pay when one breaks with tradition. And my parents were no exception.

May Reynolds, one of four teachers at Gaigue National School, lived at home on the farm with her mother and siblings on the side of Gaigue Hill, a short mile from the school. She dutifully handed over to her mother her monthly salary to help defray household expenses and put her younger sister through teacher's training school. When Arnold Meagher, a young civic guard, a native of County Offally stationed locally, asked her to marry him, she had to make a tough decision. Marriage would mean that her mother would stop receiving a teacher's monthly paycheck. Years later she confided in my sister Eileen that she prayed over the decision for a year. When she finally said yes, her mother was so upset that she refused to go to the wedding. The loss of income was no doubt the major reason, but her mother also objected to her suitor on the grounds that he was an unknown outsider from another county.

The rift did not last long. The arrival of my brother Eamonn a year later, the first grandchild born in Ireland (a granddaughter had been born earlier in the U.S.), changed hearts, though a little coolness to the outsider lingered.

Mom, Dad, and my eleven-month-old brother, Eamonn, were living in Ballinamuck when I showed up. Ballinamuck, a much smaller village than Drumlish, had a drapery shop, a post office, a church, and two pubs. It is located five miles northwest of Drumlish, one quarter mile off the road between the towns of Longford and Cavan. The name Ballinamuck is also Gaelic, *Beal Atha na Muc,* which translates as "The Mouth of the Ford of the Pig." Legend has it that a famous black pig from Ulster in the North of Ireland was passing through Ballinamuck on its way south when a native hit it on the head with a stone and killed it. The legend is vague, but this was somehow a show-stopping event, and thus the village's name came into being.

My parents, Arnold Meagher and May Reynolds shortly after their wedding in 1931. (Photograph reproduced from a family album. When the family was young, all of us kids called our parents Mammy and Daddy. That was our tradition in the heartland. Sometime after we went away to boarding school, we called them Mom and Dad, which is what I have opted to call them uniformly throughout these pages.)

But Ballinamuck has its place in history not because of the misfortune of any black pig, but because of the battle fought in the fields around the village on September 8, 1798. The village is proud of its Pikeman monument, erected in memory of the many Irishmen and Frenchmen who perished in the battle and the many Irishmen who were ruthlessly slaughtered upon surrender. As a toddler, I did not understand the story of how the Pikeman came to be. Back then, the Pikeman was simply a playmate confined to his fenced-in play-house. Long after I left Ballinamuck and was in 7th grade in Gaigue school, my teacher, The Master, told us the story in some detail that brought the monument to life. The Master was passionate in the telling with tears coming into his eyes as he told us how the British mercilessly killed defenseless Irish soldiers who had surrendered.

In 1798 there was a general uprising around Ireland against British rule, but in location after location the rebellion was quickly and savagely put down. Some rebels escaped to France and pleaded with the French Government to help the Irish cause. As part of its initial response, France sent General Humbert with 1,000 men and 3,000 spare muskets. This small force, accompanied by three Irish leaders, landed at Killala in County Mayo in the west of Ireland on August 22, 1798. Killala and the adjacent town of Ballina were taken from the British without much difficulty.

Joined by local Irish rebels, General Humbert marched inland and on August 27 inflicted a rout on the British Red Coats at Castlebar. So rapidly did the British soldiers flee before the charge of the French and the Irish that the rout is known as "the Races of Castlebar." Meanwhile, English reinforcements were rushed to Ireland. They met Humbert at Ballinamuck, overpowered him by force of numbers, and compelled him to surrender. The French soldiers were treated as prisoners of war, taken to Dublin, and after a banquet in honor of the French officers, were sent home to France. The captured Irish fighters were slaughtered on the battlefield.

The Master went on to tell us how a leader of the uprising, Wolfe Tone, a Northern Ireland Protestant attorney captured in a subsequent battle, at his trial in which he was condemned to death, explained his rationale for taking part in the rebellion:

"From my earliest youth I have regarded the connection between Ireland and Great Britain as the curse of the Irish nation, and felt convinced that while it lasted, this country would never be free or happy. In consequence, I determined to apply all the powers which my individual efforts could move, in order to separate the two countries. For that purpose, I have sacrificed all my views of life; I have courted poverty; I have left a beloved wife unprotected, and children whom I adored, fatherless. After such sacrifices, in a cause, which I have always considered as the cause of justice and freedom—it is no great effort to add the sacrifice of my life!"

This story got my patriotic blood simmering. The Pikeman monument was transformed in my mind from a play-house to a shrine demanding my deepest respect and prayers for the deceased Irish soldiers whenever I returned to the village of Ballinamuck. The Master was not a dispassionate teacher of history, or of any subject. He evoked in me a combination of fear and awe. But more on that later.

Ballinamuck's Pikeman Monument, Commemorating the Battle of 1798. (Photograph taken by the author in the summer of 2000.)

The move from the historic village of Ballinamuck was occasioned by Dad, a *Garda Siochana*, being assigned to the Drumlish *Garda* station. He had been stationed in Rathowen, fifteen miles east of Longford town on the road to Mullingar and had owned a motorbike to get to and from work. Mom rode a bicycle the mile and a half to Gaigue School, where she taught infants through second grade. She was assigned to the school in 1927, following her graduation from the Saint Louis Convent at Carrickmacross, County Monaghan. She held that assignment for forty-two years to her retirement in 1969.

I was four years old when we moved to the larger village of Drumlish. This move occasioned big changes. Dad traded in his motorbike for the family's first car, a Baby Ford with the County Longford registration of IX 1315, so Mom could drive the four and one-half miles to school. And Dad got a bicycle for his police work.

In our new village, we tried out a couple of houses (Batty Gray's haunted house at the bottom of Main Street and Burbage's new house across the street from their hardware shop on St Mary's Street) before we settled into a house on Main Street that was formerly a drapery shop, also supposedly haunted, owned by Charlie Kiernan. He was the proprietor of one of the four large hardware and grocery shops in the village. This house, with its galvanized gate (that gave my brother Eamonn and me a bird's eye view of Esther across the street), became our rented home from 1939 to 1955. In 1955, the family moved back to Ballinamuck when Dad retired and Mom inherited one of the Ballinamuck village pubs from her cousin, Mrs. Jeannie Reynolds, who died leaving no children.

Our Drumlish home had four bedrooms upstairs. The downstairs had a kitchen, a sitting room, a pantry and a large locked shop area that occupied about half the ground floor that we did not have access to. This is where the ghost hung out undisturbed in its daylight off-hours. Outside the back door, off the pantry, was a large cement tank that collected rainwater from the roof. There was a large back yard, large enough for 5-a/side soccer, flanked by a turf-shed at one end, and a garage with a hayloft above it at the other. Alongside the garage was a stall for a cow or horse. Next to the stall was a walled-off section that we used as a henhouse and a doghouse, but not at the same time. To the left of the dog/henhouse was a cemented area against the gable of our neighbor's house that we used as a handball court. A high wall separated the yard from the street. And on the opposite side, a high hedge separated the yard from a three-quarter-acre garden with eight apple trees. A path wound down to the bottom of the garden where the outhouse nestled, hidden discretely among trees whose evergreen branches brushed the ground. The earthy humor of Bob Boland (County Kerry Poet, 1888-1955) captures the function of this critical facility:

> Temple of seclusion! aptly set apart...
> Where each lone patron, with no special art,
> Relaxes for expulsion, setting free
> Imprisoned waste and the unmuffled fart.

(Lines taken from a book of his writings published posthumously entitled "Thistles and Docks.")

Most of our neighbors had similar size gardens that also had apple trees. Some also had currant and gooseberry bushes, as well as outhouses. Our outhouse was a one-holer, the standard "one-size-fits-all" economy model. Fancier models had two holes—a large size hole for adults and a smaller hole for children. When I was small, I had a fear of falling through the opening, a fear that I gradually overcame, but happily passed along to my younger brothers and sisters, warning them: "Be careful not to fall in."

The outhouse held another fear for me that had nothing to do with size. The first thing I did when I entered the outhouse was to hold my nose and peer down the hole to see if there was anything lurking there that might nip at my bare parts. I always felt very vulnerable sitting there and took care of business with dispatch. There was no dallying. In moments like these, I felt so grateful to St. Patrick for banishing the snakes from Ireland and from the ditch at the bottom of our garden.

Four children were born to Mom and Dad in Ballinamuck: Eamonn, myself, Mary and Eileen. Five more children were born to them in Drumlish: Frank, Niall, Colm, Teresa and Seamus. We arrived on planet Earth for the most part in two's, though not as sets of twins. Eamonn and I came in 1932 and 1933. Since there were but eleven months between us, I grew up in my older brother's shadow, wanting to do everything that he did and wanting to receive everything that he received. I was highly successful in copying my brother. So much so, that we were often taken for twins, a pattern that persisted until my brother went away to secondary school. We dressed alike and achieved the milestones of First Communion, First Confession, and Confirmation together. We worked side-by-side planting and weeding Dad's vegetables in the garden. As a team, we exercised Dad's greyhounds. We traded catching and harnessing our pony, Dick, every other school morning to take our mother and family to Gaigue School. We fished for trout at the Mill Dam together and stole gooseberries and red and black currants from the neighbor's garden, one of us keeping an eye out for the neighbor as the other filled trouser pockets with the forbidden fruit. We tried our hand at smoking cigarettes together, and when we ran afoul of Dad, we faced the music together.

Our fights were over small things. We fought over who got into the tub first on Saturday nights for the head-to-foot washing by Mom, over who slept on the side of the bed next to the wall, and who took the reins and drove the pony and trap to school, but Eamonn, being older, almost always won out. We fought over our button collections that we used in the game of pitch and toss and had to hide our stash of buttons from each other. But on big issues like who went to my grandmother's, there was little rivalry as I liked to go and Eamonn preferred to stay at home. So, from the age of eight to twelve, I spent most of my non-school time—evenings, weekends and summers—at my grandmother's, while Eamonn was at home. Though I followed him to the same secondary school a year later, he had made some new friends who did not become my friends, as each class more or less hung out together. From that point on, we went our different ways, except for getting together for football matches on Sunday afternoons and for major events like cutting turf on the bog each summer.

Mary and Eileen arrived in 1935 and 1936, separated by fourteen months, and Frank and Niall were born 16 months apart in 1937 and 1938. They had similar kinds of twosome relationships as Eamonn and I during the primary school years, dressing like twins and sharing major spiritual and social milestones. They also went to our grandmother's in Gaigue, but seldom did they go together. When it came time to go to secondary school, Mary went to the convent in Longford town and over a year later Eileen went to the convent in Ballymahon. Frank and Niall went to St. Mel's but a year apart, so they had much the same experience there as Eamonn and I. Whatever sibling rivalries there were in our family took place within the twosomes during the primary school years and the rest of us were not privy to what went on.

The last three arrivals in our family broke the twosome pattern. Colm and Teresa came in 1941 and 1944, thirty-eight months apart. And Seamus, the last born, came in 1946. I went away to boarding school the year Seamus arrived and was not around to share in his or in most of Colm's or Teresa's growing up.

All nine of us arrived within the short span of fourteen years, stayed in the family until age 12 or so with extended visits to our maternal grandmother's, and then went to boarding school. This meant that in our early teens we became quite independent of one another, and developed our distinct set of friends apart from the family and the village where we grew up.

Our parents seemed to accept each new addition to the family with minimum fuss and planning. Mom went to Mrs. Maguire's nursing home in Longford town for a few days and came back with a new baby, whom we all dutifully kissed. Within a week, Mom was back at her post teaching.

Many years later, I was to learn that after Niall, number six, was born, my parents decided that that was enough. Mom thought it best to mention their decision to the priest in confession. Her confessor commented: "I presume then you are planning to live as brother and sister and to sleep in separate bedrooms." There was no such planning, and absent planning, the family continued to expand. I cannot imagine our family without the last three arrivals. They were meant to be. If my parents had waited some years to get married as my grandmother wanted, then in all probability I would have missed out on life; so would my brother Eamonn and perhaps my sister Mary. A profoundly sobering thought! Now, in my autumn years, I thank my parents each day for the gift of life. Would that I had thought of doing that when they were alive.

Mom had that quiet strength and resourcefulness of someone very much in tune with the source of all strength and being. She gave unstintingly to each one of us. If she had favorites among us, her secret was well kept. She made each of us feel special, so that we all felt like favorites. This impartiality she maintained to the end, dividing her earthly goods evenly among all nine children, though some of us had long scattered across the seas and my sister Mary had nursed her in her final years.

Mom stood five feet five and one-half inches, had dark brown hair and was a slender 115 pounds. Her every pound was built for lasting wear and endurance. I never heard Mom complain of her lot, though in terms of work she had plenty to complain about. In our village there was no electricity, no plumbing, and no washing machines. Besides teaching five days a week, Mom somehow found the time to hand wash our clothes using a wooden washboard, hang them out to dry and complete the drying in the kitchen on a line over the hob, iron them, darn the toes and heels of our socks, darn the elbows of our jerseys worn threadbare, bake a half dozen cakes of bread daily and keep a husband and nine kids fed, healthy and relatively happy.

As we grew older, we lightened her burden somewhat by helping with the daily chores. But when we got old enough to be of real help in our early teens, both girls and boys were sent off to boarding school, leaving Mom to fend for the little ones. During school hours, we had a babysitter for those too young to go to school. The sitter, Lizzie O'Hara, became over time like a member of the family. She came to live with us full-time, fought with us kids like a tenth child, and was a big help to Mom. Before Lizzie became a part of the family, she had lived with her brother on a small farm a mile or so outside the village. Her parents had passed away and she did not marry. It was a big change from a home with no children to a houseful of kids that treated her more as one of themselves than an adult. With Mom's understanding help, she made the transition, and stayed with us about ten years until the family moved back to Ballinamuck. Lizzie returned to the farm to live with her brother.

Mom seldom raised her voice to us. She exerted her influence by example. She worked tirelessly, prayed endlessly, fasted during Holy Week and was a daily communicant, except when her teaching clashed with the daily Mass schedule. She never had a mean word to say about anybody. Her deep respect for each person was reflected in the warm tender smile she had for everyone. She explained to us that the doctor talking to himself was the doctor "discussing with himself his patients' problems." When Gandy Ellis came to the door one Friday with kippers for Dad from his father's stall, Mom greeted him by his formal baptismal name of Anthony. He beamed with satisfaction that she knew his real name and did not greet him by his nickname of "Gandy." She was probably the only person other than his mother to bestow on him the dignity of his real name. Whatever gentleness and sensitivity we may have as individuals and as a family are due principally to Mom.

Dad, being a policeman, was the disciplinarian in the family and used the stick, or the threat of it, to keep us in check. But his bark was worse than his bite. His conniption fits when we got out of line were many, but the whippings were very few. He was five feet eleven inches and of slight build. He had problems with his stomach, and consumed bottles of milk of magnesia and stomach powders. Noise irritated him, so when he was in the house, we had to be quiet as mice, which was against our natures. Our frequent lapses were a constant source of tension. As a result, we grew up trying to avoid our dad as much as possible.

In later years, when both he and we tried to draw closer, there was an invisible barrier that always seemed to prevent closeness from happening. He was a good dad with one problem habit—his chain smoking. On several occasions, he tried to give up smoking. To the relief of all of us, these attempts did not last long, as he was extremely irritable without his cigarettes. On one of these attempts to quit smoking, his eyesight seemed to deteriorate so badly that he could no longer read. His doctor, Dr. McGarry, urged him to get back on cigarettes right away, which he did. His eyesight quickly returned to normal, and so did life in our house.

Dad loved fresh vegetables, and under his direction our garden produced a goodly supply of potatoes, cabbages, carrots, parsnips, turnips, beats, peas, onions and lettuce. To provide fresh milk for us, he bought a cow, which each of us learned to milk morning and evening.

For a period of some years, Dad bred and raised greyhounds for the track. It was the chore of the boys in the family to walk and run the greyhounds daily. So after school, we would take them on long walks outside the village to a long field. My brother, Eamonn, would run to the other end of the field while I held the dogs as they strained their leashes to follow him. When he was near the other end, I would let the dogs go and they would race each other to him. He would hold them until I called them and they would race back to me. We repeated this a few times, which gave the dogs and us plenty of exercise. We then walked the dogs home. This exercise of running and walking was supposed to prepare the greyhounds for the race-track. We never went with Dad to the dog races, so we never knew how successful our efforts were. Nor did Dad ever share with us whether or not he made money when he sold the pups bred from his favorite bitch, Lilly, or when he sold grown dogs that we helped train. Since he terminated his greyhound project after about seven years, we figured he was not too successful.

Dad was staunchly patriotic and anti-British. As a young man he grew up in daily fear of the British special police forces recruited in England and Scotland to augment the ranks of the Royal Irish Constabulary. They dressed in khaki trousers, dark green tunics, and black belts, and were nicknamed Black and Tans. They ran rampant through the country in 1920 and 1921 in a police war, destroying the property of anybody suspected of opposing British rule or supporting Irish rebels, and killing anyone they suspected of guerilla activities. These special forces were meant to enforce the law of the land, but were themselves not subject to the rule of law.

In revenge for the assassination of British intelligence agents in Dublin on the morning of November 21, 1920, the Black and Tans opened fire that afternoon on a defenseless crowd attending a football match at Croke Park in Dublin, killing twelve spectators and players, and wounding sixty. This notorious act of revenge against innocent people got much public attention, but similar acts on a smaller scale were regular occurrences.

An American Commission, established to investigate conditions in Ireland under the Black and Tan campaign, found that: "The Imperial British Government has created and introduced into Ireland a force of at least 78,000 men, many of them youthful and inexperienced, and some of them convicts; and has incited that force to unbridled violence." The British Government's own investigative Commission wrote in its report: "Things are being done in Ireland, in the name of Britain, which must make her name stink in the nostrils of the whole world." Given the campaign of terror unleashed by the Black and Tans and the 700-year history of British oppression of the Irish, Dad's anti-British sentiments were understandable to say the least.

Dad was an avid reader who loved his morning *Irish Independent*, one of the island's two daily newspapers, which he got from the post office across the street. He was considered by his peers to be good with words and to have a literary bent, and he did a good job of writing obituaries for the local newspapers for both my grandmothers.

Despite his anti-British political leanings, he was partial to British weeklies, which he considered a little too adult for his children to read. He would hide them under the mattress of his bed, where we retrieved them whenever we wanted to know what was going on across the Irish Sea. We always made sure to return them to their hiding place, so that the security of the location was never compromised.

Doing crossword puzzles was one of his favorite ways to relax, and he fancied himself an authority of sorts on the English language. He also followed horse racing as well as dog racing, and wagered a bet once in a while. But he kept his win/loss record very much to himself.

Dad's reluctance to share his life with us may have resulted from his training and role as a policeman, where he felt there were many aspects of his work he could not share with us. But I suspect that his reluctance to share may also have arisen from the fact that he was from another county and never felt truly at home among my mother's people. Dad hailed from County Offally and, because of the distance, seldom went home. The few occasions that I saw him open up with people were on visits to his mother, my grandmother, in the town of Birr, County Offaly, which was his home town.

When Dad and Mom retired from the pub in Ballinamuck, which was their second retirement, they bought a bungalow on the outskirts of Longford town. Dad named the house "Corvil." We were in the dark as to where the name came from. Since Dad did not offer an explanation, we respected his secret and did not ask for one. It was only long after he was gone that we found out that the name had been associated with the O'Meagher clan country in northern Tipperary.

From early Christian times in the fifth and sixth centuries, the O'Meaghers patronized and sponsored monastic settlements, including the monastery at Sean Ross in Ikerrin, near the modern town of Roscrea in northern Tipperary. The grants of land that the O'Meagher clan gave to the monastery at Sean Ross evolved into the parish of Corville in the 12th century, when the organization of the church changed from a monastic system to the diocesan and parish systems that we know today. Dad was quietly very proud of his family clan heritage. Unfortunately, he did not verbalize his pride to his children.

Nor did he share with us that as a young man of eighteen he changed the spelling of his last name from the anglicized spelling of Maher to the more traditional Gaelic spelling of Meagher. In his application to become a policeman in 1924, he entered his name as Meagher. But his birth certificate, correctly or incorrectly, spelled it the other way, and someone back then crossed out Meagher on the application and wrote in Maher above it. Since some of Dad's brothers spelled their last name as Maher, we grew up believing that they had changed their name. But the copy of Dad's application to the *Garda Siochana*, and his birth certificate that I received from the *Garda* archives, tell a different story. Dad was the one who changed the spelling of his name from the spelling on his birth certificate.

My parents lived from paycheck to paycheck. I was never aware of any financial crisis. Our credit was always good at Ned Cleary's store where we purchased our groceries and had a constant tab. We always had plenty to eat, though everything that appeared on the table disappeared quickly. Besides oatmeal porridge or stirabout, soup was a daily staple, with oxtail soup on Saturdays being a special treat. A cardinal table rule was that we could not ever take more on our plate than we could eat. We could go back for seconds after everybody had a first helping, but to leave food on our plate was at least a venial sin that merited mention in confession. To this day, I feel a compulsion to finish what is on my plate no matter what it is.

At meals, I do not recall ever seeing leftovers. Even the large basket of potatoes, their skins cracked open in broad smiles, in the middle of the table, which was a staple at dinner, always dwindled to nothing. My brothers and I ate seven or eight of these laughing spuds each at a sitting. While eating one potato, we peeled a second, and had our eyes on a third. Without potatoes we would have assuredly gone hungry at times. Mom could never have baked enough bread to take their place. No wonder our ancestors had a famine when the potato crop failed! As part our daily nourishment, Mom insisted that we have a tablespoonful of cod liver oil, a ritual we hated.

Saturday was wash day. On Saturday afternoons we went to confession, whether we needed to or not, and got a spiritual washing. Later, after the family rosary and before the kitchen fire, we got a physical washing. Unlike the spiritual washing, there was no doubt whatsoever about the need.

Mom boiled a couple of large pots of water, brought in the galvanized bath tub from the pantry, half filled it with hot water before the fire, then poured in cold water from the cement tank until it met the elbow test. Each of us in turn, beginning with the oldest, got into the tub for a head to foot washing administered by Mom. The oldest went first, for it was not unknown for the youngest to pee in the tub. Mom lathered us from head to foot with carbolic soap. We complained bitterly when the soap got into our eyes and often tried to bolt from the tub. But Mom's firm hands held us there, and with the corner of a towel, cleared away the soap from stinging eyes. The water was changed only a couple of times during the process, as the hot water was limited. But each head was rinsed off with a saucepan of fresh warm water, so as to wash out all carbolic residue. We dried off before the turf fire.

We were then packed off to bed so that we would be fresh clean inside and out for Sunday Mass the next morning. But sleep did not always come right away. It was usually prefaced, at least among us boys (with four of us in one room sharing two beds), with strenuous pillow fights that were brought to a halt only by Mom's intervention. We usually protested that we were only playing, but more often than not it was very serious play, and we were secretly glad that parental authority intervened. Better that than have to give in to an older brother, or worse still have to give in to a younger brother. I usually fell asleep counting the crows on the tall trees behind Batty Gray's house.

chapter 3

gaigue primary school—a typical day

And still they gazed,
And still the wonder grew,
That one small head could
Carry all he knew.

—Oliver Goldsmith (1728-1774)
Irish Playwright, Novelist and Poet
Born in County Longford

In winter, when the trees are bare of leaves, Gaigue National Primary School is within sight of my grandmother's farmhouse. In summer, the full foliage of trees and bushes hides one from the other. The month of May saw the school and the farmhouse gradually disappear from the other's view.

I spent a considerable amount of time on my grandmother's farm. It was a second home for me. I attended Gaigue National School, where my mother taught, which is about a mile from my grandmother's house as the crow flies. And that is the route I took each morning scurrying through hedges, across stone walls and over ditches in the shortest distance available to an agile twelve-year-old boy determined to be on time for school. I can't recall ever walking to school from my grandmother's. I always ran to school, not because I overslept, but because it was always a race to complete all the chores and still get to school to avoid punishment for being late—four to ten strokes of a cane, depending on The Master's humor.

The Master's humor at the beginning of the day was a major concern to all his students. It was a major concern to me, for nothing I hated more than having to nurse swollen hands for hours at a time. Starting out with the use of the dreaded cane did not bode well for the rest of the school day.

As I finished breakfast, a quick glance at the clock in the windowsill showed that it was four minutes to 9 a.m. and the start of school. Stuffing a slice of brown buttered bread into my mouth, I grabbed my satchel and my lunch consisting of two oatmeal cakes placed between pages of my jotter, and bolted out the door. Shep was waiting outside to jump on me and give me a parting lick, for which he got what was left of the slice of bread hanging from my mouth.

The first quarter mile to school was a straight run down the lane through the rows of daffodils, now on their last legs with tousled heads bent close to the ground. Between the thick hedge on one side of the lane and a mossy bank on the other side I flew, my nimble feet barely touching the ground, to the first stone wall alongside the fort. Three round small stones on a top stone of the fence verified that the Gormans: Jimmy, Paschal, and Vincent, who were my closest neighbors, had already passed this point. Maybe I could catch up with them. I increased my speed and made mental notes on the movement of birds as I sped along, observations that would help me pinpoint the location of their nests when I had more time for discovery.

The Gormans were climbing over the last fence onto the road alongside the school when I caught up with them. The schoolmaster, Peter Duignan, we called him The Master, was turning the corner on his bicycle about 125 yards up the road at Philip Brady's. The Master was of small stature, about 5 feet 8 inches, of trim build with a rather large head, and a long bony freckled face of ruddy complexion topped with a mop of red sandy hair. He dressed nattily, was very businesslike in the classroom, never greeted his students, never gave compliments, and his stern school face never smiled, except when talking with visitors. In riding his bicycle to school, he almost always wore a topcoat and a cap.

This morning we had beaten The Master to the school, which meant that we were on time no matter what time it was on the school clock. When we entered the classroom, the clock on the wall over the fireplace read six minutes past nine. There would be no cane slogging (colloquialism for beating) this morning for being late, for The Master himself was obviously a little tardy. All of us hated to see the school day start with someone being slogged for running nonstop to school. This usually meant a bad day for all. It established a mood of uncertainty as to what the day held in store now that the cane was out of its hiding place in the cupboard at the back of the classroom, and was on The Master's desk ready for use.

The hated cane, out of its closet, set a mood of opposition between students and teacher and dampened any enthusiasm we might have for learning. Such a mood was normally broken only by outside intervention—such as one of the three women teachers in the four-room school coming by to speak with The Master, who was also the school principal; or the regular lunch break at noon; or a visit from the Parish Priest, who was the school administrator and who came by weekly, usually to talk with The Master, but often to quiz us on our catechism. Such interventions were always welcome for they broke the downward spiral of mean spiritedness, and the cane disappeared from The Master's desk back into the closet.

When these interventions did not take place, we usually had a few bad hours with students growing un-cooperative and sullen, and The Master taking out his frustration and anger in bursts of cane slogging. When he got really mad, he stuck his tongue out of the right corner of his mouth and bit down on it with a savage look of determination in his eyes. How we dreaded that look! This did not happen every day, but it happened with enough frequency to be a matter of constant concern and worry. And every student had a personal caning "horror" story or two to tell.

My most memorable "horror" story of a cane slogging by The Master happened when I was in the fifth grade in Mrs. Murphy's classroom. I can vividly recall The Master coming around the corner at Philip Brady's one misty morning at about fifteen minutes to nine to see Paschal Gorman and myself jump over the fence from the meadow across the road from the school. He waved at us to wait for him, and when he came to a stop and threw his leg off his bicycle beside us, he demanded to know what we were doing in the meadow, contrary to school rules. We knew that the field was out of bounds for students, except when the teachers assigned students the task of gathering ferns for the fireplace in the summer months. We obviously had no fern with us but we felt that we had a very legitimate excuse.

We had arrived early in our classroom that morning to find that a jackdaw had slipped down the chimney into the classroom overnight. In a fruitless effort to get out, it had flown at the windows knocking over and breaking several clay flower pots, leaving dirt and broken pots and plants in a mess underneath each window. We dutifully caught the pest (jackdaws had a bad press and were generally detested and lumped together in the same category with rats and foxes), wrung its neck, as we had seen the neck wrung off chickens at home and were returning from dispatching the body in the bushes in the meadow across the road when The Master turned the corner at Brady's.

In response to his query, we enthusiastically told him what had happened and how we had quickly taken care of the intruder that had wrought such havoc in our classroom. He listened intently to our story and said simply, "Come with me."

Paschal and I looked at each other a little confused, as The Master did not seem pleased with our heroics. We followed him into his empty classroom. Since it was a little early, the students had not yet arrived. He flung his cap on the desk and without taking off his topcoat, he snatched the cane from the cupboard, stuck his tongue out of the right corner of his mouth, bit down hard on it with a grimace, and not saying a word, beat us on both hands until the sweat poured down his face, and he seemed unable to beat us anymore. When our hands sagged under the weight of the cane, he beat us on the knuckles from underneath to keep our hands up. We lost count of the strokes. Our hands burned with pain. He dismissed us with the admonition: "Never do that again."

We returned to our classroom, where other students and the teacher were finishing cleaning up the jackdaw's mess. When they heard our tearful story, they were appalled. They did not want to believe us, but our hands, now swollen to about twice their normal size, were convincing evidence. Mrs. Murphy went into a long conference with the teacher next door, who was also my mother. There were tears of anger in their eyes when they examined our hands. Nothing much was said to us. To my knowledge nothing was ever said to The Master. He was the school principal, and the principal in matters of student discipline was above reproach, at least in my school. I never complained to my parents or to my grandmother about a beating at school. If I did, I ran the risk of getting another beating, or some other punishment, or at least a severe scolding, for the presumption was that I misbehaved or did not do my homework. People in general, including myself, believed that the cane was a necessary tool of learning and discipline, so it was better to suffer silently than to complain.

On this damp May morning, we all piled into the classroom with the seventh grade students in the front of the room closest to The Master's desk, and the eighth grade students at the back of the room closest to the door. A couple of eighth grade boys made a fire using a few sticks and some paper as kindling for the turf. During the cold winter months, we always had a fire in the classroom. Each student brought two sods of turf to class each day, which kept the fire going. A few fathers brought a cartload of turf directly from the bog at the beginning of the school year so that their children would not have to carry the two sods daily to school. On this spring day a fire was at the discretion of The Master, and he choose to have one, which was a good omen.

All eyes were on The Master searching for any telltale expression that would give a clue to his humor and what the day had in store for us. We took the making of a fire as a positive sign. Nobody could be in bad humor for long with a fire crackling in the grate.

There was no set schedule for when each subject was taught. That depended entirely on the whim of The Master. There were a few dreaded subjects that almost always exposed our ignorance and brought on the anger of The Master. And invariably ended with almost all of us getting a few strokes of the cane, or being lifted up by the ears, or getting our jaws stretched, or our faces slapped. The most punishment prone subjects were spelling, recitation of poems we had to memorize and the memorization of answers from the catechism.

But by far, the most feared subject was spelling. For each misspelled word we raised one finger above our heads. Some of us often had fingers on both hands reaching for the rafters. No one ever wanted to reach the critical point of having all ten fingers pointing toward the ceiling, for that triggered the settling of accounts.

To this day I can close my eyes and vividly see The Master standing on the desk above my head meting out punishment on my shaking hand with a grin of satisfaction on his freckled face. Some students were spitting on their hands or sitting on them to prepare them for the cane, as if that would somehow ease the pain. While others quietly prayed that we would take our punishment without doing something foolish as take the cane from The Master and break it into *smidereens* (little pieces), as some of the boys threatened to do, but never did.

In dire situations when the number of fingers raised for missed spellings got perilously close to ten, the only thing that could save us was direct divine intervention with the priest or the school inspector dropping by for a visit. This happened only once in my memory, resulting in general amnesty, with The Master, red-faced, attempting to explain to his visitor what was going on. The relief on our faces no doubt told our visitor that he was indeed something more than a welcome guest. He was a savior. This one amnesty served as the wellspring of hope for divine intervention at all subsequent settlings of accounts, hope for divine intervention that never again came.

These spelling quizzes were often marathon sessions covering several chapters of the English reader. At the end we received one stroke of the cane for each raised finger, unless we were caught cheating on the number of fingers raised, when the number of cane strokes depended solely on the discretion or lack of discretion of The Master.

Although Gaelic was the language of the school and all subjects, except English and catechism, were taught by means of Gaelic, I cannot recall ever having a spelling test in Gaelic, which was The Master's pet subject. In fact, Gaelic was the pet subject of the primary school system. We spoke Gaelic throughout the school day, even during the unsupervised lunch break. But outside of school we spoke English almost everywhere, including home. In primary school all of us were more or less bilingual in Gaelic and English, and took much pride in our ability to converse in Gaelic.

When I was at my grandmother's, I almost never spoke Gaelic except to the animals, who seemed to be equally unmoved by Gaelic or English. My grandmother and my uncle did not speak Gaelic, though their daily conversations were peppered with Gaelic words and phrases. When I was at home, I spoke Gaelic to my mother and at times to my brothers and sisters. Dad did not speak Gaelic, and whenever he was around, the language of the home was English. When we played ball or other games with the children in the neighborhood or when we went on errands to the shop, we spoke English. Commuting the four and a half miles to school with my mother, brothers, and sisters in the pony and trap was always a "Gaelic only" one hour and fifteen minute journey, which invariably included five decades of the rosary in Gaelic.

Our pony, Dick, was one animal that seemed to respond better to exhortations in Gaelic than English. He also had a sense of the sacredness of holy places, and slowed down to a crawl going by the church. My mother said he was a real knave, but nonetheless indulged his reverence for the sacred and would not permit us to use the stick on him in such instances.

Dick was also a quiet but determined supporter of conversation with the world at large, and would come to an abrupt stop whenever my mother greeted anybody as we left the village. For that reason we tried to avoid meeting the people coming out of morning Mass. Whenever we failed to leave on time to avoid this, as sometimes happened when the Mass was short or we had problems catching Dick where he grazed overnight a mile outside of town, the passing of the church was a tedious, embarrassing, stop and go operation that made us want to slide down into the belly of the trap and hide. It also made us quite late for school.

On this school day, when we had all settled in our appointed places, The Master surprised us by asking had any of us found any new wild flowers for the classroom's wild flower collection. Of course we did. Flowers and flowering grasses and weeds were bursting out all over. It was that time of year. Going to and coming from school, we were always on the lookout for wildflowers. We immediately produced several specimens from between book leaves and jotters. These were assigned to a few students to be appropriately catalogued. The flowers that could not be identified were prepared for mailing to somebody in a department of government in Dublin whose task it was to know all about wild flowers and to respond to such requests.

The rest of us were given geometry problems to solve. This augured well for a cane-less and perhaps even a productive day. Resolving geometry problems became group efforts with The Master guiding us and keeping us on the right course. On this day lunchtime came all too soon.

The first sign that lunch was fast approaching was the selection of one of us boys to get The Master's lunch. This was a coveted assignment. It took about a half hour to run to The Master's home about one and a quarter miles away, eat the hot lunch and cake prepared by his gracious wife, and return just as the students were exiting for their lunch break. The lunch at The Master's home was always a special treat. The only qualifications for the assignment was the ability to execute the errand within a half hour or so. Although The Master had a bicycle at school, and all of us in the seventh and eight grades could ride a bicycle, the option of using a bicycle simply never came up. We ran such errands whether at home or at school.

Lunchtime was a time for a game of soccer in the school playground. We picked sides and played like demons in our bare feet until the bell signaled the end of the lunch period and the victors. Shoes were not allowed. When not muddy, the playground was a hard, craggy, uneven surface, good for hardening the soles of our feet and on occasion splitting a toe open. The rubber ball used was normally no larger than a fist. The ball game was more important than lunch, so lunch was gulped down or forgotten about until the bell sounded. Then it was usually too late to do anything but take one big bite and toss it over the wall. It was a no-no to return to the classroom with our mouths full. That was almost as bad as being late for school. It could put The Master in a mean mood and trigger a bad afternoon. From The Master's perspective, lunchtime was first and foremost for lunch, and then for soccer. Reversing the order was inexcusable.

This afternoon was spent reading, writing and a little oratory. A few of us read aloud to the classroom with The Master critiquing our enunciation. He urged us to put life and meaning into what we read, like everyday conversation.

This was not easy but we enjoyed trying. It was easy enough to put feeling into some poems like Joyce Kilmer's "Trees" or "The Daffodils" by William Wordsworth, but works like Edgar Allen Poe's "The Raven" or Thomas Gray's "Elegy Written in a Country Church Yard," we stumbled over and butchered time after time. It was difficult to get our tongues around some of the words and our minds around some of the meaning. Words without meaning generated little feeling.

The Master encouraged us to memorize speeches, such as Padraig Pearse's eulogy at the grave of O'Donavan Rossa in 1915 and to re-enact the eulogy before the classroom. We were better at the political speeches for here feelings seemed to come naturally. On this day it was my turn to give the speech and whether my attempt at oratory was going well or poorly I do not know, but The Master ordered me out of the classroom and up on the wall that surrounded the school.

The class spilled out onto the playground. "Now let us hear you," The Master challenged. I filled my lungs to capacity and bellowed with all my vocal strength as if to reach the ears of my grandmother a mile away across the fields:

> "It has seemed right, before we turn away from this place in which we have laid the mortal remains of O'Donavan Rossa, that one of us should, in the name of all, speak the praise of that valiant man, and endeavor to formulate the thought and the hope that there are in us, as we stand around his grave...."

Some of my classmates snickered, but I pretended not to notice and continued with Pearse's oration trying to put meaning into every word:

> "Life springs from death and from the graves of these patriot men and women spring living nations. The defenders of this realm have worked well in secret and in the open. They think that they have pacified Ireland. They think that they have purchased half of us and intimidated the other half. They think that they have foreseen everything, think that they have provided against everything; but the fools, the fools, the fools!—they have left us our Fenian dead, and while Ireland holds these graves, Ireland unfree shall never be at peace."

Three o'clock came while I was still on the wall. The raising of the noise level in Mrs. McQuaid's room next door told us that school was over at least next door. The Master never seemed to be in a hurry to dismiss his charges. Without the appropriate signal from The Master any premature activity that indicated we were through for the day only prolonged school. I had no choice but to continue hollering to the amazement and amusement of Mrs. McQuade's pupils. They asked each other, "What has he done to earn this kind of punishment?"

When The Master was ready, he signaled that I get down off the wall. School was over. We had survived another day. This had been a good day— a good day being defined as a day when the cane never left the closet and not one of us was pulled out of our seat by the ears.

Our school days were spent in both fear and awe of The Master. We were in awe of his learning and in fear of his commitment to make us learn, particularly when that meant beating the learning into us. He not only gave us the beginnings of an appreciation of Irish history but also the beginnings of an understanding of Ireland's literary heritage, introducing us to the works of poets such as Oliver Goldsmith, William Yeats, Thomas Davis, Thomas Moore, Padraig Pearse, Robert Joyce and Padraic Colum. But as with most subjects, this appreciation was seriously compromised if not tragically lost to many young minds by the use of the cane. In my own case, though I liked poetry and what these writers had to offer, I had a real difficulty in seeing the beauty of anything that was beaten into me. And sad to say pride in Irish writers and their contribution to literature was something I had buried in my subconscious until I met students and professors on the University of California, Davis Campus with a genuine admiration of Irish men and women of letters.

The Master was an educator of his time, an educator with a cane, who took great pride in coaching and beating his students to bring the highest academic honors to the school. He was singularly successful in this, winning the coveted Carlisle and Blake Premium award for excellence in teaching on more than one occasion.

Then there was a darker side, where he seemed to take delight in inflicting pain and caning us until he was unable to continue. When he stuck his tongue out of the right corner of his mouth, the beatings were usually out of proportion to the transgressions of his students. In the case of the jackdaw, he had never expressed a concern for jackdaw life before that event or since. That beating, as well as many others, would seem to have been impulsive, resulting from some need to express his anger or frustration caused by something that was unrelated to school, or at least to that one event. If what we did was so bad, surely he should have talked to our classroom teacher about it, but as far as we knew, he never did.

The Master loved gardening. The half-acre surrounding his house was a showcase of flowers and vegetables. He was seemingly a good husband and father of seven children, six girls and a boy. Although, in the classroom, he treated his own children no different from the rest of us, caning them and lifting them out of their seats by their ears.

I have no easy explanation for his unpredictable brutality in the classroom. He was just that way, and since he was the only Master that I had known in primary school, perhaps that was the way Masters behaved. His unpredictability kept us on our toes from 9:00 a.m. to 3:00 p.m. It also prepared me to take in stride similar treatment from the priests in secondary school, though incidents of brutality were much less frequent.

Twelve lines of the 430-line poem entitled "The Deserted Village," by Oliver Goldsmith, summarizes my feelings towards The Master both then and now over fifty years later. The poem, first published in 1770, presents the poet's rather idealized reminiscences of the Irish village of Lissoy where he spent his early boyhood years. Goldsmith was one of The Master's favorite poets. We had to memorize extracts from the poem including the following:

> Beside yon straggling fence that skirts the way,
> With blossom'd furze unprofitably gay,
> There, in his noisy mansion, skill'd to rule,
> The village master taught his little school.
> A man severe he was, and stern to view;
> I knew him well, and every truant knew;
> Well had the boding tremblers learn'd to trace
> The day's disasters in his morning face;
> Full well they laughed with counterfeited glee
> At all his jokes, for many a joke had he;
> Full well the busy whisper circling round
> Convey'd the dismal tidings when he frown'd.
> Yet he was kind, or, if severe in aught,
> The love he bore to learning was in fault.

The day was still young. There were seven more hours before darkness fell. On Thursdays, some of us went directly to my mother's classroom, where we had an hour of instruction in Irish dancing for sixpence a person per session. We were taught to dance the reel, slip jig, double jig and, for the more advanced, the hornpipe. We were also taught group dancing in the four-hand, three-hand and eight-hand reels, and for large groups set dances like the "Walls of Limerick."

We demonstrated our step-dancing expertise in competition with one another and with kids from other schools at local Feis (Gaelic for Irish step-dancing competition), where we vied for first, second, and third place medals. Most of us boys could boast of only a few medals, but the girls sported strings of medals, often wearing them on their dance costumes. I enjoyed the Irish dancing. It was a skill that I was proud of, and to this day can dance a double jig with the right encouragement. Our dance teacher was a young man from Donegal, Sean McLiam, who made a living going from school to school on his bicycle to conduct these dance lessons. Irish dancing was part of the post-independence revival of Celtic culture and traditions.

On other days, we dispersed quickly, for many had chores awaiting them at home. My grandmother would usually tell me at breakfast what she had in mind for me to do after school. This was accompanied with the usual admonition not to dally on the way home. But there was one springtime ritual that, despite admonitions, I always made time for on the way to my grandmother's back up Gaigue Hill.

In springtime, on my commute to and from school, I gave special attention to the nesting activities of the birds. I strove to have at least one nest of each kind of bird that I watched over and observed through the entire cycle of nest building, laying of eggs, hatching the eggs, birthing of the scaldings (chicks), feeding of heads with wide open beaks, and first lessons in flying. I tried to make the rounds of these nests, about fifteen of them, daily if possible. I was reluctant to share my nests with others lest they scare the birds, or be secret bird egg collectors and rob the nests for their collections. I was over-protective of my nests.

Some birds such as pigeons built very shabby nests of a few criss-crossed twigs, and it was a miracle how the eggs stayed on them. Other birds like the tiny wren built lavish round homes of moss with a cozy layer of white down feathers on the inside with one small hole for an entrance. It was a treat to share a moment of the day with these artists of nature, observe their progress, count their eggs, give a helping hand with feeding the young with a worm or two, and watch the first nervous, unsuccessful attempts at flight.

These were special moments enjoyed best alone with the birds at the end of the school day. These special moments were particularly therapeutic on bad days when my hands still ached a bit from The Master's cane.

chapter 4

village fair and market days

To Meath of the pastures,
From wet hills by the sea,
Through Leitrim and Longford,
Go my cattle and me.

—Padraic Colum (1881-1972)
Irish Poet, Born in County Longford

The village of Drumlish was a built-up stretch of shops and houses along a road that went to other places. People from beyond the parish of Drumlish did not usually come to my village. Rather, they passed through it on the way to the larger towns of Longford and Cavan. Like many rural villages, Drumlish became a destination once a week on market days when men and small animals poured in from the countryside in their carts. This was particularly true once a month on fair days, when the village became a crowded, bustling, smelly throng of farmers and jobbers with sticks, cattle and horses with swinging tails warding off flies, a noisy assortment of small animals confined to carts but determined to be heard, vendors, stunt men and three-card trick men.

The village at the back of the fort would not have made the better maps of Ireland; it certainly would not have existed, as I knew it, without the sustaining support of fair and market days. I was not aware of it then, but the weekly markets, and particularly the monthly fairs, were the backbone of my village's existence. They supported the village's four large hardware and grocery shops that sold lumber, farm equipment, hardware, groceries, whiskey and Guinness in barrels and half-barrels to go, as well as for consumption on the premises.

The hardware shops made their own blend of loose teas from large 150-pound plywood chests of Assam black tea imported from the foothills of the Himalayan Blue Mountains in India, and Ceylon tea imported from the tea gardens of what is now the island of Sri Lanka. These shops were hives of activity on fair days. Most sales of animals were finalized at their bars over a pint of Guinness porter. And sellers of animals did not go home empty-handed. They filled their carts with goods for people and animals on the farm. And if a farmer had a particularly good day, he might spring for an extra piece of farm equipment, or some lumber to fix up or add to some of the farmhouses.

The lumberyard of McQuade's shop had many storage sheds, and there I often played hide and seek with my friends. At times we squirted at one another with quart-ize bottles of soda water, the ones with the short snouts used to add soda water to the whiskey and sodas. We shook the bottles and squirted the contents in a stream of fizz and soda water some twenty feet. We had great fun at the shop's expense. But most shop employees looked the other way or joined in the fun.

The weekly markets and monthly fairs also supported three additional pubs. One of them was owned by Maggie O'Connell, whose pub was two houses up the street from our house. Customers at Maggie's could get a quiet drink on fair and market days, away from the hustle and bustle of animals and people. Some customers and villagers were known to get a quiet pint from Maggie after hours and by special arrangement. Pat Kane, the father of Annie Catherine Kane and a retired postman, who lived in the thatched cottage between our house and O'Connell's pub, had that kind of special arrangement. Pat liked a quiet pint. Though he lived next door to the pub, he could not go there without somebody knowing about it and word getting back to his wife, who was very much opposed to Pat having a quiet pint now and then. There was a six-foot wall separating Kane's and O'Connell's back yards, which we could see from our bedroom window. From time to time a pint of Guinness would appear atop the wall. Within minutes, a pair of hands from both sides of a head with Pat's crumpled hat on it would reach up and seize the pint. This would seem to have been a fairly regular occurrence, and went unhindered and, I presume, undetected for many a day by Mrs. Kane. Some would say many a year. Unfortunately, technology in youthful hands found a way to interfere with a gentle, retired postman having a quiet pint. There is no such thing as a perfect arrangement in an imperfect world. The black pint with its white frothy cap on the six-foot wall was too tempting a target. My younger brother, Colm, used a pellet gun to knock the glass off the wall on more than one occasion, and lived to boast about it.

Although O'Connell's pub was but two doors up the street from us, it was the one shop in the village that I had not seen the inside of. A partition inside the front door blocked the view to the inside from the street, and since the pub only sold Guinness and whiskey for on-the-premises consumption, I never had any reason to go inside. The elderly couple who owned it had no children, so I could not very well go in to ask somebody to come out to play. I often tried to kick a ball into the shop so I would have an excuse to go inside, but with no success. The ball invariably bounced off the partition and back onto the street. Mrs. O' Connell would come to the door in a black bib that touched the ground to see what was going on. But by then, I was away down the street kicking the ball against the walls of other houses, as if to show that the ball hitting her partition was an accident. I am sure she had her misgivings, yet she never complained to my parents.

The market days and fair days also supported the three smaller grocery shops, including Ned Cleary's where we got our groceries. Market and fair days supported Charlie Kiernan's and John Brown's drapery shops; Dick Reilly's bicycle shop, where we got new chains for our bicycles, as chains were always breaking down when we stood on the pedals going up hills; John Kane's shoe and boot shop, where my family got our boots and shoes; John McGowan's paint shop; and of course Bessie Dooris' and Annie Catherine Kane's sweets and ice cream shops.

But without the weekly markets and the monthly fairs, the village could scarcely exist. On market days, local farmers, their unbuttoned topcoats waving in the breeze, sold chickens, ducks, geese, turkeys, and a scattering of pigs and calves. They had a few drinks in the pubs and took a few items home from the shops for their families.

On fair days, cattle, horses, and pigs of all sizes and ages crowded into the village's one wide street and one short cross-street. Carts, parked wheel to wheel on either side of the street, offered pigs, big and small, calves, and a variety of chickens, ducks, geese and turkeys, particularly coming up to Christmas. Cattle, too big to fit in carts and horses and their owners bunched in groups on the middle of the street, and made passage a slow, time-consuming process. Jobbers or buyers, also in unbuttoned topcoats, moved among the cattle and horses, looking into the mouths of the horses to tell their age and slapping the cattle on their rumps with hand or stick to test their reaction.

Each jobber and owner carried a stick, some quite distinctive. Most of them were made from the blackthorn or sloe shrub. These sticks were as much symbols of the roles of their owners, as they were implements useful in controlling the animals.

Fair days had much larger crowds. In addition to more animals, farmers and jobbers, fair days also attracted an assortment of vendors, entertainers and hucksters. Vendors had stalls displaying kitchen-ware, clothes and sundries. These stalls did a brisk business among farmers who had sold their livestock.

For us kids, the entertainers were the big attraction. There was a strong man, who balanced a cartwheel on his chin. To demonstrate his control, with the heavy wheel on his chin and his arms spread wide, he strolled around the circle that the people made for him by jumping out of his way. Most men could not lift the cartwheel off the ground, never mind hoisting it up on their chins and balancing it there until the crowd got tired of looking at the feat. For his next stunt, he lay on the road, placed a large flagstone on his bare chest, and invited onlookers to attempt to break the stone with a large sledgehammer. There were plenty of eager takers, but nobody was able to break the stone.

But the strong man's best stunt was to break a bunch of Guinness stout bottles on the sidewalk, take off his coat and shirt, lie on the broken glass with his bare skin, and invite some of the heaviest men in the crowd to stand on his bare chest. Many were glad to oblige, and I could hear the glass being crunched under their weight. He then got up and proudly showed his back with pieces of Guinness bottles embedded in the skin, but the skin was not broken and there was no blood. Was his skin made of leather? Even the adults had their mouths open in awe. After each stunt, he passed his hat around the crowd for contributions. After the Guinness broken bottle stunt, he seemed to get the largest contribution, for his hat was bent out of shape with the weight of the coins, mostly large copper pennies.

There were the three-card trick men, who plied their game on a small folding table that could be placed quickly in the middle of a crowd, and just as quickly taken away should there be a policeman sighted in the area. These men did not have a good reputation. The police regarded them as swindlers and were constantly on the watch for them. But they knew how to play the crowd and pander to its gambling instincts. The three-card game or trick looked simple enough, almost too simple. A man at a little folding table showed onlookers three cards, one of them a Queen. He then put them face down on the table. He moved them around and asked for anyone to bet that he could find the Queen. The bet was even money. To get the men milling about really interested, a shill blustered his way through the crowd with not a little commotion, slapped a crumpled pound note on the table and confidently announced, "Begorrah, I can find the Queen."

The crowd was suddenly quiet. Everybody was straining to get a good look at the cards as they were shuffled from left to right, to center to right, to center to left. Was the eye as quick as the hand was slight? The man who shuffled waited for the wagerer of the pound to decide where the Queen was. Onlookers gave conflicting advice.

"Its in the middle;"

"Its the card on the right."

An elderly man leaned toward the wagerer and whispered, "The Queen is the card on the left."

The wagerer scratched his head, reached for the card in the middle, changed his mind and turned up the card on the left. Sure enough it was the Queen. The man at the table put a crisp new pound note on top of the wagerer's crumpled pound. It was that simple. Others reached into their pockets to finger their possible wager.

The man at the table urged the crowd on: "If you don't speculate, you won't accumulate. Come in your barefeet, go home in a motorcar. This could be your big opportunity. Please stand back, do stand back, and let the gentleman see the table."

Several men, thinking that they were the "gentleman" being addressed, moved closer to the table. The man at the table assured them, "Everybody, everybody will have an opportunity to win, but only one can bet at a time. Who wants to be the next lucky man?"

Several moved forward, including the man who had just won the pound. The man at the table told the man who had won to give others a chance, that the day was young, and that he would have other opportunities later.

A young man in his late twenties or early thirties stepped forward, fingering a few pounds. The crowd encouraged him to bet it all. "Sean, *a Mac*, go for the motorcar," urged a voice from the edge of the crowd. "Go for it Sean, speculate!" encouraged another.

After some hesitation, he put two pounds on the table. The man shuffled the cards, showing the Queen to Sean and to the crowd a couple of times in the process. A blind man could almost pick the Queen. Everybody was sure where it was. Sean was also sure. Without hesitation his hand went straight to the card on the right. "That's the one, Sean. That's it. I saw it with my two eyes," roared two of his buddies almost in unison.

The card on the right was everybody's choice. Sean turned the card over.

There was a loud collective intake of breadth. It was the seven of spades.

The man at the table leisurely turned over the card in the middle. It was the Queen of spades.

How could it have gotten there? Everybody saw it, or more correctly, thought they saw it move to the right on the final shuffle. Sean wanted to bet another pound, no doubt his last pound. But the man at the table urged him to let others have a chance first, which Sean did reluctantly. Others tried their luck, and all but one lost. It was hard to tell if the second man who won was also in cahoots with the man at the table.

The crowd was becoming somewhat annoyed at the inability of wagerers to win.

"It is just too one-sided to be fair," shouted someone over the grumbling.

He seemed to sum up the general sentiments. Somebody mentioned the police. Within seconds, the man and his table disappeared. The crowd remained for a while debating if it was a game of chance or skill, but there was no clear resolution of the issue. Nor was it clear who mentioned the police. No policeman showed up. Was the police sighting also part of the act to enable the three-card trick man get away from a crowd that could easily become hostile? It seemed that way.

But I will never know for sure. I tried the three-card game later at home with my buddies in the neighborhood. With some practice, even my amateur skills could fool them most of the time, which convinced me that the hand is quicker than the eye. If only the neighborhood kids had real money instead of buttons! It was indeed a game of skill, but the game was stacked heavily in favor of the one shuffling the cards.

As the day wore on, the animals became more resigned to standing in one place with tails swishing rhythmically to ward off persistent flies. Farmyard smells became more potent, and the floors of the pubs became a funky mixture of sawdust and manure carried in from the street on boots heavy with dirt. And farmers came down on their asking prices, not wanting to run the risk of having to walk home their weary and hungry animals.

On these fair days, youngsters like myself made a few pennies minding the animals while owners dropped into the nearest pub to close a sale or simply to take the edge off their thirst. Or, as my grandmother would say, to "wet their whistles."

It took most of a week to clean up after fair days, with each shopkeeper cleaning the street in front of his shop and helping out in areas where responsibility was ill-defined.

chapter 5

favorite village hangouts

How often have I paused on every charm,
The sheltered cot, the cultivated farm,
The never-failing brook, the busy mill,
The decent church that topped the neighboring hill.

—Oliver Goldsmith (1728-1774)
Irish Playwright, Novelist and Poet
Born in County Longford

If the graveyards, fairy forts, and the dark spaces of night were the places in the village of Drumlish that scared me, there were many other places that attracted me. Roger's mill, the busy village mill, was one of my favorite hangouts. It was one of the oldest structures in the village, built in the early 1840s prior to the great famine. It crushed the oats that gave the people and my family our daily oatmeal porridge, or stirabout. The mill was at the other end of town at the bottom of a hill, a long half-mile from our house. A large wooden water wheel on the outside wall of the mill turned the machinery that crushed the oat grain. The mill had a dam from which a constant stream of water was channeled through a specially constructed mill run with sluice gates to turn on the water that operated the big wooden wheel.

The mill served the village of Drumlish and the surrounding countryside for over a hundred years from the 1840s to the 1950s when the big mill wheel stopped as farmers turned to more modern methods of processing their oats crop. When I watched it work in the 1940s, the mill was busiest in the months after the grain crops were harvested. From October through February, the mill yard was full with horse-drawn carts bringing sacks of oats to be crushed and other carts taking home sacks of oat-meal ready to be turned into stirabout. We were very proud of the mill. It operated even during the dreadful potato famine years of 1845 to 1848, when its output diminished the local suffering and death caused by the potato crop failure. People remembered its contribution and strongly supported its restoration in 1995. It is the only mill of its kind still standing in County Longford.

For me, the mill dam was always a good spot to catch trout. I often went fishing at the dam on Saturdays with my brother Eamonn, or with Vincent Reilly whose dad owned a pub in the village and whose garden bordered ours. We dug worms from our gardens to use as bait and put them in a jam jar with a little dirt to keep them from crawling out. Our best worms were large dark-red crawlers dug from the edges of the dunghill. The trout usually went crazy over them. We used corks from Reilly's pub on our fishing lines, which bobbed in the water when the fish were biting. All bottled Guinness stout and ale then had corks, which were as plentiful as bottle caps are today. A quick jerk of the rod and line at the right moment, when the cork bobbed, would hook the trout, and then it was a simple matter to haul them in.

The Village Mill, recently restored, that crushed the oats that gave us our daily stirabout. (Photograph taken by the author in the summer of 2000.)

We fried the trout on the pan as soon as we got home and the largest trout was always set aside for Dad, who loved fish. Whenever we could get some, fish was a Friday dish. It was then a mortal sin to knowingly eat meat on

Fridays. And mortal sin was the most dreadful thing that could happen to a young soul, or to any soul. With no refrigeration, trout caught at the dam could not wait for Fridays. None of the shops sold fish. On Friday mornings Frank Ellis usually had a box of salty kippers on the street corner up from the water pump, until he sold out. Mom always tried to get some for Dad, but she was not always successful. Frank only had one small boxful resting on a small stool and it was first come first served. And his schedule was not always predictable. When there were only a few kippers left in the box, Frank traded places with the box to rest his frame. He looked like an old woman resting by the roadside, with his topcoat draped all around him in a heap as he waited for the last kippers to be sold.

When the fish were not biting at the mill dam, we stopped into the mill for a visit with the workmen, who were drying or crushing oats. The room next to the kiln, where they dried oats before crushing them, was warm and cozy. The men gathered there to sit on the bags of grain, with the owners' initials painted on them with tar, and chatted and smoked. The kiln was fired by turf brought by the farmers whose oats were being dried. On cold days men came by just to get warm. It was a neighborhood meeting place for men and boys.

We almost always met some other boys from the village, including Jim and Micky Rodgers, whose parents owned the mill, the Mulleadys, the Blacks, the McWades, the O'Reillys and the Davises. In late summer, we challenged one another to a game of chestnuts. I carefully picked the best chestnuts, as they fell from the chestnut trees, down the street from us at McKeon's. I seasoned and hardened the chestnuts on the hearth before the open fire, being careful not to get them too hot or too dried out, for then they would crack and lose their value as a potential conqueror. Each of us had our prized "conqueror" chestnut on a string. In a test of skill and chestnut endurance, I tried to hit the other guy's conqueror with my champion conqueror. The chestnut that survived the contest was the new conqueror. Someone would challenge the victor with his prized, carefully selected and husbanded chestnut. When there were no more challengers, the surviving chestnut was declared the conqueror for that day. It was sweet victory to linger over the scattered, broken remains of fallen chestnuts, some of which had experienced their own gloating moments of conquest and victory.

When chestnuts were out of season, we pitched and tossed buttons as substitutes for pennies. I had a jarful of buttons hidden in the turf-shed. I added to or subtracted from my stash as needed. When buttons were missing from family clothes, Mom often wanted to look through my collection. I usually succeeded in avoiding a parental search for missing buttons by offering a couple of similar, but not identical buttons, which demonstrated a willingness to cooperate while heading off suspicions that I had taken the buttons. The buttons were stand-ins for money and we used them not only to pitch and toss but also to buy and trade among one another items such as pencil sharpeners, whistles, and erasers.

Another of my favorite hangouts was Gunshinan's forge. It was one of the few places in the village that had something going on at all times and that welcomed onlookers, even kids. Located in the middle of town adjacent to the church, it was another gathering place for men and boys. I dallied there mostly on Saturdays on my way home from weekly confession. The blacksmith, Bernie Gunshinan, was a big-hearted little man, who suffered kids in his forge as long as we knew enough not to get in harm's way or impede his work. He even allowed us to pump the bellows to fan his coal fire, as long as we did it only at his bidding and in support of his blacksmithing. Bernie made iron shoes for horses, asses, and cart wheels. He also made iron gates, but only when he had no animals or cart wheels to shoe.

Bernie, clad in his leather apron that looked like it was as old as the village, greeted me with his usual Saturday question:

"What is the Canon handing out today?"

"Three Our Fathers," was my honest reply.

"Ah, he went light on you. Did he hear everything you tould (told) him?"

"I believe so," I assured him.

"He is becoming a little hard of hearing, I think, and a pushover in his ould (old) age. You youngsters should have to confess to the curate. I hear he is handing out rosaries for ordinary everyday garden type sins," Bernie asserted with a wry smile.

I avoided the curate whenever I could, because more than likely he would recognize my voice, and there was the risk of holding back something when I felt that the priest knew who I was. I also wanted to avoid having to say a whole rosary for stealing a few gooseberries. If rosaries were being dished out for stealing gooseberries, I wondered what the going penance was for a mortal sin. None of my friends seemed to know, and I was too embarrassed to ask Bernie. He might think that I had committed one and was trying to find out what the consequences would be.

I squelched my curiosity and, instead of pursuing my fascination with the dreaded mortal sin, simply said, "I would rather take my chances with the

Canon," quietly hoping that the matter would end there. Bernie seemed to sense my uneasiness, smiled, and addressed a few soft-spoken words to the horse he was preparing to shoe.

On Saturdays, there were always a couple of horses and once in a while an ass waiting their turn to be shod. The process of making a set of shoes for a horse or ass was always fun to watch. Bernie started with a straight bar of iron. He stuck one end of it in the fire and pumped the bellows that fanned the coal fire to a white-hot glow. This was when he allowed us small folk to pump the bellows, as it freed him to prepare the horse's hooves for the new shoes. With his back to the horse, he took the horse's hoof between his legs. With the hoof placed firmly against his leather apron, he first stripped the hoof of its old shoe. He then pared the hoof with a special hoof knife of any loose or broken pieces of hoof that might make for an uneven fit with the new shoe.

By this time, the end of the bar of iron that was in the fire was red-hot. He put the red-hot end on his anvil and with a couple of precise blows with a special tool, he cut off the makings of a horseshoe. He stuck the piece back in the fire, took it out when it again became red-hot and placed it on the curved pointed end of the anvil, and beat it with a hammer into a U shape. He kept alternately heating it and hammering it, with sparks flying every which way in a mini-fireworks display, until it looked like a horseshoe. He then took the horse's hoof between his legs for a trial fit with the red-hot shoe. The sizzle, smoke, and smell of burning hoof was not very pleasant, but Bernie saw what was needed to be done to assure a good fit. He then put the shoe back in the fire, and when it was red-hot again, he hammered it into its final shape. He again shoved it in the fire, pumped the bellows a few times, retrieved the shoe, put it on his anvil and made six nail holes in the hot iron, three on either side of the U-shaped shoe. He then plunged the hot shoe into a trough of water, where it hissed a couple of seconds and gave off a puff of steam. It was now ready to go on the horse's hoof.

Bernie again took the horse's hoof between his legs and with six specially shaped silver-looking, rust-proof nails nailed the iron shoe to the hoof. With his hammer, he flattened the tips of the nails that protruded through. He then used a large rasp to file the hoof so that it was even with the horseshoe and looked like the neat tight fit that it was.

It always amazed me that horses and asses were usually calm and unconcerned throughout the entire process, even through the nailing of the shoes on their hooves. The making of four shoes took about an hour and a half. My visits usually lasted at least that long.

The forge had a very relaxed atmosphere. Bernie worked methodically as he chatted with the owner of the horse or ass, or others who dropped in to get a coal for their tobacco pipes, to light a cigarette, or simply to chew the fat awhile. The forge's garage-like sliding doors opened onto the street. Almost every male, young and old, who passed by, stopped in for a bit. It was just the neighborly thing to do.

The village had two dance halls, Batty Gray's and McWade's, that doubled as places for plays and movies. My parents forbade us to go to dances because dances were regarded as adult entertainment. We had to wait until we were eighteen, which seemed like forever. The most that I did was occasionally sneak a peek in the door or listen to the band from my open bedroom window and dream what it was like to waltz around the dance floor with a girl, to have her sit on my knees between dances and chat, as I saw the men do when I peeked in the door.

Most of the movies were cowboy movies and cost fourpence, or the cost of two half-inch ice creams. We had movies once a month or so. Stage plays were less frequent, but usually took place at night when it was past my bedtime. Once in a while, when the actors in the plays were locals, there was a children's matinee on Saturday. Most of the fun was knowing the people who were on stage pretending they were somebody else.

But I preferred the movies, for at plays we had to be quiet. At the movies, we could holler and shout at the characters and nobody seemed to mind. For both movies and plays, we sat on long wooden benches, and jostled one another to get to sit in the first two rows. That way we did not have to look over or around others.

All of us kids did our share of hanging out at the two village sweet and ice cream shops. Proprietors Bessie Dooris and Annie Catherine Kane competed for our pennies. I did my share of comparison-shopping before I spent the much-fingered, warm, large coppers that were wearing a hole in my pant's pocket. A good deal was two pieces of paper-wrapped sweets for a copper (penny) and a half-inch thick slice of ice cream between two wafers for tuppence (two pennies). I took my business to the shop that had the thickest half-inch, which varied with the mood of Bessie and Annie Catherine, moods that were frustratingly unpredictable. The size of the ice cream we received not only depended on mood, but also on where they were located in the cutting of the block of ice cream. The beginning often produced a more generous slice; at the middle tended to be a more conservative cut; or at the end could mean getting all that was left in the block, when what was left was too little for two slices. Because of this unpredictability, I often waited outside the shops until Bessie and Annie Catherine left from behind the counter, hoping to get a better deal from Bessie's husband, Paddy, or from one of Annie Catherine's brothers, Stephen or Jimmy. The wait paid off about fifty per cent of the time, and since I had all kinds of time and very little money, the waiting, or "hanging tough" with my pennies, was worth it.

A forbidden pastime was the game of pitch and toss at the crossroads with the grown men on Sunday evenings—something much frowned upon by my parents. Whenever I could sneak out of the house, I pitched my saved pennies at a small stone, called a spud, on a sandy section of the crossroads. The owner of the nearest penny to the stone got to toss all the pennies in pairs while others bet on them coming down heads or tails. The tosser got to keep all the heads and the tails went to the owner of the second nearest penny to the spud. This person also tossed the pennies in the air in pairs while others bet on the outcome. This continued, with the tossing of the tails going to the owner of the next nearest penny to the spud, until all the pennies came down heads. Then the process was repeated with another pitch of pennies to the spud. I did not have the money to bet (except when I got altar-boy tips from the priests from England and America when they were home on vacation), but I often had the pennies to try my luck at pitching. Sometimes I was lucky and got near enough to the spud to toss some pennies and came home with twenty or so pennies ahead. But mostly I sneaked back into the house penniless, wondering if I had sprinkled a few drops of holy water on my pennies, would I have had better luck?

chapter 6

a gaelic football match

...in dreams begins responsibility

—Edna O'Brien (1932-)
Irish Novelist and Pacifist

Ireland boasts of four team sports that are considered part of the nation's Gaelic heritage and culture: football, hurling, camogie (a game similar to hurling played by women) and handball. These games are sponsored and controlled by the Gaelic Athletic Association (known locally as the GAA), an amateur sports organization founded in 1884 to preserve and cultivate the national games. The Association has grown into a powerful national movement with nearly a million members in a total population of four and one-half million and has played, and continues to play, a major social and cultural role in Irish life.

While the Association is credited with organizing, standardizing and vitalizing the national games, giving birth in the process to over 2,800 sports clubs across the country, it has been criticized for being too nationalistic in forbidding its members to play or attend non-Gaelic games, such as soccer, cricket and rugby. But this ban on so-called "foreign" games did not affect us much in rural areas, such as Drumlish, where the only games played on an organized basis were the national games.

Gaelic football is Ireland's most popular sport. Soccer is second in popularity, and hurling is third. The first records of Gaelic football are contained in the Statutes of the City of Galway on the island's west coast dating back to 1527. But it was in the 1880s that the game was standardized and modern rules were established by the Gaelic Athletic Association. (The game of soccer was standardized in England some 20 years earlier in the 1860s.) Gaelic football is played only in Ireland and by Irish emigrants in large metropolitan areas such as New York, Boston, San Francisco, Los Angeles, Chicago, London, Manchester and Melbourne. The All Ireland Championship Final of Gaelic Football is televised by CNN for a worldwide audience each year in September.

In Gaelic football, a team consists of 15 players: a goalkeeper, three full-backs and three half-backs, two midfielders, three half-forwards and three full-forwards. Their positions on the field of play are as follows:

	Goalkeeper	
Right Full-back	Full-back	Left Full-back
Right Half-back	Center Half-back	Left Half-back
Midfielder		Midfielder
Right Half-forward	Center Half-forward	Left Half-forward
Right Full-forward	Center Full-forward	Left Full-forward

The ball used is made of pigskin and is a sphere like a soccer ball but smaller, about 4/5 the radius. The playing field, or pitch, is 140 to 160 yards long and 84 to 100 yards wide with goalposts at either end. The goalposts are shaped like the capital letter "H." A goal (three points) is scored when a player puts the ball between the uprights and under the crossbar. A point is scored when a player puts the ball between the posts and over the crossbar.

Gaelic football is often described as a combination of soccer and rugby, though it predates both games. Players may catch the ball with their hands as in rugby or American football, but can only carry the ball four steps without committing a foul. To avoid committing a foul, players, after taking four steps with the ball, must then bounce the ball, play it from hand to foot as they run with it, pass it to a teammate, or kick it toward the opposing team's goal. Players may not pick the ball up off the ground—they must tip it into their hands with a foot. Players may jostle or shoulder one another off the ball, but may not push an opponent in the back.

A Gaelic football game currently consists of two 35-minute periods (when I was growing up a period lasted 30 minutes) with no time-outs or stoppages, except for major injuries. The game is officiated by a referee (the only official with a whistle), two linesmen and four umpires, two at each goal. In all matters, the decision of the referee is final.

In our family of six boys, football was an addiction. We regularly got into trouble for over-indulgence that neglected schoolwork and chores, such as walking Dad's greyhounds or planting and weeding our vegetable garden.

Pigskin footballs were often hard to come by, so we often had to make do with balls made of rags or blown-up pig bladders. We got pig bladders from our grandmother's farm. But they did not last too long, even though in summer we banned the use of boots or shoes whenever the ball was the bladder of a pig. Years later, I discovered that we had something in common with Pacific Islanders who played a form of soccer also using pig bladders for footballs.

Incessant practice and dreams of someday representing our parish and our county on the football field paid off. My oldest brother, Eamonn, became a star half-back of Longford County and Leinster Provincial all-star teams. Four other brothers, Frank, Niall, Colm, and I, also played for Longford County. Frank, Niall, and I had the honor of captaining football teams for St. Mel's College where we attended secondary school. And my five brothers, Eamonn, Frank, Niall, Colm, and Seamus, constituted one-third of the Drumlish Parish team in the Longford County championship in the summer of 1966.

Though I played football at the inter-county and inter-high school levels competing with teams from around the country, it is the games at the local level between competing parishes that present the most vivid memories. And these memories are of games when I was not yet old enough to be a player and had to be content with being a partisan spectator dreaming of some day representing my home parish. I can recall as if it were last week the excitement provided by a game between my home parish of Drumlish and the neighboring parish of Mullinaghta in the second round of the league championship. The year was 1943. I was ten years old, and World War II was in full swing.

Because of the war and stringent gasoline rationing, all private cars, vans, and trucks were mothballed (only priests and doctors got coupons for gasoline). Everybody, including players and officials, came to the game on bicycles, sometimes two and three to a bicycle. Players could be easily spotted with a pair of football boots strung over their shoulders as they pedaled through town with kids like myself providing them an entourage.

The game was at three p.m. on a Sunday afternoon. This schedule permitted players and spectators to bicycle up to twenty-five miles after 11 a.m. Mass. The playing field was a pasture at the edge of the village provided by the McKeon family and a mere ten-minute walk from our house. I left the house at two p.m. with a tanner (sixpence) in my pocket, which I had saved from money I had received from my grandmother, and I joined the one-way flow of traffic to the game. I left early so that I could be with the home team as they togged-out (put on their playing outfits) and got ready for the game.

Admission to the playing field down a narrow tree-covered lane was a tanner for adults and thrupence (threepence) for school children. Pre-school children with parents or adults were free. I paid my thrupence and held firmly on to the other thrupence which I would use to buy something from Frank Ellis' stall that had an assortment of sweets, chocolate bars, apples, and lemonade, as well as badges with the colors of the two teams. Frank's stall was an essential part of local sports events, particularly for us kids. While Frank staffed the ass cart that easily converted into a stall, his son, Gandy, who was about my age, plied the sidelines with a basketful of goodies shouting, "Colors and chocolate." I envied Gandy's easy access to so many sweets.

The playing field was regulation size with two goalposts and nothing else by way of amenities. The rest of the week it was a cow pasture and was dotted with unfriendly cow patties. Patches of long grasses had been cut the previous day, which gave the field the sweet smell of new-mown hay. Drumlish club officials had marked the sidelines, the penalty box, the 21-yard line at each goal and centerfield with whitewash, which would last for the day, unless a heavy shower intervened. Since there was no seating, spectators came early to get the best standing positions along the sidelines. Spectators and players stacked their bicycles along the hedges and ditches leading to the pitch, beating down the lush growth of weeds and tall grasses. They took with them their bicycle pumps lest they be stolen, and some took them for use as offensive or defensive tools in the event of a fight. Bicycles were very seldom stolen, as they could not be easily hidden in a small town, where everybody knew what everybody else possessed.

Players togged-out in the ditches or behind bushes. Drumlish players used the bushes on the right side of the field, and Mullinaghta players used the bushes on the opposite side. Each player had to provide for himself football boots and white shorts or togs. The clubs provided the jerseys and knee-length socks in the club colors. Fifteen players and two substitutes togged-out for each side. The substitutes were used only as replacements for seriously injured players.

The Drumlish Brass and Reed Band tuned up behind the goalposts with a bunch of small kids beating on the big drum. The drummer hoisted the drum on his chest, which was the signal for the band to line up to lead the players around the field prior to the start of the match.

In a corner of the field, the referee, surrounded by his support staff, togged-out in a white jersey and socks to distinguish him from the players. His staff did not change clothes. The only indication of their official capacity was a small flag that each carried. The two linesmen had white flags, which they raised to indicate to the referee that the ball had gone out of bounds. The umpires had red and white flags. They raised the red flag to indicate that a goal was scored and raised the white flag when a point was scored. They crossed the two flags to indicate that an apparent score was disallowed.

These signals were important to everybody, as there was no public address system to communicate scoring or decisions made in relation to scoring. At five minutes to three, the referee with the game ball in hand went to the center of the pitch and blew his whistle. This was a warning whistle to the two teams that the game was about to begin. Our team gathered around the club president for a few final words of advice. He reminded his players of the strengths of the other side and what they had to do to neutralize or overcome these strengths. He emphasized that each player represented his parish and that the whole parish was relying on him to give his best effort for the entire match, not just for forty or fifty minutes, but until the final whistle blew. He wished them luck. Players let out a cheer and lined up single file behind the band, together with the opposing team, for the parade around the field. The band led them to the center of the field where the referee was waiting.

All thirty players lined up at midfield. The band went to the sideline. The referee asked that the team captains identify themselves. He tossed a coin and while it was in the air the captains called heads or tails. Mullinaghta won the toss and decided to defend the goals on the west side of the field and play with the wind for the first period. The referee counted the players. He then cautioned them, saying that he would not tolerate any unsportsmanlike conduct, and that he would enforce the rules strictly. He motioned for the goalies and backs to take up their positions. Then with his back to the midfielders and forwards, he blew the whistle and threw in the ball. The game was underway.

Since this was a senior league game, there was no age limit for players, and parishes fielded their best possible teams. Sometimes, when clubs had the money, they brought players home from England for the game. But that kind of expenditure was usually reserved for the county final. This was but the second round of a six-round competition. In this match, each side fielded a combination of youth and experience. Our most experienced player and the captain of our team was Jim Hannify, a county player, who some said was past his prime. But he was still able to give opposing teams headaches in the position of midfielder or as full forward. Now in his late thirties, he was slower to get to the ball, but when he got the ball in his hands, he could score. Our side's strategy was simple—give the ball to Hannify. The Mullinaghta side was very much aware of Hannify's threat, so he would be closely marked (guarded).

Drumlish players got the ball from the throw-in, took it down the field, passed it to Hannify around the 21-yard line, who tapped it (kicked it with a light touch) over the crossbar for the first point of the game, which got the home crowd cheering. Within a couple of minutes Mullinaghta responded with a point, then another, and another. Mullinaghta dominated play. It looked like Drumlish could do nothing right. Drumlish players were beaten to the ball almost every time, so that the ball seemed to be stuck in the Drumlish defense end of the field. Hannify switched with one of his players and moved to centerfield. But he was outrun every time by the younger players; so the Mullinaghta possession of the ball continued, scoring a goal and two more points amid several misses. It seemed like Mullinaghta players, Reilly and the Rogers trio, were everywhere the ball was. The ball seemed to follow them. It looked bleak for the home team. The crowd was dumfounded into silence.

Toward the end of the first period, our boys took the ball to the Mullinaghta goal and Mick Sorohan had only the goalie to beat. As he was about to take a shot at goal, he was tripped. The whistle blew. It was a penalty kick for Drumlish. The referee placed the ball right smack in front of the goals on the 14-yard line. With a penalty, only the goalie could defend. Jim Hannify was selected to be the kicker.

Necks strained along the sideline to see the action. The referee moved all other players behind the ball. Hannify bent down and checked his right football boot. He was right-footed. The referee blew the whistle. Hannify moved slowly but deliberately to the ball, looked at the left corner of the goals, and shot the ball into the right corner. The goalie did not even smell it. A huge cheer went up from the Drumlish spectators. Their caps and bicycle pumps flew into the air.

The score was now one goal and one point, or four points, for Drumlish to Mullinaghta's one goal and five points, or eight points. It was a match again with the crowd urging on its players. Mullinaghta quickly took the ball to the Drumlish goals, but their shot at goal went inches wide. The Drumlish fans gave a coordinated sigh of relief. From the kickout, Drumlish got the ball and were pressing toward the Mullianaghta goal. The whistle blew.

Players and spectators wondered what the foul might be. But there was none. The referee called for the ball. It was the end of the first half. Some Drumlish spectators shouted at the referee to get a real watch. But others said he was doing a fair job and should be left alone.

Players went to their respective sidelines and huddled with their mentors for the 15-minute break. The band, surrounded by a great host of kids, struck up some old favorite tunes at the back of the goals. I wormed my way into the inner circle of Drumlish players and club officials. Despite the score, there was a general air of optimism. Everybody and his mother was doling out advice: "Stay closer to your man," "You got to anticipate where the ball is going," "You got to get loose from your man," "Pass the ball to Hannify," "Move Hannify back to full forward, where he can do the most damage."

The club president asked for quiet. He told his players that they were lucky to be trailing only by four points, that the Mullinaghta players were beating them to the ball almost every time, and that if they continued in this mode there was no way on God's earth they could win. He told them that they must hustle and get to the ball a step ahead of their opponents. He confirmed that Jim Hannify would return to the full forward position and pleaded with the other forwards to get the ball to him. He told them that they could win, that they had but a half hour to make amends for the poor showing of the first half that, luckily, was not fully reflected in the score. He then had a couple of private words with Captain Jim Hannify. He also had a few whispered words with right half-back, Paddy Brady, whose man beat him to the ball every time in the first half.

I overheard one of the other players explain to a teammate that Paddy had to take "a dive"—meaning that at the first opportunity where he was involved with the ball, he had to go down and feign injury so as to be replaced by one of the substitutes. This was contrary to the rules and the spirit of the game, where all starting players must finish the game unless incapacitated by serious injury. It was also generally known that when club officials disagreed on the selection of a player, they often agreed to replace him with a substitute if he was playing poorly. We would have to wait and see if this was the situation in Paddy's case and if the whisperings were being interpreted correctly.

The referee blew his whistle for the start of the second half. The goalies and backs went to their field positions. The forwards and midfielders lined up at centerfield. The referee threw in the ball and the second period was underway. Mullinaghta got the ball and moved it down the left side of the field, passed it to their full forward, who kicked it over the crossbar for a five-point lead.

At the kickout, the ball went down the right side. Paddy Brady beat his man to the ball for the first time and sent a long kick across the field right into Hannify's hands, who took a quick shot at goal. But the goalie punched it wide for a 50-yard free kick for Drumlish. The kicker dropped a high ball into the square in front of the goals. The ball bounced off the up-stretched hands of defenders and forwards, and into the waiting arms of Joe MacNally. He turned his back to the goal and the players bunched in front of him, and kicked it over his head for a point. Four points again separated the sides.

The full-back kicked the ball out the right side of the field. Paddy Brady and his man bounced off each other as they tried to get to the ball. Neither of them succeeded and the ball went out of bounds. But Paddy was on the ground wriggling in pain, whether feigned or real it was hard to tell. He did not get up. A couple of Drumlish club officials ran to his aid. After a cursory look that was a little too fast, they beckoned for a substitute to come on and informed the referee of their decision. Paddy limped off the field assisted by the club officials. The play resumed with a Drumlish sideline kick.

The ball went back and forth up and down the field several times without a score or even the ball going out of play. Finally, a Drumlish forward kicked a point attempt that seemed to go wide but was flagged a point. The referee checked with the umpires, and there was agreement that it was a point as no crossed flags went up. There were about fifteen minutes left to play and Mullinaghta still led by four points.

Drumlish backs Tom Murphy and Barnie Dillon seemed to come alive. Now the ball seemed to seek them out. Time after time, they broke up Mullinaghta attacks on the Drumlish goals and sent the ball back down the other end of the field to their forwards. They responded with five unanswered points, three by Jim Hannify and two by Mick Sorahan to tie the match with five minutes left on the clock. With the kickout Drumlish got the ball again and got it to Hannify. He sidestepped the full back and had only the goalie to beat. From about twelve yards out he shot the ball directly at the goalie, who stopped it, but it bounced off his hands over the crossbar for a point. Another sigh from the crowd as they were holding their collective breath anticipating a goal. But Drumlish now had the lead by the slim margin of one point. Drumlish supporters were going wild.

Mullinaghta reshuffled some of their players in the hope of getting something going. The reshuffle seemed to confuse the Drumlish players, for Mullinaghta marched down the field and looked threatening, but their right full forward was fouled on the 21-yard line. That would be an easy free kick over the crossbar to tie the game again. But the Mullinaghta kicker had other intentions. He gave the ball a short low kick to his full forward, who got the ball and passed it to the kicker, who rammed it by everybody for a goal. A great moan went up from the crowd. This seemed like curtains. Mullinaghta gambled. They passed up a sure point and went for the winning goal. They were now up two points with less than two minutes to play.

With the referee looking at his watch, Hannify ran out for a word with his midfielders. Whatever he said, one of them got the ball from the kickout and kicked it to the right side of the field where Mick Sorahan was all alone waiting for it. He ran with it hand to foot towards the goal and passed it to Hannify, who managed to cut free from the fullback and was about to take a shot at goal when he was pulled down from behind. The ref's whistle signaled a foul. The ref had a short conference with the umpires to determine if the foul was committed within the penalty area. Every Drumlish spectator hollered "a penalty." A roar of approval went up as the ref signaled for all players to move back behind the ball, which he placed on the 14-yard line.

There was no doubt who was going to take the penalty kick. Hannify stepped into position. A hush descended upon the crowd as it seemed to stop breathing. This could be the last kick of the game. Could Hannify repeat what he did at the end of the first half? His experience kept him composed. The ref blew the whistle. Hannify kicked a bullet but right at the goalie. The ball bounced off him and Hannify, who had kept running at goal, blasted the ball past the goalie on the second try. The Drumlish crowd went wild and flowed onto the playing field.

The ref had to ask his linesmen and umpires to clear the field, as there was a minute left to play. It took them five minutes to do so. When the game resumed, Mullinaghta in a desperate effort took possession of the ball and expertly passed it through the Drumlish backs as if they were statues. A forward took a shot at goal but Barnie Dillon blocked the kick. A Mullinaghta forward got it again on the rebound and took a shot at a point that would tie the game. It was impossible to tell from where I stood whether or not it had gone between the uprights and over the crossbar. After consultation with his partner, the umpire signaled wide to a great cheer of approval from the crowd. With the kickout, the ref blew the long whistle that ended the game. The final score was Drumlish two goals and seven points for a total of thirteen points, Mullinaghta two goals and six points for a total of twelve points.

Drumlish players carried Hannify off the field, giving him some protection from the mauling hands of jubilant supporters. Celebrations continued until a heavy shower sent everybody scurrying for shelter. Frank Ellis pulled an oilcloth over his cart and crawled under it. Many of us just got drenched. But the joys of victory crowded out any feelings of discomfort. And anyway, for me, home was only ten minutes out the lane and up the road a-piece.

On my way out the lane, I put my hand in my wet pocket and felt my thrupence. In my total absorption in the game, I had forgotten to spend it.

chapter 7

the war years—world war ii

Said the king to the colonel,
"Thy complaints are eternal,
That you Irish give more trouble
Than any other corps."
Said the colonel to the king,
"This complaint is no new thing,
Sire, your enemies have made it
A hundred times before."

> —Sir Arthur Conan Doyle (1859-1930)
> Creator of Sherlock Holmes, in Tribute to
> the World War I Fighting Record of Irish
> Troops in the British Army.

We had barely settled into Kiernan's house in Drumlish when Germany invaded Poland on September 1, 1939. I was six and one-half years old. We felt the start of the war within weeks. Imported foods and clothing vanished from the shops as stringent rationing was introduced for many food items, clothing, and petrol. Private motoring ceased. I was just getting used to seeing a few cars on the roads, when motor vehicles were mothballed and horse drawn vehicles got an extension of their lives. Bicycles became the most common way of getting from place to place. McGirr's bus, which ran daily, except Sundays, between Arva and Longford passing through Drumlish, was now the only motorized vehicle to take people to Longford town. It was usually standing room only, and on Saturdays people hung out the doors.

Dad mothballed our Baby Ford in the garage, where it became a playhouse for us. He replaced it with a pony and trap, which took us to school much more slowly. Unlike the Baby Ford, Dick, the pony, had to be caught in the open field and harnessed each morning and afternoon. It was an adjustment for all of us, but especially for Mom, who had to get us all ready for school. And then, for over an hour had to coax and sweet talk Dick to get us to the school on time. Each day was a new coaxing challenge.

Tea, butter, sugar, flour, bread and clothes were severely rationed. The ration books had separate pages for each item, which had to be presented to the shopkeeper in order to buy the items. In large families like ours, the kids got equal rations with adults, so we had a surplus of tea and sugar. We shared this surplus with our grandmother and our aunts. We seldom had to go without rationed foods. The exception was white flour, which was impossible to get. Dad liked white bread, so Mom put the regular wartime brown flour through a sieve of cheese-cloth to get white flour. This was a slow, tedious process, whitening everything in close proximity. The resultant white bread was hidden from us kids and reserved for Dad alone. He appreciated every slice. I envied him, perhaps for the extra attention he got, for I had no particular yearning for white bread.

Mrs. Anna Payton of Drumlish and daughter in their pony and trap, similar to the way we traveled to school during the war years. (Photograph courtesy of Co. Longford Historical Society.)

With our Baby Ford in storage, there were no Saturday trips by Mom to Longford town, and there were no special treats of bananas and oranges. Within weeks of the outbreak of the war, the government, under emergency decrees, froze all incomes and required farmers to cultivate all available land and to produce as much turf as possible. Turf replaced coal to heat homes, empower industry and keep the trains running. Close to ninety-eight per cent of Ireland's coal came from England, where all of the coal was now needed to support the war effort. The other two per cent came from a few small deposits of anthracite coal in the counties of Leitrim, Kilkenny, and Tipperary, but the quality was poor.

Merchant shipping was also seriously curtailed due to the increasing number of merchant ships being sunk by German U-Boats. About ninety-five per cent of all imports to Ireland were carried by non-Irish vessels with British ships carrying over sixty per cent of the shipping tonnage. Only five per cent of Ireland's shipping tonnage was Irish owned. Traditionally ninety per cent of Irish exports went to England. As the war progressed, with the closure of European markets to England, there was an increasing demand for Irish beef, pork, fowl, and farm produce at very favorable prices, which had a very positive effect on small towns and villages like Drumlish. With most motorized vehicles mothballed, farmers had little option but to take their livestock and produce to the local fairs and markets where jobbers supplying the British market were quick to buy.

After the war and the return of motorized vehicles, Drumlish and similar villages across Ireland experienced a steady decline of their fair and market days. In the 1950s the fair and market days disappeared altogether from most towns and villages.

In the fall of 1939, by government decree, all road signs were taken down, ostensibly to make it more difficult for invading forces to find their way around the country. Large concrete obstacles were built on the roads leading into all major towns to slow down the movement of tanks. Drumlish did not fall under the category of a major town and hence had no concrete obstacles. But I saw them on the Battery Road leading into Longford town. These obstacles consisted of large concrete structures placed on the street in a zig-zag fashion with steel shafts like railroad tracks protruding from them. All vehicles, except bicycles, had to slow to a crawl to get through them.

As a family, we did our part to cope with the shortages brought on by the war. Dad made sure that we used every inch of the garden to grow vegetables. We cultivated vegetables even under the apple trees. We got a cow so that we could have our own milk. We cut and harvested our own turf. Dad rented a small plot of land outside the village where we planted extra potatoes.

I listened each evening to the war news on Radio Eireann and on the BBC. Though the news was censored by both the British and Irish Governments, each broadcast had details of battles in the air, on land, and at sea that riveted me to the wireless (radio). Of particular interest to my dad and to me were the broadcasts of Lord Haw Haw, a renegade Englishman, who broadcast Nazi propaganda to his countrymen from Bremer, Germany. Lord Haw Haw was the nickname given to William Joyce by his British listeners because he put on an aristocratic accent in delivering his pro-Nazi propaganda. William Joyce was born in Brooklyn, New York, to an English mother and an Irish-American father. The family moved to England in 1921. William was trained by the Jesuits in Galway. In 1939 he went to Germany, where he became one of Propaganda Minister Joseph Goebell's radio stars broadcasting from Germany on the New British Broadcasting (NBBC) station. After the war, he was put on trial for treason in the Central Criminal Court, better known as London's Old Bailey, and was found guilty. He was hanged on January 3, 1946.

Though I did not believe much of what Lord Haw-Haw said, his propaganda appealed to the anti-British feelings that were part of my upbringing. In primary school, my Irish history classes were a long litany of British injustices to and oppressions of my ancestors. Dad regarded Churchill as someone who could not be trusted and who would re-impose British oppressive rule on Ireland if he got half an excuse.

At the beginning of the war, I was ambivalent about a British victory, though over 50,000 of my countrymen were fighting Hitler in the British Royal army, navy, and air force, and legions of Irish workers crossed the Irish Sea and poured into English munitions factories. Irish labor and Irish soldiers made a considerable contribution to the British war effort. I certainly did not want Hitler to win, but I had feelings of satisfaction in hearing our old enemy, Britain, get trounced. When America entered the war, I was for a United States victory, and acquiesced in a British victory as a necessary, lesser evil.

In 1939 and 1940, we heard frequent rumors and were fearful of a German invasion of Ireland. We were also fearful of Britain retaking the south, or at least retaking Ireland's southern ports. These ports had been returned to Ireland in 1938 by the then British Prime Minister, Neville Chamberlain, in keeping with his Munich policy of appeasement. Irish playwright George Bernard

Shaw argued in the British press that Ireland's southern ports belonged to Europe, to the world, and indeed to civilization, and should be borrowed by the Allies for the duration of the war. Dad said that he was full of nonsense.

After the United States entered the war in December, 1941, we were fearful of an invasion by United States troops. But despite persistent pressures from many quarters for Ireland to join the Allies, including pressure from the British, United States, and Canadian Governments, the Irish Government, under the leadership of the Taoiseach (Gaelic for Prime Minister) Eamonn de Valera, maintained an uneasy but steadfast neutrality, vowing to fight to the death any invaders be they German, British, or United States forces.

Dad said that that kind of talk was pure rhetoric, for at the outbreak of the war in 1939, Ireland's armed forces totaled a paltry 7,600. During the course of the war from 1939 to 1945, Ireland's defense forces swelled to 250,000 and became a highly efficient army, that in post-war years, has served with distinction as part of the United Nation's peace keeping efforts in Cyprus, Israel, and the Congo.

After the United States entered the war, de Valera, who was born in New York but grew up in Bruree, County Limerick, repeated Ireland's policy of neutrality saying that, "We can only be a friendly neutral." When 240,000 American GIs landed in Northern Ireland in 1942, de Valera's Government quietly worked out secret arrangements for cooperation with the Allies should Germany invade Ireland. But those arrangements only came to light after the war's end.

De Valera, or Dev as we affectionately called him, was our hero. He eloquently stood up to Winston Churchill's repeated threats to take over the Irish southern ports. Typical of the war of words between the two leaders was their exchange a few days following the end of the war.

In the course of his victory speech of May 13, 1945, Churchill said:

> "Owing to the action of Mr. de Valera, so much at variance with the temper and instinct of thousands of Southern Irishmen who hastened to the battle-front to prove their ancient valor, the approaches which the southern Irish ports and airfields could so easily have guarded were closed by the hostile aircraft and the U-boats.... However, with a restraint and poise to which, I say, history will find few parallels, His Majesty's Government never laid a violent hand upon them, though at times it would have been quite easy and quite natural, and we left the de Valera Government to frolic with the Germans and later with the

Japanese to their heart's content." (As quoted by Tim Pat Coogan in his book *Eamonn De Valera: The Man Who Was Ireland*, pages 610-611.)

Excitement grew as Dev deliberately waited four days to respond. Pubs filled to capacity and neighbors gathered in each other's homes to listen to Dev's radio response. I had my ear glued to our radio. After a lengthy review of the war years, Dev replied directly to Churchill:

"Mr. Churchill makes it clear that in certain circumstances he would have violated our neutrality and that he would justify his action by Britain's necessity. It seems strange to me that Mr. Churchill does not see that this, if accepted, would mean that Britain's necessity would become a moral code and that when this necessity became sufficiently great, other people's rights were not to count...this same code is precisely why we have the disastrous succession of wars.... By resisting his temptation in this instance, Mr. Churchill, instead of adding another horrid chapter to the already bloodstained record of the relations between England and this country, has advanced the cause of international morality an important step... Mr. Churchill is proud of Britain's stand alone, after France had fallen and before America entered the war. Could he not find in his heart the generosity to acknowledge that there is a small nation that has stood alone, not for one year or two, but for several hundred years against aggression, that endured spoliations, famines, massacres in endless succession, that was clubbed many times into insensibility, but that each time on returning consciousness took up the fight anew, a small nation that could never be got to accept defeat and has never surrendered her soul?" (Ibid, page 611.)

My listening heart swelled with pride. Sir John Maffey, the British Representative to Ireland remarked:

"Mr. de Valera assumed the role of the elder statesman and skillfully worked on all the old passions in order to dramatize the stand taken by Eire in this war." (Ibid, page 612.)

At the time, reflecting the general sentiment of my dad and my elders, I was intensely proud of de Valera's defiant stance of neutrality. I was unaware of the long-term and even short-term consequences of this policy of neutrality.

In later years, I became aware that while neutrality, in the short-term, saved the country from being a target of German bombing raids, it isolated Ireland from the mainstream of European and world economic and cultural events. Long-term, neutrality hindered Ireland from becoming integrated into the world of nations. And it was not until 1955, ten years after the end of the war, despite strenuous efforts on its part, that Ireland was welcomed as a member of the United Nations. Short-term, by refusing to join the war on the British side, de Valera avoided an outbreak of hostilities and a possible civil war with a very militant Irish Republican Army (IRA), who were vehemently opposed to such a move, as were the vast majority of the Irish people. Long-term, by pursuing a policy of neutrality, Ireland declared to a skeptical world in a very forceful way that it was an independent sovereign nation, despite the fact that it was almost totally dependent on Britain for manufactured goods to conduct the business of its daily existence.

Since independence in 1922 to the outbreak of World War II, Ireland had done nothing about fostering a shipping industry or about establishing a central bank to handle foreign currency. It relied on Britain to provide these essential services. During the war years, Ireland was forced to acquire and refurbish a motly fleet of some fifteen ships to get grain and vital supplies to its people, and to establish the Central Bank of Ireland to conduct the nation's finances.

The war years in many respects forced Ireland to set out on the road to become economically and financially independent and to stand on its own two feet. I found myself in agreement with the sentiments of an anonymous poem of the 19th century:

> Too long our Irish hearts we schooled,
> In patient hope to bide;
> By dreams of English justice fooled,
> And English tongues that lied.
> That hour of weak delusion's past,
> The empty dream has flown;
> Our hope and strength we find at last
> Is in ourselves alone.

Dad would concur totally.

chapter 8

a day on the bog

The sounds of Ireland,
that restless whispering
you never get away
from, seeping out of
low bushes and grass,
heatherbells and fern,
wrinkling bog pools....

—John Montague (1929-)
Irish Poet

Ireland is one of the boggiest places on planet Earth. Bogs are as plentiful in Ireland as lakes are in Minnesota. Peat of some kind underlies nearly a quarter of the island's surface area. On our daily four and one-half mile trek to school from the village of Drumlish to the townland of Gaigue we passed through the middle of two bogs and skirted another two. In the countryside, bogs are never very far away. Bogs are so much a part of life that it is said "you can take a man out of the bog, but you cannot take the bog out of the man." I proudly wear the badge of being a bog man, but it has taken much time and great distance to cultivate and acknowledge that pride.

The bog is a place of vast silence, save for the whispering of bog breezes, turf drying, midges flying, whirligigs skiing across bog pools and dragonflies, with wing spans as wide as a human hand, hovering guard over stagnant ponds. The bog had a few very distinctive sounds that occasionally shattered, and accentuated the whispering. There are three sounds that I can still hear when I close my eyes and transport myself back in time and space: the mournful wail of the curlew; the shrill ear-piercing cry of the snipe when disturbed; and the joyful caroling of the skylark uttered from a tiny fluttering form high up in the sky, a sight and sound that inspired the English poet, Shelley, to write in 1820, words that we had to memorize in primary school:

> Hail to thee, blithe Spirit!
> Bird thou never wert,
> That from heaven or near it,
> Pourest thy full heart
> In profuse strains of unpremeditated art.

Apart from these unique sounds, the bog was a wilderness of whispering, a quiet zone. But this did not mean that the bog was devoid of life. Besides the birds and the insects alluded to, the bog was home to the hare, red grouse, the meadow pipit, bees gathering gourmet heather honey, whirligigs which skimmed across the open water of bog-holes as if on patrol, frogs that kept mum in the daylight hours, butterflies, moths, beetles and a host of insects that fed on plant nectar and on each other among the bog mosses, heathers, bog rosemary, bog cotton and bog grasses. The vast carpet of purple heather, extending to the horizon, treeless and bushless, had nothing upon which the eye could focus except the dark gashes in its side, whence last year's crop of turf had been extracted.

Bog accumulates and grows at about one centimeter annually in shallow, waterlogged, oxygen poor basins where, because of poor activity of microscopic organisms, plant production exceeds the rate of plant decomposition. Composed of eighty per cent water and twenty per cent plant fibers, the bog is made up of a surface layer of living vegetation resting on layer upon layer of partially decomposed and compressed vegetation accumulated over thousands of years. The top layer, consisting of a thick carpet of bog mosses with heathers, cotton, sedges and grasses protruding through it, floats on a bed of up to nine or ten feet deep of soggy plant material.

This soggy, floating mass is a living archive, preserving in its many layers of plants, seeds and pollen much information for our understanding of the development of peoples, cultures, economies and climates. The bog is like a giant sponge that receives, stores and preserves information about the past.

Bogs have yielded some of Ireland's most spectacular archaeological finds, including tools, weapons, items of worship, ornaments of gold, stone and wood, animal traps, boats, well-preserved human remains and blocks of butter. The bog was the closest equivalent to a refrigerator. The cold antiseptic peat offered to my ancestors a way to preserve things. Somebody explained all that to me at one time, but that was more than I ever wanted to know at that time about bogs.

When I was growing up, my only interest and the only interest of my family in the bog, was not as an archive of history, but as a source of fuel and heat to cook our food year around and to keep us warm in the winter. With bog being eighty per cent water and given Ireland's damp climate, it was a real challenge to harvest and produce from the bog dry, quality fuel.

For centuries the bog was and continues to be a vital fuel resource. There is evidence that the bog provided fuel in pre–Christian times. Pliny's Natural History describes the cutting and harvesting of turf in the first century A.D. by Celtic peoples in northern Europe. In medieval times in Ireland, turf was burned in monasteries, manors and in the huts of the people. As wood became scarce with major forest clearances in the sixteenth and seventeenth centuries, turf became widely used as a domestic fuel. Absent trees, coal, gas, oil and electricity, the bog provided the only fuel to cook and the only source of heat for the bleak winter days and long winter nights of my youth. During World War II, bogs were called upon to provide for the entire fuel needs of the country, replacing over 2,000,000 tons of British coal annually. Turf was used for industrial as well as domestic needs. Turf fueled homes, steam engines, factories, power stations and trains.

Turf was a critical crop that had to be harvested each summer of my youth in the 1940s and 1950s. Each family farm owned a section of the nearest bog. Since our family did not own a farm, Dad rented a section of bog from a family that did. And harvesting a year's supply of turf was a principal summer task for the older boys of our family.

Three of my brothers—Eamonn, Frank, and Niall—and I arrived in the bog on our two bicycles (two to a bicycle) around 9:00 a.m., packing a few tools and the makings of our mid-day meal. We had dropped off two flatbed wheelbarrows a few days earlier and had hidden them in a bog hole.

Our section of bog was like most of the other bog sections, about forty feet in width and stretched to the base of a hill about one third of a mile away. The bog had a high bank and a low bank separated by a bog hole—an area of water three or four feet deep. Think of the high bank as a giant sponge or a giant pound cake forty feet in width and extending back for one third of a mile. Each summer we cut a slice of this pound cake about six feet from front to back, forty feet in width and about nine feet deep. That rectangular slice of pound cake or high bank (2,160 cubic feet) provided our family with sufficient fuel to cook and to heat the house for a year. The low bank was the ground where the bog had been harvested in previous years. The bog hole of water in between the high and low banks was the hole that remained after last year's section of bog was harvested. Our task was to harvest another 2,000 cubic feet or thereabouts, and do so while keeping the water, which was on all sides, at bay.

To minimize the water problem, we decided to first harvest half the width of the high bank, or twenty feet instead of forty feet. Once we got down below the waterline in our cutting operation, we had to complete the task during that day. Otherwise, water would undoubtedly seep in overnight and prevent further cutting in that hole. The deeper we went, the older and more compressed was the peat, which made the hardest and best burning fuel. So our goal was to go as deep in the bog as possible, to even reach sand or rock bottom, which we never achieved. Usually at about eight or nine feet, we came upon trunks or limbs of trees, which opened up cracks through which the water gushed in and ended further cutting in that hole.

Having decided upon a plan of action, our first task was to dig off the top heathery scraw, and most of the white turf, to get to the brown turf and the black turf underneath. We dumped the top three feet or so into the hole left from the previous year, thus filling it up and adding another six feet to the low bank. The first three feet of high bank was too young and too little compressed to make good turf. It would dry light as a feather and burn much too quickly; so we discarded it into the hole to continue the process of compression to make good turf some hundreds of years in the future.

With the high bank cleared of the top three feet of bog, we set about cutting turf. We used a long-handled tool, called a *sleaghan* (pronounced "slawn") in Gaelic, to cut the wet peat into rectangles of about 5" x 10" x 4". The *sleaghan* was a tool with a long wooden handle and an iron head consisting of a flat blade with a wing on one side. With a single movement of the *sleaghan* we cut the peat on two sides and slid it off the end of the tool throwing it to Frank or Niall on the low bank, who caught it and placed it on the wheelbarrow. When they had a load of forty-to-fifty of these wet rectangles of peat, they pushed the wheelbarrow out to the end of the low bank, dumped the load in a heap, and returned for another load. Each depth of the *sleaghan* we called a floor.

Eamonn, my older brother, and I took turns cutting floors of turf and strategizing on the best course of action to contain the water, and get as deep as possible for the blackest and best turf. We also took turns relieving our younger brothers, Frank and Niall, giving them a rest, for wheeling the wet turf to the farthest end of the low bank was muscle building, fatiguing work. By mid-day we were close to the waterline and hungry. Once below the waterline we could not afford to stop, for the water was a constant threat. It was a good time to break to eat.

With three feet of scraw taken off the top, Jack McHugh and Patsy Fallon, using a *sleaghan* and flat wheelbarrow, are cutting the first floor of turf in Mosstown bog, Co. Longford. (Photo: courtesy of the Co. Longford Historical Society.)

We built a fire of old dried pieces of turf, boiled bog water for tea in one saucepan and boiled two eggs each in another saucepan. When the water boiled in the tea saucepan, we added a small handful of loose tea, let it draw a few minutes, and then added sugar and milk. Thank goodness, we all liked our eggs however they came out. On the bog we could not be fussy about our eggs. We gulped them down together with buttered slices of our mother's homemade soda bread, and washed all down with mugs of strong, hot tea. The bog water made the tea stronger than normal with a distinct peat flavor. Food on the bog always tasted better than it did at home. The bog air and the hard work stimulated our appetites.

Mealtime was a time for relaxation and fun. We threw wet lumps of peat at egg shells set up as targets, and when we tired of that, we threw them at one another. We looked for nests of curlews and snipe, and we searched amongst the dense growths of heather for bilberries, a small blue berry that grew on low-lying scrubs, and were ripe for picking in July. The bilberries served as a desert. And we visited with neighbors working their sections of bog to see how they were doing and how they were coping with the water problems.

With the realization that we had to cut all the turf that we could from this hole before we could quit for the day, we set about the more delicate task of cutting turf below the waterline. We tried to drain off as much water as we could surrounding the hole that we were about to make and kept a close watch for tree limbs or cracks, which we would have to circumvent. As we went lower, the cutting became more difficult and slower. We now had to throw the cut turf up to the boys on the bank. The deeper we went, the peat became more compressed, heavier, and more brittle, which demanded more skill in cutting and delivering regular shaped turf to the person with the wheelbarrow. Irregular shaped turf or smaller pieces were simply more difficult to handle and harvest.

As we got closer to nine feet deep, one of us cut and the other baled out water with a saucepan. It was a race against the water and its allies, the hoards of midges that came out to eat as the sun went down. As the day became evening, midges, tiny flying insects smaller than the head of a pin with wing spans of less than two mm, took special delight in biting hard-working, sweating people, particularly in bogs. Like their relatives, the mosquitoes, it is the female midges that bite. Although only four of the thirty species of Irish midges bother people, it did not seem so to us. Swarms of blood-thirsty hungry females came at us in small dense clouds. Like the hordes of northern European tribes that attacked the Roman Empire in the fifth Century, the midges' strength was in their numbers. The attacks of these largely unseen, silent tormentors became almost intolerable.

As the boghole got deeper, each new floor of peat uncovered major water problems. And with the midges biting furiously, I often wished for the water to come rushing in. I was tempted to put a nick in the side of the hole to put a quick end to our misery. But the bottom turf was worth every effort. They dried hard and black as coal and burned almost as good. We refused to be run off by armies of blood-sucking midges. We used every strategy known to us and put up with the scourge of the midges so as to harvest every piece of black turf before the water forced us to abandon the hole. Towards the end, standing in water knee-deep and flailing the air to keep the midges at bay, we cut turf out of the sides of the hole, salvaging every last sod. The abandoned hole quickly filled with water, and would remain that way with midges and dragonflies hovering above it until the next cutting the following year.

At day's end, we were pleased with our achievement. And when Dad came by to inspect our work, he could see by the amount of turf that lay in small wet heaps on the low bank that he had already got his money's worth out of the rented section of bog. The next day we would repeat the same approach for the second twenty feet of high bank.

The other steps in the harvesting process: spreading the heaps of wet turf once they had a skin on them so they could be moved apart without breaking them into smaller pieces; footing the turf or placing two or three upright with one to two sods on top to accelerate the drying process; clamping the turf or making little ricks waist high from three or four wheelbarrow loads to enable the wind to blow through them and dry them more thoroughly; and finally, carting the turf home to the turf-shed. All these activities would be left for other days on the bog.

Tired but contented with our work, we peddled the few miles home on bicycles not built for two. But we were not too tired to join other boys from the village in a game of football in progress in Kiernan's meadow at the foot of our garden until darkness fell.

Mom was annoyed that we put off eating the supper that she was solicitously keeping warm for us on the hearth alongside the dwindling fire. But she knew that we had earned a little diversion, and her disposition softened when the food quickly disappeared into hungry mouths.

chapter 9

Boy-girl Relationships

There is nothing half so sweet in life
as love's young dreams.

—Thomas Moore (1779-1852)
Irish Poet

I stole my first kiss, a playful peck on the cheek, at the age of twelve, and my first real kiss on the mouth was stolen from me at age fourteen. But before we get to the details of these milestones in my relationship with girls, I need to tell you that in my village, boys and girls did not have the opportunity to experience a relationship with the opposite sex until after secondary school. Irish society imposed a celibate life on its youth and was quite successful, at least within the limits of my experience in my village and my county. So what do I have to relate? Not much really, except some small happenings and awakenings at the fringes of what might have been, at another time and place, a relationship.

In the 1930s and 1940s, I attended the amalgamated Gaigue elementary school and sat side-by-side with girls from infants through the eighth grade. Interaction with girls was limited to the classroom, as girls and boys had separate playgrounds. We played soccer and the girls played hop-scotch and tag. As an extracurricular activity, I danced set dances with girls in the Irish dancing classes, which took place in my mother's classroom after school once a week. There was keen competition between girls and boys for recognition from the dancing instructor, and at the local parish and county *Feis* where we competed against one another for medals.

At one such *Feis*, I got third prize medal for the double jig, beating my classmate, Imelda O'Conner, whom many regarded as a much better dancer. Some of the other girls teased me saying that I got the medal just because I was a boy, a clear case of discrimination to favor the disadvantaged. In their minds, the judges gave me the medal to encourage more boys to take up Irish dancing. I did not buy that. I asked Imelda what she thought. She graciously said that she did not give her best performance that day, and that I won the medal fairly. We continued to be friends. Because of my daily interaction with girls in school and at home (I had three younger sisters), I took the pre-puberty boy-girl relationship in stride with no memorable bumps along the way.

In the seventh and eighth grades, I had a growing awareness of male-female differences. I began to look at girls not only as classmates but how they dressed, how they carried themselves, how they interacted with others, and in particular, how they treated me. I admired the McEntee sisters: Alice (deceased), Sheila, Rosaline, and Philomena. One was in the class ahead of me, one was in my class, and two were in classes behind me. All four seemed to me to be special. They were always dressed attractively and were friendly without being forward. They were the kind of girls I could admire without thinking bad thoughts. They had a civilizing effect on the rest of us. I like to think that they also had a civilizing effect on The Master. I never saw him mistreat them as he did most of us.

The McEntee girls were from the village of Ballinamuck, where their parents owned a drapery shop, the only store in the village besides the pub. It was one of the joys of going to church in Ballinamuck with my grandmother and uncle Michael to see the graceful forms of the McEntee girls in their Sunday finery and matching hats march into church single file with their mother in the lead and their dad bringing up the rear. The front door of the church was placed at the side, so that those entering had to parade before the entire congregation to get to their pew. All heads turned to watch the mini-procession. As my grandmother said, "It was a cure for sore eyes." I wanted to shout, "Hello, Sheila; Hello, Alice," but thought better not to, and whispered instead to my grandmother, "Sheila, the second girl, is in my class in school." To which my grandmother replied, "*Whist a mhac*," which demanded my unequivocal silence. I wonder what she would have said had I shouted out their names.

When I came to the U.S. in 1957 and saw the Lennon sisters on the Lawrence Welk Show, I was instantly reminded of the McEntee girls—form and grace in motion.

When I was in the seventh grade, I had a crush on a girl in the class ahead of me. She lived next door to the McEntee family in Ballinamuck. Maire

91

Reilly was more even-tempered, more physically developed, and to my eyes, prettier than the other girls in my school. I sat two rows of seats behind her and she was always in my line of vision. She wore glasses and always spoke softly. She lit up my day with her smile. But I kept any feelings I had a closely guarded secret from her and even from myself. It was only when I learned a couple of years later of her marriage to an older man that I realized there was a little jealously in my heart. I still think of her as my first crush.

Now back to those milestones. My first kiss was part of a kissing frenzy that broke out one evening when the seventh and eight graders from my village had gathered at 7:00 p.m. for a Gaelic language session with Drumlish school teachers, Paddy Felle and Kit Halpin. When the teachers did not show after a forty-five minute wait, there was a spontaneous outbreak of boys and girls trading kisses on the school playground that lasted for a half-hour or so before we went home. I expected teachers and parents to conduct an inquiry, but days and weeks passed and nothing happened. I presume that since all present partook of the forbidden fruit, no one squealed, and since we were home at the regular time, no questions were asked.

I must have given and received kisses from twenty different girls, some of them more than once. I tried to steal a kiss from a girl whom my older brother Eamonn was kissing. He gave me a look that could kill. I quickly moved on and sought out girls who were not in the act of kissing. Eighth grade boys like my brother were having prolonged kisses with the same girl, while I flitted like a butterfly from girl to girl kissing them lightly on the lips and on the cheek, and quickly moving on to the next target. I was more interested in quantity and wanted to kiss every girl there, while the older boys seemed to be more interested in quality—prolonged quality.

I was twelve years of age, and like the other seventh and eighth graders, enjoyed the outbreak. What triggered it I do not know. Like myself, I presume that over ninety-five per cent of the girls and boys had never kissed the opposite sex, other than family, before that evening. When left un-chaperoned, somebody let loose the kissing bug and we all got infected. That was the most excitement I had along those lines for many years to come.

In the days that followed, I thought often about what happened. I wondered how those prolonged kisses felt and had I missed out on something. But I kept my wondering to myself. I did not feel that I could share it with anybody. I never discussed what happened that evening with any of my friends—not even with my brother Eamonn. This is the first time I have talked about it, and I feel like I am violating a long-kept secret. I never kissed any of those girls again. I never had the opportunity.

My first memorable kiss was stolen from me by a second cousin while I was churning in the dairy at my grandmother's. I was fourteen and had completed my first year of secondary school. It was a firm kiss, right on the mouth, and caught me by surprise. It was different from the innocent kisses in the school playground two years previously. It was as different as sunlight is from candlelight. I had matured a little and my cousin was a couple of years older. I was unsure what it meant and did not know how to react. I was confused. I wanted to grab her and return the favor. But I knew that would be wrong. I was afraid what it might lead to. One part of me said do it. Other parts said keep on churning or the butter will spoil. Her warm, wet lips tasted tantalizingly good and that was before Tic-Tacs. I continued churning and made very good butter.

But her kiss resonated within me. All that day I kept thinking what if I had returned her kiss? For several days I licked my lips and could still taste the kiss. It had staying power. It packed a wallop of something or other. Was that what was meant by passion? Unlike the playground kisses, I can still sense it.

When I was thirteen years of age, I went to boarding school exclusively for boys, where football became my consuming interest and girls were put on the back burner. We had no contact with girls during the school year. We even had little to no discussions about girls. Girls were simply not an important part of my secondary school years from thirteen to eighteen.

Once in a while there was a flurry of excitement when somebody goofed and we met the girls from the convent on a school walk through town. On such walks, the girls marched in pairs all dressed alike in their uniform skirts, blouses and jackets with their prefects at the head of the line and two nuns bringing up the rear. We also marched in pairs with our prefects at the top of the line and a priest at the end, but we did not have uniforms. Boys who knew some of the girls shouted out their names, and they hollered names back, much to the discomfort of the two nuns nervously fingering their rosaries who accompanied the girls, and the priest with us who tried to keep the two groups to separate sides of the street. But the excitement was fleeting, at least for me, for I did not know any of the girls. Any vicarious interest soon dissipated, succumbing to the all-absorbing topic of football.

Throughout secondary school, girls were simply not around. There were no dances or social events that brought secondary school boys and girls together. The schools did not sponsor any such events, nor did the church promote such gatherings. There would seem to have been a concerted effort to keep boys and girls separated, at least through the end of secondary school, which was the way it was for generations. Whether that was good or bad depends on one's perspective. My peers and I accepted what our society dictated as correct. We had no movies or magazines that presented another way. And what we did not know did not bother us.

In the summer before my last year of secondary school, my sister Eileen introduced me to a friend of hers, Ita McGee. Ita and Eileen attended the same convent school for girls in Ballymahon, a town in the southeast of Longford County. I met Ita at her brother-in-law's store near Ballinamuck. We chatted awkwardly and briefly outside the shop. But her eyes were saying more than her words, and there was a bounce to her step as she first walked, then skipped, and then ran the last few strides into the house that left my heart a-tingle. I wanted to see more of her, but there was no follow-through. There were no telephones available to us, and I never had any experience putting my feelings in writing. And with feelings such as these, I would not know where or how to begin. But the determining factor was that boy-girl relationships before eighteen were discouraged by society as a whole and were difficult, if not impossible, to pursue. Ita lived in another part of the county and our paths did not cross again.

Looking back, there was a dearth of boy-girl relationships in my growing up, even in my day-dreaming. Thinking of girls sexually was construed as having bad thoughts, and dwelling on them for any length of time, particularly enjoying the thoughts, could easily lead to the dreaded mortal sin that was always material for confession. When Ita McGee popped into my mind, as happened many times after our fleeting exchange of a few words outside her brother-in-law's shop, I had to pop her back out again as quickly as I could. For "girl thoughts" had to be suppressed as bad for the soul, and suppress them I did as best I knew how. The social pressure of going to Mass and Holy Communion regularly was more urgent than the attraction of girls, and kept such desires submerged.

My only real kiss to age eighteen, and the one with any umph to it, was the churning kiss when I was fourteen. And that one was stolen and should not count. Even if it does count, I had a one-kiss youth, which an American friend dubbed pitiful. To my statement at the beginning that Irish society imposed a celibate life on its youth, the same friend said that that was a sad understatement. No wonder Irish men and women married late in life, or became priests and nuns, or entered the cloister, or became lifelong bachelors and spinsters!

While the entire society, including parents, the church and school, discouraged boys and girls getting together before eighteen, the church did promote dances for people over eighteen. The church in Ballinamuck built and owned its own dance hall. Dances were held there on Sunday evenings twice a month from 7:30 p.m. to midnight.

Would my grandmother allow me to go to the church-sponsored Ballinamuck dances after I turned eighteen? Whatever about my grandmother, with seven younger brothers and sisters at home I knew my parents would have major objections.

part 2

farm

chapteR 10

my gRandmotheR's faRm

There was a place in childhood that I remember well,
And there a voice of sweetest tone bright fairy tales did tell.

—Samuel Lover (1797-1868)
Anglo-Irish Novelist,
Songwriter and Painter

"Gaigue Upper: Mrs. Mary Reynolds, 3 shillings; Mick McQuade, 2 shillings and sixpence; Michael Hurson, 2 shillings...." Father McCarthy's un-amplified voice filled every corner of the T-shaped Ballinamuck church. There was none of the usual coughing, clearing of throats, shuffling of feet on the stone floor, sniffing of noses with lingering colds, whimpering of children. The priest was announcing from the altar the quarterly offerings of each family of St. Patrick's Church. Mrs. Mary Reynolds was my grandmother, my mother's mother. She headed the list of the twelve families of the Townland of Gaigue Upper because she was responsible for collecting the townland's quarterly offerings to the church.

When Father McCarthy announced the offerings, there was an intensity of listening that quieted all who would interfere with his voice being channeled into wide-open, attentive ears. My grandmother stopped twiddling her thumbs and channeled the priest's voice directly to her memory bank, whence she recalled with complete accuracy what each household gave and whether it differed from the last time.

Families did not change their offerings lightly. Any increase or decrease signaled a significant change in family fortunes. In subsequent days and nights my grandmother, and no doubt many others like my grandmother, who kept close track of such things, made it their business to find out the reason or reasons for the change. Changes in offerings were rare occurrences. For

99

families, who might have good reason to increase or decrease their offerings, were reluctant to do so, for it would draw unwanted attention to their economic condition.

At the reading of the offerings, I too listened intently, particularly for Gaigue Upper, because I often collected the shillings from each of the other eleven families, braving the opposition of unwelcoming dogs. It was satisfying to me to hear the families' names and their contributions acknowledged, though I was somewhat disappointed that the priest did not acknowledge the efforts of those who collected the offerings.

The quarterly offerings publicly recognized from the altar every family as existing and contributing. It was a public accounting of each family's stewardship. And from what I know of one typical family from among the Ballinamuck families, I have no doubt that the vast majority were good stewards, not only in respect to the church, but in respect to their land, animals, and other possessions. They were quiet caretakers of the earth. My grandmother's and uncle Michael's sense of commitment to future generations on the farm was unheralded, but it was at the core of their every decision.

The special way of living and coping that I knew on my grandmother's farm in the 1940s has virtually disappeared from rural Ireland, but it should not be forgotten. It was a span of life and time rich in unhurried hard work, community cooperation and sharing, and in an abiding faith in God, in the devil, and at the edges beneath the surface, a quiet but firm belief in the magical and the Little People.

My grandmother, Granny to her grandchildren, was a widow when I lived with her in the 1940s. My grandfather died in 1913, twenty years before I was born, when his children were quite young. There were eleven children born to my maternal grandparents. Two children, Kate and Kathleen, died as the result of a deadly strain of influenza. Of the remaining nine children (five girls and four boys), two boys and one girl emigrated to the United States, one boy emigrated to England, and the other five remained in the home County of Longford. Michael, the only boy who stayed at home, worked and inherited the farm.

This dispersion of my grandmother's children was fairly typical of large Irish families. Emigration from Ireland started with the exodus of scholar-monks to monasteries and the courts of kings and dukes throughout Europe in the 7th through the 9th centuries, expanded with Cromwell's conquest of Ireland in the middle of the seventeenth century, accelerated with the great famine of 1845 to 1848, and continued to the economic boom of the 1990s.

In my parents family of nine children, three of us emigrated to the United States, three emigrated to England, and three stayed in Ireland.

Grandfather and Grandmother Reynolds with 7 of their 11 children: back row standing left to right, Francie, Bridgie and John (ordained a priest); front row, Annie, Michael, Maggie and May (my mother). Nellie and Sonny were not yet born. This photo was taken early in the first decade of the 20th century. (Photograph provided by Ann Reynolds, daughter of my uncle Michael.)

Granny raised her nine children on her forty-two-acre farm, located on the side of Gaigue Hill. Like all her neighbors, she was a subsistence farmer. She grew everything that people and animals on the farm needed to live. She raised cattle including six to eight milking cows, pigs, chickens, ducks and turkeys. Occasionally she raised geese and the more exotic birds, such as bantam and guinea hens. She grew potatoes, oats, occasionally wheat and barley, hay and an assortment of vegetables, including cabbages, turnips, carrots, parsnips, onions, lettuce, red beet and rhubarb.

Granny was very proud and very solicitous of her 40 x 20 foot flower garden in front of the house, where she cultivated chrysanthemums, irises, crocuses, fuchsia, dahlias, carnations, geraniums, hydrangeas, gladiolas, peonies, tulips, sweet peas and a wide variety of roses. She also had an assortment of herbs including several mints, French tarragon, lemon verbena and parsley. In one corner of the garden was a reading seat over which was a bamboo arch draped in climbing roses. The reading seat was meant principally for her son, Father John, when he came on his visits from the U.S. It was a quiet spot where he could read his daily prayers, the divine office. But I never saw Father John, or Granny, or anybody else sit there. When my grandmother was in the garden, she was taking care of her flowers.

One of my regular chores after school was to weed her flower garden. It always seemed to be in need of weeding. The flowers grew in abundance but so did the weeds. The garden had eight flowerbeds and small boxwood hedges bordered the paths that separated the beds. The boxwood hedges had to be clipped, the weeds pulled from the beds and from the paths, and all the weeds, hedge clippings, and grasses gathered into a wheelbarrow and dumped at the back of the dunghill. It took two evenings after school to do a good job. I had to be very careful not to pull up any flowers with the weeds. Granny knew where every flower was and I could not get away with being careless, even in a single instance.

The farm had a horse named Bob for heavy farm work such as ploughing and mowing, though these tasks were normally done by two horses with the other horse being borrowed from Philip Brady, a neighbor. And the farm had a pony named Dolly, with its chief task being the transportation of the family to and from Mass on Sundays, and to and from funeral removals from home and burials. These took place once or twice a month.

The farmhouse and farmyard that I knew was a happy home for people and animals. The people's two-story building had three bedrooms upstairs with the kitchen, sitting room, and dining room on the ground level. The people lived, cooked, and ate in the kitchen, with the sitting room and dining room used sparingly and for special occasions, such as stations, weddings, and parties for visiting Yankees. My uncle John, the priest from America, used the sitting room to say daily Mass when he came on vacation for six weeks to two months every four or five years after World War II was over. Granny always threw a party for her priest son, inviting her extended family and the neighbors to celebrate his homecoming with plenty of food, good music, singing and dancing that went to the wee hours of the morning. I tried to be at my grandmother's when Father John was home and sometimes succeeded, for there were always visitors coming and going and an abundance of fancy food that I seldom saw at other times, with plenty left over for kids. His homecoming was always much anticipated by the entire family, but his leave taking was heartbreaking, and my grandmother's was a sad, sad place for several days thereafter.

The farmhouse formed one side of a fifty-foot square farmyard with buildings on all four sides. Opposite the back door of the people's house was the byre with stalls for eight cows and a loft that sometimes held hay or straw, two cats, and bats. The pigsty was beneath the loft and to the right of the byre. The pigsty had an enclosed mini-yard with four small apartments opening on to it and a galvanized gate leading to the main farmyard. One apartment was for the mama pig, the sow. Piglets and pigs of various sizes occupied the others. When the apartments were not occupied by pigs, they were used to house baby calves and ducks.

The dunghill from which the farmyard cock crowed daily was at the back of the byre. On the left side of the yard, attached to the people's house, was the dairy. Next to the dairy was the stable with stalls for Bob and Dolly with the barn as a second story facing the haggard (an enclosed open-air area close to the farmhouse, where the sheaves of grain were stacked, awaiting the arrival of the thresher). The cart-shed was to the right of the stable. The turf-shed and a walled small flower garden formed the fourth side of the square farmyard on the right.

The hen house was outside the farmyard proper at the back of the cart-shed. And opposite the hen-house was the *sheugh* (a small pond), fed by a spring, that provided drinking water for the animals, a pond for the ducks and water to wash the potatoes. My uncle Michael built a cement trough near the sheugh to meet the daily need of washing potatoes before boiling them for human and animal consumption. A smaller sheugh, also fed by a spring, was located about twenty yards from the first sheugh, and since it had less traffic, it was a favorite hangout of the ducks.

The outhouse, a one-holer, was set apart as if the cluster of farmyard buildings did not want to be associated with it. It straddled a ditch about thirty yards beyond the second *sheugh*. The outhouse usually had a supply of pages from the *Longford Leader*, the weekly county newspaper, cut up in squares. If I desired a softer reading material, I had to bring my own, which was not easy to come by. When we ran out of pages of the *Longford Leader*, which happened often, we used dock-leaves, the soft-textured broad leaves of a plant that grew in abundance close by the outhouse.

This is my grandmother's farmhouse, photographed from the air in the 1960s. The extension at the back of the house was added and the turf-shed at the right of the house was also added to since I knew it in the 1940s. (Photograph provided by Ann Reynolds, daughter of my uncle Michael.)

The hay shed was at the front of the house beyond the flower garden to the right, and separated by the people's house from the farmyard and the animals.

The spring well, a source of sparkling cold water the year around, even on the hottest days, was to the left of the flower garden. The runoff from the well rapidly cooled and set my grandmother's jelly, a special after dinner treat. Shep, the dog, had his house in the hayshed—a hole in the wall of hay.

Granny's farmyard was the setting for many of my most vivid and cherished childhood memories—a compact arrangement of buildings no doubt designed to minimize human labor in catering to the needs of animals and people.

On my grandmother's farm the only items needed from the outside were clothes, shoes, lamp oil, the *Longford Leader* which cost thruppence, and an occasional roast beef or mutton, or a leg of lamb. Money for these items was generated by selling cattle, pigs, turkeys, chickens, eggs and butter. All the produce grown on the farm was consumed on the farm by the people and the animals. A small percentage was withheld to be sown or planted the following spring.

Since taking care of all the animals and the crops was more than my grandmother and uncle Michael could handle, my brothers, sisters, and I helped with the farm chores. It was convenient for us to drop up to my grandmother's, when school let out at 3:00 in the afternoon, where plenty of work as well as a change of pace awaited us. All of us kids got our turn working on the farm. When we went, we usually went to work, so it was usually the older boys who went there on a regular basis. But all of us, girls and boys, got our turn under the demanding, yet caring, eye of our mother's mother.

Granny was a major influence in my young life and in the young lives of my brothers and sisters. She stood five feet four inches tall, about the same size as my mother, but much heavier. How much heavier I do not know for she invariably wore a long black dress that draped to her insteps, hiding her real frame. She wore her gray hair braided in a ball at the back of her head. She had false teeth that only came out at night. I became aware of their existence when I brought her a morning cup of tea in bed. I saw the teeth in a shallow bowl of water on the dresser. Her mouth looked like someone had taken a big bite out of her and pulled the skin over it to cover up the hole, leaving a deep hollow around her mouth.

Granny was soft-spoken even with her teeth in, but she was used to having her desires and wishes put into effect, so she took no nonsense from anybody.

Granny was a woman of deep faith in God with an equally deep belief in the devil. Her belief system could be described as an 80/20 blend of Christianity and Druidism.

When St. Patrick converted Ireland to Christianity in the Fifth Century, he first converted the local kings and chieftains. But there was an accommodation with Druidism, which explains why, unlike all other conversions of nations to Christianity, there was no blood-letting in the conversion process in Ireland. Conversion was by persuasion and compromise, and the majority of the people retained some of their druid beliefs in the magical, along with their druid festivals and customs.

Over the centuries, these druid beliefs and customs were subsumed into the Christian belief system. But remnants of Druidism remained. Belief in the magical and in the Little People were still very strong in the Irish countryside, and were very much part of my grandmother's faith and of my growing up. So my grandmother would warn me against offending the Little People in one breath and invoke the holy names of Jesus and the Virgin Mary in the next. At her quiet insistence, we would pray the rosary each evening with the same regularity as the sun setting, and before she rolled into bed each night she would sprinkle herself with holy water praying softly, "for myself and all belonging to me, for the dying and the dead this day, and for the suffering souls in purgatory."

Devotion to and praying for the "suffering souls" (also called the "holy souls") in purgatory was an important aspect of daily prayer. Because their time in purgatory could be shortened by the prayer and penance of the living, we were constantly reminded of our obligation to the "holy souls." They had their own feast day on All Souls Day, November 2nd, when we bombarded heaven with penance and prayers for their speedy relief and ascent to heaven.

By the time I knew my grandmother, most of her life was behind her. Others recall her work as a midwife to mothers in the surrounding townlands and her generosity to the less fortunate. She had reared nine children on her own and had successfully conducted the operation of the farm after her husband passed on in 1913. When I knew her, she felt she was beginning to lose the total control over life on the farm that had been hers for over two decades.

She complained to me, "Your uncle Michael is ignoring my wishes and is deciding on his own in which fields to plant the oats and the potatoes."

I was taken aback by this. I did not know what to say. I knew my uncle Michael, who was by this time in his early forties, to be a very hard worker and very level headed in all that he did. So I just listened sympathetically and said nothing. I figured out later that this was all that was expected of me, to be a good listener. But I was now aware of a tension between two people I idolized.

Uncle Michael stood five feet nine inches with his boots on. He was slender, but every muscle of his body was hard as nails. His blue eyes smiled from under bushy eyebrows. He approached his work and life with a steady methodical determination that bespoke self-confidence and a mastery of his profession. He had a warmth and a gentleness not normally associated with a rough and tumble hard working farmer. I never saw him lose his temper with an animal or with any of us kids. In fact, I never saw him lose his temper at anybody or anything. He was temperate even in his smoking, smoking only one or two cigarettes a day, and drinking only a pint or two of Guinness on special occasions like weddings, funerals, threshing day when the threshing was done, and on fair days when he had a successful sale of pigs or cattle.

He accepted my imperfect work without criticism and taught me how to do farm chores by example. He lent a hand when he could, otherwise he let me do the job my way. In the fields, I worked alongside him and struggled to keep up with his steady pace. When he saw that I was tiring, he would take a break, or suggest that I do some chores at the house saying that he would be along shortly. This was his way of easing the burden of work without any suggestion of failure. The result was that I worked all the harder to show no fatigue and to keep up with him, and never lag behind as long as I physically could avoid it.

He was a man of few words. We often worked for hours without any verbal exchange, but nonetheless I felt that we were communicating. Words did not seem important. At meals and in company, he let his mother, my grandmother, do most of the talking. He was content with a back seat. But when it came to work, he always took the lead. I enjoyed working with him, as working alongside him was never simply a chore.

I also felt a sense of accomplishment working for my grandmother. I took care of all her pet chores, weeding her flower garden and weeding and thinning her vegetables. And she sang my praises to everybody who came by the house. She would say to others, "He is the best *gossun* (Gaelic for young lad)," and I would scamper off to do her bidding, determined to justify her praise.

My day on the farm began sometime between six and six-thirty when my grandmother awoke and called out, "It is time to be up, a *mhac.*" When I was younger, I often slept with my grandmother. Her bed had a down mattress, which wrapped me in its folds and gave me a sense of being in a cozy cocoon. When I got older, I slept in a press bed in my grandmother's bedroom, which had a mattress almost as hard as a wooden bench. Sometimes I slept with my uncle in his bedroom.

The press bed, which folded up like a cupboard when not in use, was by far the most ascetic and was much easier to leave when the wake-up call came. I was usually up and out in a minute or two, rarely needing a second wake-up call. The freshness of a new day seemed to have its own special powers of attraction, beckoning me to participate in its unfolding.

My daily routine on the farm started with uncovering the live coals from the ashes that had been piled on top of them the night before, slowing their burn, and preserving them to be the start of a new fire the next morning. I built new turf around the surviving coals on the open hearth. Then fetched fresh water from the spring well adjacent to my grandmother's flower garden, and hung a kettle of the well-water over the slowly awakening fire. With a whistle or two, I aroused Shep from his bed in the hay shed and together we set off up the hill at the back of the house to bring down the cows for milking.

In the late spring and summer, I loved (as did all of us kids) to go barefoot. My bare feet gave me direct communication with the soft earth and its carpet of moist grasses, and I felt in tune with it. It was fun to kick droplets of dew from blades of grass and from daisies that glittered and danced in the morning sun. Shep and I made fresh paths across the dew-laden fields as we raced each other from field to field. The morning sun, already a few hours old, was pushing straggling clouds behind the trees and over the horizon, gaining total mastery of the sky. The fields and hedges were alive with bees and smaller insects foraging for food, and birds gathering building materials for their nests. Spring was bursting out all over, and the words of Gerard Manley Hopkins, a nineteenth century Jesuit priest and poet, were dancing in my head:

> Nothing is so beautiful as spring–
> When weeds, in wheels, shoot long and lovely and lush;
> Thrush's eggs look little low heavens, and thrush
> Through the echoing timber does so rinse and wring
> The ear, it strikes like lightnings to hear him sing.

But the cows were still resting contentedly, chewing their cud. They seemed to have a morning preference for the fields farthest from the house. Tady's field was the highest field on Gaigue Hill and the furthest from the farmyard, and that was their field of preference for breakfast. The field got its name from Tady Farrell, a hedge school teacher, who lived in a hut in that field during the Penal Days when there was a price on teachers' heads. The field was far from roads and the reach of British authority, and afforded a measure of security to the outlawed teacher and his clandestine hedge school.

On this morning as usual, the cows greeted me with indifference and the dog with disdain. But we never had trouble establishing who was boss, and Shep quickly aroused them and rounded them up for the trek down to the farmyard.

Shep appreciated the responsibility of bringing the cows together and policing them down the hill, and I took advantage of Shep's expertise to linger on the warm spots where the cows had lain. It was not unlike putting my cold feet in warm water. I ran from warm spot to warm spot, lingering awhile in each, and then scampered to catch up with Shep and his charges. In the months of July and August, on the way up the hill and on the way back, I was on the lookout for mushrooms that sprung up overnight. I knew from experience where they might be. It was easy to spot their white caps, and I was often rewarded with a find of a handful or two.

On reaching the farmyard, the cows went to their appointed slots in the byre. I secured them in their stalls lest they wander back out and up the hill. On the way to the house across the farmyard, I patted Shep for a job well done. He showed his appreciation of my recognition of his skills by jumping up and licking my face profusely. Shep came in with me to the kitchen and lay down by the fire. He was not usually allowed into the house, but neither of us would tell. Early morning, before my grandmother got up, was our special time together.

By now, the kettle was singing. I wet a pot of tea using two teaspoonfuls of loose tea, being careful to first scald the teapot with boiling water as my grandmother insisted. She could taste the difference. Whenever I had newly picked mushrooms, I peeled them. Mushrooms have a sweeter taste when peeled. I pulled out some flat coals from the fire, placed the mushrooms directly on the coals, and put a pinch of salt in the well of each mushroom where I had removed the stalk.

A "cuppa tay" (cup of tea) in bed in the morning was part of my grandmother's daily routine. I prepared a cup of hot tea with milk and sugar, a slice of home-baked brown soda bread with butter and jam, and on occasion a special treat of mushrooms hot off the coals with their wells filled to the brim with their own juices. My grandmother appreciated the "cuppa tay" in bed and welcomed it almost as if each serving was being done for the first time. She made me feel important.

With a bounce to my step, I grabbed the milking buckets and munched on a slice of bread well coated with butter and jam, which I shared with Shep on the way to the byre. I also had my portion of the special treat of mushrooms, which I didn't have to share with Shep, and would not want to even if he liked them. To my young taste buds, the mushrooms were the "chocolates" of the farm.

Milking six to eight cows by hand took about an hour. Singing or whistling as I milked made the cows more cooperative and the task seem easier. The two farm cats usually came by for a share of the fresh warm milk, which they enjoyed from the lid of a can or a discarded chipped saucer in an empty stall.

One of the cats, the less timid of the two, the one with the white star on her forehead, relished getting a streak of milk direct from the cow's udder. Seldom was the streak of milk on target, but as long as it landed anywhere on or near her, she was happy to lap it up. The other cat watched the proceedings from a distance and preferred her milk from a saucer, thank you! My brother Colm insisted that because of the spray of milk which usually greeted the cats, they entered the byre at milking time with their eyes shut.

Shep waited outside in the farmyard for the cows did not like him near their heels. Sometimes my uncle Michael helped with the milking, but he was often busy with preparing the horses or machinery for the day's work ahead. It was a matter of great pride to me to be entrusted with milking the cows and handling all the farmyard chores. I responded to this trust by doing the best job possible.

The next task after milking was to separate the cream from the milk using the separator machine in the dairy. The skim milk I used to feed the newborn calves, and to mix with potatoes and grain for pigs, chickens, turkeys, ducks and, of course, Shep. All these boisterous creatures, great and small, greeted me, or more accurately, greeted the food with enthusiasm that was at times overwhelming. They proclaimed their ravenous appreciation using all the notes in the scale from low base grunts to high pitched squawks and jostled one another and me to get their share. Their enthusiasm at the beginning of a new day was part of what made each day special.

Each animal had a special story to tell. The mother hen with her brood of chicks needed to be segregated and protected from the rest of the animals if they were to get a fair share. I always saved some choice morsels for them. It was the same with the mother duck and her brood of ducklings, who kept her charges at the edge of the throng, and nodded her head in gratitude when I singled them out for special attention.

The orphaned very young calves needed the help of a finger to enable them to drink the milk. They had no teeth and simply sucked my finger as a substitute for their mama's teat. Offering my finger as a surrogate teat was just part of the daily chores. To prevent the baby calves from sucking on things that might be harmful to them, we outfitted them with a *guban*, a mug made of tin with holes punched in the bottom to allow for easier breathing. The tin mug or porringer was placed over the calf's mouth with string from holes in the top of the porringer tied around the calf's ears to keep it in place. I took this contraption off to feed the calf and replaced it when the calf had sucked the last drop of fingered milk. The calf fought against its re-imposition with all its young strength, which was formidable. The calf shook its head with utter abandon, no doubt pleading, "For God's sake don't put that contraption on my young face. I hate it! I hate it! Have you no compassion? I am only a baby!"

I was listening to the pleadings too intently. But the thought of an injured or dead calf snapped me out of it, and I did the right thing. Baby calves, like all babies, do not always know what is best for them, particularly when they are apart from their mothers.

Besides putting the *guban* on baby calves, the only other morning task that I was somewhat uncomfortable with was testing the ducks to see if they had laid their eggs before I let them out. My grandmother always asked if I had performed this chore, as if she had reason to believe I would skip it. I must have somehow voiced my reservations about it. I would count the number of duck eggs, many of them hidden in the straw bedding, and determine how many ducks were holding back to lay their eggs in a nest hidden in the bushes and ditches around the farmyard. Then I would test each duck to identify the culprits and not let them out until they dutifully laid the eggs. This, of course, was a follow-up task for my grandmother.

Local gossip warned that this activity of testing the ducks, or as we called it "trying the ducks," stunted the growth of the finger used. I really did not believe this, but nonetheless took no chances and tried to mitigate the effects of this occupational hazard by distributing the hazard among all fingers, except the thumbs and little fingers, which were awkward to use and anyway were short enough as they were.

On occasion, on weekends, I would forego the testing and then watch the ducks from a perch in a tree to see where the culprits were laying their eggs. I discovered a number of nests this way, and upon consultation with my grandmother usually let the ducks continue with their secret nesting until they hatched the eggs and proudly waddled back into the farmyard with a new brood of darling ducklings. The entire farmyard seemed to be in awe of the parade of little waddlers.

With the farmyard chores completed, I reported for breakfast prepared by my grandmother. Breakfast consisted of oatmeal porridge or stirabout, as we called it (the name, I surmise, coming from the need to stir porridge a lot as it was cooking), and fresh milk. My grandmother made the stirabout the night before and was normally eaten cold for breakfast. It was more crunchy when cold, particularly the stirabout closest to the sides of the pot, and it tasted better cold with the warm fresh milk.

In addition to stirabout, I had bread and butter and the tops of two boiled eggs. The tops came from the two boiled eggs of my grandmother and uncle Michael. My uncle's top was usually larger and had some of the yoke. My grandmother's top usually consisted only of the white of the egg. My grandmother sold eggs weekly. It was one of her few sources of cash, so she was conserving of them in every way.

Shep was the last to see me off to school each morning and the first to welcome me home each afternoon. Shep seemed to know the time of my return, and patiently waited for me at the top of the lane. After Shep bestowed the usual wet licks of welcome, my grandmother appeared from her garden to give me special instructions on the weeding chores she had planned for me. On occasion there were surprise assignments. One such assignment was taking the blue cow to the bull. I was to eat without delay my share of the noonday meal that was kept for me in a pot by the fire. The weeding of the garden would be put off until another day.

Few farms could afford to own a bull. So one bull served the farms of a few townlands for a fee. Our bull was in another townland about two miles away by narrow lanes with gates that had to be opened and closed.

A cow in season is a wild unpredictable animal. She will go through hedges and jump ditches to get to a mate, and all other cattle along the way are potential mates. The challenge was to keep the cow pointed in the direction I wanted her to go and keep the forward momentum such that she did not have the opportunity to jump to the left or to the right. The opening and the closing of gates with one person to control the wild animal were delicate maneuvers. Other hazards I encountered were neighbors' dogs, which scared the dickens more out of me than the cow. I prayed that we not meet cattle in the lane, or worst of all, another cow in a similar state of wild desire. Even in the best of circumstances I needed to be in several places at once—behind the cow, on the left side, on the right side and at times in front of the cow as she took the wrong fork in the lane or headed through the open gate of a neighbor's farmyard.

With lots of agility, much sweat and a little luck, we both made it to the bull's place. The bull's owner responded to my shouts announcing our arrival and helped me drive the cow into an enclosed part of the farmyard. Then he led in the bull, a handsome white-faced massive hunk. The bull first looked at me. I shook my head and wondered what to do next. But the bull, with a swish of his tail and a swagger to his gait, turned towards the cow. He knew his role. He took care of business with dispatch. The transformation in the cow was instantaneous. The wild animal was replaced with a placid hump-backed cow. The bull's owner slapped her hard on the hump, and the hump disappeared.

I flung an arm around the blue cow's velvety neck and together, like friends after sharing an exhausting experience, we trudged contentedly home, relieved that the ordeal was over.

When we got to my grandmother's, it was time to start the evening chores, which were more or less a repetition of the morning chores with the milking of the cows and the feeding of the animals. When the chores were finished, there was time for a game of handball against the barn wall with uncle Michael, and we watched the bats at dusk display their echo-location skills. We threw a ball or stone in the air to see how quickly the bats flew towards it to check it out and having somehow determined that it was not an object of their desire, they veered away from the falling ball or stone. They never seemed to tire of checking out objects that disturbed the air within the range of their sensors. We tired of it before they did.

With darkness almost imperceptibly chasing the light away, I closed the doors to the hen house and duck house for there were night-prowling, fowl-hungry foxes in the area. I brought in a creel of turf for the night and early morning fires. My grandmother was already on her knees fingering her rosary beads. Uncle Michael and I quickly got our rosary beads from the nail by the window and joined her for our nightly prayer.

After the rosary, which invariably encouraged sleep, much to the dismay of my grandmother, I had a bowl of hot stirabout and fresh milk, gave my bare feet a cursory washing, and was ready for bed.

It was a full day. But the day was no fuller for me than it was for the blue cow or any of the other creatures that dwelt on the farm, including my grandmother and uncle Michael. I felt strangely grateful for darkness and the night, conditions that I normally feared. Sleep came almost the instant I hit the hard mattress of the press bed.

chapter 11

a shopping trip with my grandmother

Better keep yourself clean and bright.
You are the window through which you must see the world.

—George Bernard Shaw (1865-1950)
Irish Playwright, Essayist, Lecturer and Philosopher

My grandmother and I got along very well, except on her infrequent Saturday shopping trips. On these occasions, she insisted that I come along. I did not know how to tell her that I dreaded the experience, because of what I felt was her old-fashioned approach to shopping and her insistence on saving pennies on my bus fare. While I saw her actions in these instances as stingy and felt ashamed, she saw them as thriftiness and felt great pride in her bargaining prowess.

On shopping trips to Longford town, Granny loved to go from shop to shop, dragging me along as she bargained with the shopkeepers to get the lowest prices. She treated every purchase no matter how small as if she was buying a pig or a calf and believed that the marked price was only the initial asking price, and that the real price had to be haggled and negotiated, downward of course. For that reason she always asked for the shop owner, for she knew that only the owner could give her the best bargain.

On these tortuous outings, she invariably bought me a pair of socks. She never asked me what I would like. I really did not want her to buy anything for me for that only meant a haggling session. My wish was that she give me money to buy something myself, which would be chocolate, toffee or ice cream. But that never happened.

On this Saturday in August, uncle Michael drove my grandmother and me the two miles to the bus stop at Gaigue crossroads in the pony and trap. McGirr's bus was not known for being on time. Sometimes it was late, very late. And sometimes it was early, even a half-hour early or more. When it was early, it did not wait on passengers. So to be sure to catch the bus, we had to be at the bus stop forty-five minutes ahead of the scheduled arrival time.

Granny was on edge until the small group waiting at the crossroads assured us that the bus had not come. She sat in the trap until we saw the bus approaching. It was a forty-minute wait.

The bus was only a quarter full. There were plenty of seats. On getting into the bus, Granny tried to hide me from the bus conductor with her shawl. She had me sit on the inside window seat, not as a protective measure, but as a cost-saving one. When the conductor came by to collect fares, she pushed me down between the seats saying, "Juke down, *a mhac*," so that I would appear small enough to qualify for the half-fare for a child half my age. The conductor took a long hard look at me, and out of pity for me or out of fear of a fight with my grandmother, which he knew he would not win, he reluctantly accepted the one-and-a-half fares proffered.

The problem was that I had to remain crouched down for the entire trip of over eleven miles with multiple stops along the way to pick up passengers. The conductor took a long look at me each time he passed by our seat. I was mortified with embarrassment. I would have to endure the same ordeal on the return trip with the same conductor eyeing me with what I felt was a mixture of pity and scorn.

It was 11:00 a.m. when we climbed down out of the bus outside the Longford County Courthouse. The conductor was nowhere in sight, so I came out from hiding behind Granny's shawl. The first shop we went into was a men's drapery shop. Granny asked to speak to the owner. An energetic balding man in his fifties was quickly at her side asking, "How can I help you today, Mam?"

Fingering a pair of dark gray socks and pushing her hand down to the toe as if looking for some moth holes, she asked, "What is your best price for a pair of these overpriced socks for this *gossun* here?" She was pointing at me.

Sensing a bit of a challenge but eager to make a sale, the owner responded, "For you I will take three pennies off the marked price of that very fine pair of socks, the best socks in the shop."

He did not know that haggling was Granny's strong suit. After a deliberate pause, she asked, "What would the reduction be for two pair?"

Unsure of where this was going and wishing to bring the sale to a quick conclusion, he said, "Mam, I will give you the second pair at half-price."

She had him on the ropes, and followed quickly with, "What would the reduction be for three pair?"

He knew he was beaten. He threw up his hands in total surrender or exasperation, which, I do not know, and said, "Mam, to you all additional pairs are at half-price."

Granny beamed. She could not resist a bargain. To my surprise, the owner too was smiling. He evidently enjoyed the haggling, even though to my mind he came out second best. He seemed to have a grudging respect for my grandmother's bargaining abilities. They shook hands like old friends and he asked her to drop in the next time she was in town. Granny replied, "You will have to give me a better deal on socks." They both laughed heartily.

I got four pair of socks, but in no way did I feel blessed. Even 100 pair of socks were not worth the embarrassment to the point where I wished that the ground would open up and swallow me. In contrast, Granny was elated and triumphant. The half-price socks gave a big boost to her day, and oddly enough, that seemed to make the store-owner happy too. He evidently did not regard my grandmother's haggling as an annoyance and a boderation (colloquialism for vexation). The rapport between them left me somewhat confused, but did not diminish my discomfort.

This was an ominous start to the day and I did not want to reflect on what the rest of the day would bring. The bus did not leave until 4:00 p.m. and it was just as well that Granny did not tell me how she planned to spend the day.

The next stop was the butcher's shop. Granny made it clear to the owner that she was interested only in beef and lamb. She wanted to take home a roast for Sunday's dinner. She engaged the butcher in a conversation about the various cuts of meat for over a half-hour. Meanwhile, several patrons came, got what they wanted, and left. She finally settled on a small leg of lamb, but did not want to pay the going price. The butcher said that he could get that price from the next person that came in looking for a leg of lamb. When he relented and threw in with the lamb a few good beef bones to make soup, Granny felt that she had gotten a bargain. She asked the butcher to put her name on the package and to keep it for her until later in the day, which he was happy to do. She did not want to be carting the meat around town.

Saturday was market day in Longford. We walked to Ballymahon Street where the market was concentrated and got a close look at the carts of pigs, calves, chickens, ducks and geese. Granny wanted to know what the going prices were, so we listened in to the bargaining of buyers and farmers haggling over prices. I tired of this quickly, but Granny could have spent the entire afternoon there. After about an hour, that included a second round of haggling from the same buyers with no resulting sale, even Granny was ready to move on.

Cattle market in the town of Longford. Markets on the streets of towns were replaced by cattle marts in the early 1960s. (Photograph courtesy of the County Longford Historical Society.)

Since we were only a short distance away from St. Mel's Cathedral, Granny decided that we should pay a visit. The campanile tower of the cathedral rose above all the other buildings of the town and the bells of the tower rang out on the quarter hour. On the way, Granny said that I should jump at the chance to go to confession, which took me by surprise. I had never been to the Cathedral and I felt that a few prayers would be enough on the first visit. Anyway, I did not have big enough sins for a Cathedral confession. I tried to explain how I felt, but Granny quietly insisted that I go. Perhaps she had detected my uneasiness with her shopping and bargaining techniques, and concluded that there was something weighing upon and clouding my mind that distorted my understanding and saw confession as a way of correcting this. She said that confession would be good for me, that we all needed to have our souls cleansed, and that I would not have to go at home. She was so insistent that I felt I had no option. I fervently prayed that the priests were taking their dinner break and that I would not have to go.

The Cathedral was awe-inspiring both outside and inside. I felt very small as we climbed the six steps past the great round pillars to the entrance. The main door was huge, big enough to admit a giant. The interior was massive, with ceilings much higher than I could throw a stone. The two churches that I knew in Drumlish and Ballinamuck would both easily fit inside it. Everything was big: big pews, big statues, big high altar and big pulpit high up on the wall. And the few people moving around or quietly praying looked so small. If the intent was to inspire awe and the submission of all who entered, it certainly succeeded with me. I felt puny and submissive. Is that what God wanted? A subdued and submissive people! I wanted to return to the market square and the noises and smells of the animals. There I was more in my element. Here in the Cathedral, unlike the smaller churches in my parish, I felt strangely ungrounded.

I kept gaping all around me until Granny beckoned me to join her in the left side aisle where one of the confessionals inserted in the wall had a few people around it. "The priest is in there," she whispered in a voice that echoed off the walls and rumbled around through the Cathedral's great empty spaces. "Get yourself ready for confession." I did as I was bid. I tried to examine my conscience to see what sins I had committed, but I could find nothing worthy of a Cathedral confession. So I settled on the usual short list of *pecadillos*. Would the Cathedral priest see me as wasting his time? The grown man ahead of me was taking a long time. He must have something big to tell? I envied him. My sins were of the everyday variety, so ho-hum. I pushed aside the temptation to make up a decent sin like stealing 10 shillings. But what if I had to pay it back? Then what would I do? I did not have that much money, and if I saved up to get it, to whom would I pay it? The man ahead of me finally came out, bringing an end to my confession plotting. He came out smiling and certainly did not look like a man who would commit a mortal sin. So why was he in there so long? Was he smiling because he had a weight lifted off his soul, and felt like jumping over the moon?

Granny motioned me to go in. Inside the confessional, waiting my turn, I rehearsed the telling of my sins, resisting the temptation to make them any bigger or worse that they were. Did other people face the same problem of trying to magnify their sins, or were some faced with the challenge of minimizing them? I was not sure which was the tougher problem. Was the man in ahead of me trying to make his sins bigger or smaller? Or did he just tell them as they were? Whatever the case, it certainly took him a long time to get his story off his chest. And the result left him all smiles.

From the moment the priest pulled back the shutter on my side of the confessional, it took me less than a minute to do what I had to do. I confessed my usual short list of sins: lying, disobeying my parents, and fighting with my brothers and sisters. I got my penance and was out of there. To my surprise and relief, the cathedral confession was no different than back home. The priest accepted my sins without question and the penance was the same— three Our Fathers. It was a big to-do about little.

As I said my penance, I watched out by the corner of my eye to see if Granny went to confession but she did not. On our way out of the Cathedral, I plucked up enough courage to ask her why she did not go. She seemed surprised by my question but answered that the next day, Sunday, was not her sodality Sunday. That was the second Sunday of the month. It was the custom for men to go to communion on the first Sunday of each month, the women of the parish to go to communion on the second Sunday, and children on the third Sunday. The fourth Sunday was nobody's Sunday and everybody's Sunday. Communion on Sunday morning was always prefaced by confession on Saturday afternoon or evening. The result was that communion and confession were monthly events for most people. That was a big change from earlier days when people generally felt that they were unworthy of communion and stayed away most of the time. They went to church but not to communion. The sodalities got them back to receiving communion with some regularity. But, like my grandmother, people resisted going more often than what was prescribed by custom.

Our next stop was Donlon's on the corner between Ballymahon and Dublin Streets for tea and biscuits. I was certainly getting up an appetite. But this was not meant to be a meal, just a bite to keep us until we got home. Granny ordered for us both a small pot of tea and two scones. She tried to bargain down the price of the scones but the shop owner merely smiled and said, "That will be one shilling and sixpence, Mam." Granny reluctantly paid up. And complained to me all the way to the bus about that costly cuppa tay.

We picked up the lamb from the butcher's and got to the bus at 3:30 p.m. Although it did not leave until 4:00, to be sure of a seat Granny felt that we had to get there early. The bus conductor was not on the bus, so I did not have to hide my size. There were only a dozen or so ahead of us, so we got to choose seats up front in the third row. By 3:45 p.m., all seats were filled, and the conductor was packing people in the aisle. By 4:00 p.m., people were hanging out the door. When the bus driver came, he could not get in. The conductor ordered the people around the door to get out, which they reluctantly did. The conductor also got out. The driver got in and those who got out scrambled back in.

The conductor went up and down outside the bus asking people to crunch down the aisle. He tapped the window where I was sitting and asked me to stand, which I did, to allow another person to sit beside Granny. It was awkward standing alongside the window but not as bad as crouching down underneath the seat to make myself appear smaller. The conductor then pushed himself inside and closed the door. At least this time everybody got in. The last bus on Saturdays was always packed like sardines in a tin. Sometimes the bus took a load as far as Drumlish and then went back for those left waiting. The conductor took fares as people got off.

A big crowd got off at Drumlish and I got my seat back for the rest of the journey. Uncle Michael and the pony and trap were waiting for us at Gaigue Crossroads.

chapter 12

making hay where the corncrake sang

...Save for a cry that echoes shrill
From some lone bird disconsolate;
A corncrake calling to its mate;
The answer from the misty hill.

—Oscar Wilde (1854-1900)
Irish Playwright, Poet and Novelist

The early morning mowing left the meadow cut in neat swaths, row upon row, heavy with thick fresh green grass at one end and lighter at the other end with the heads of partially dried tall grasses. The smell of freshly mowed hay filled the air. Bees buzzed busily as they gathered the last offerings of honey from the fallen flowers. Corncrakes called from uncut meadows a few fields away. The sun and the wind conspired to push the last remnants of clouds from the sky. The sun climbed higher and higher replacing the cool breezes with dancing gusts of warm air. This meadow, with a little luck and hard work, would become a premier crop of hay. Uncle Michael and I shared an unspoken determination to make that happen.

"To make hay while the sun shines" was no mere figure of speech on my grandmother's farm. It was a basic law of economic survival. Even in summer, sunny days were infrequent. Overcast and rainy days were all too frequent. So uncle Michael had to forecast the weather with some degree of accuracy or watch the winter feed of cattle and horses rot in the field. To minimize risk, he mowed and harvested one meadow of about two to three acres at one time.

The best hay was cut and harvested the same day, but that was a rare exception. Most cut meadows took two to four days to dry sufficiently well to be cocked. To take advantage of the full day's drying, uncle Michael got up shortly after sunrise about 4 a.m. He never had to set an alarm clock. He had an internal clock that enabled him to awaken at the selected time. By 5 a.m., he was out in the meadow starting to mow the dew-laden tall grasses with two horses pulling the mowing machine. He first cut a swath all around the edges of the meadow, and then cut inward toward the center mowing on all four sides. That way the horses never had to stop, but kept going for the two hours or so that it took to mow the entire meadow.

Peter Courtney and his horses mowing a meadow at Ballymacormack, Co Longford. This picture, taken in 1955, demonstrates the way hay was cut on my grandmother's farm. (Photograph courtesy of Co. Longford Historical Society.)

Meadows were the habitat of many creatures. The most interesting dweller of the tall grasses was the elusive corncrake (scientific Latin name: *crex crex*), celebrated in ancient Celtic manuscripts and in more modern times in verse and on stamps. The corncrake is a member of the rails (*rallidae*) family of birds, somewhat larger than a quail and smaller than a domestic chicken, 26 cm or 11" in size. In Germany, it is known as the king of the quails-*wachtelkonig*. Its color scheme is speckled brown, not unlike that of the grouse, and it eats insects and seeds. The corncrake is a regular summer visitor to agricultural habitats in western Europe.

The cloistered monks who wrote the Book of Kells at the end of the 8th century featured the corncrake in their pictorial presentation of the capital letter "V," where a corncrake and a heron are intertwined; in the 1880s, Oscar Wilde penned the lines quoted at the outset; and in 1997, Ireland issued a four-pence stamp in the corncrake's honor.

The corncrake, a seasoned international traveler, made a round trip annually each April or May to my grandmother's farm from distant tropical, southeast Africa. Travel from Europe to southeast Africa by people was unknown before 1497. Concrakes had been traveling regularly between Europe and southeast Africa since the 8th century and beyond. And no doubt in the fall of 1497 on their return to winter in their tropical second home, they were surprised to see the European Vasco da Gama sail up the east coast of Africa on his way to India, the first human being known to make such a voyage. Did corncrakes nod to each other and say, "It has taken a long, long time for people to do what we have been doing for ages, if not eons, traveling to and fro between Europe and southeast Africa"?

Having traveled so far to my grandmother's farm, the corncrake had every right to make its presence known repeating its call over and over, often for hours at a time. On most starry nights in June and July, the staccato two-note crake-crake of the corncrake carried across several fields—like the call of a very hoarse and very determined drake, but with a cadence that had its own peculiar enchantment.

The corncrake is no songbird. It was no doubt banished from time immemorial from daytime performances. The call of the male duck and the braying of the ass are musical in comparison. The corncrake's distinctive call is close to the sound produced by pulling a wooden golf tee or any piece of hard wood across the teeth of a comb. I often lay awake with an open window mesmerized by the clarity and forcefulness of its cry, as it repeated its rasping mating call to the heavens untiringly late into the night. It was a strangely comforting sound, a jarring strident lullaby, which at any other time would grate on the nerves. But at night when all other creatures of the farm were silent, the corncrake's voice was music and was soothing to mind and body.

We know that we project our voices best when we bounce sounds off our hard palates. Whatever the corncrake did to produce its signature sound, it certainly had great powers of projection, for the call carried across the meadow through the hedges and the open window, and onto my pillow as if its owner was sitting on the windowsill. We were told as kids that it made its unique call by lying on its back and rubbing its feet together. We had serious doubts about this but we never got close enough to confirm or refute it. The secret of how it made its raucous two-note song was protected by the night and the tall grasses.

The mowing of the meadow presented one of the few opportunities to catch a glimpse of this often heard but rarely seen creature. This was a bird, though a long-distance flier, that preferred to run in the meadow rather than fly. So it ran to the center of the meadow in front of the mowing machine. I always tried to be in the meadow when the last half dozen swaths or so were mowed, for only then would the corncrake emerge from the tall grasses. If I was lucky enough, I saw one dash to the cover of the tall grass in the ditch surrounding the meadow and disappear. Trying to catch one was out of the question. They were so fast. My limited goal was to get a fleeting look at the speeding brown grey form with a touch of black and red on its wings. That was an accomplishment that I could boast about to my friends at school. Besides, there was the personal satisfaction of getting to know, however fleetingly, the composer and producer of my nightly lullaby—a very shy and reclusive performer. When I think of Gaigue Hill and my grandmother's farm in summer, I think first of the corncrake and its unique persistent call emanating from the meadow's tall grasses. Unfortunately, changes in hay management and in hay cutting techniques in the last two decades have destroyed the corncrake's habitat. The bird is now an endangered species and is no longer heard in Ireland's meadows except in a few protected areas such as the Shannon Callows, Northern Donegal County, and parts of County Mayo.

The next day, upon completion of the morning farmyard chores and breakfast with my tops of two eggs, my uncle and I selected a rake and a pitchfork each from the barn and proceeded to the meadow. It was nearing 10 a.m., and the top part of each swath of cut grass was already somewhat dry. Our first task was to turn over the heavy end of each swath to expose the damp green underside to the sun and wind. So we marched around the meadow, row after row, turning over each swath with a quick flip of the rake. When we got the right rhythm going, the rows flipped over in one continuous rolling motion like falling domino rows. Neither of us wanted to be the first to break the continuum, so we kept a steady pace traversing the same steps as the horses and the machine earlier the previous morning. We did not have the stamina of the horses so we stopped a couple of times, once when we unearthed a bees' nest. We had to scramble to avoid being stung. In tipping over a swath with my rake, I pulled the moss-covered top off a nest that the bees built in a hollow in the ground. They angrily ran us off. We gave the nest a wide berth and continued further down the row. The unturned section of swath marked the nest. We continued to turn the swaths.

I was on the lookout for other bees' nests for a meadow this size usually has several nests, but they were well hidden, and I found no more. We reached the center of the meadow shortly after noon. We must have slowed down towards the end for it took us longer than we had figured. We returned to the unturned section and to the bees' nest. Most of the bees were out working the cut flowers. I painstakingly removed part of the honeycomb with the pockets of honey, moved a few yards away, and squeezed out the honey onto my tongue. Fresh honey has its own special taste. I had learned from experience not to be too greedy. If I moved slowly, the bees would let me have some honey without a fight, but not all. So I took some and left some. I gingerly replaced the comb in the nest and covered it with moss as best I could.

These bees' nests seldom lasted more than a few days after mowing, for the neighborhood crows also liked the honey. They liked the unborn bees even better.

While we were discussing our next steps in the harvesting process, grandmother's football whistle rode the wind to us through the trees. It was the call to dinner, the noonday meal. We more or less knew what we were going to have to eat. The evening before, my uncle and I had dug some new potatoes, the first of the season. It was traditional that the first meal of new potatoes be colcannon and traditions were important to my grandmother.

Colcannon was an easy meal to prepare for there was only one dish— new potatoes. The new potatoes were peeled and boiled. When the boiling water was drained, the potatoes were mashed with a pounder—a piece of wood that was thick and rounded on the end. The round end was used to pound the potatoes into a mush-like consistency without lumps. We added a white sauce made of corn flour, hot milk, chopped scallions, chopped parsley, and a little salt, and pounded some more until we had mashed potatoes of the consistency of modern-day creamed garlic potatoes. Each person got a stacked plateful with a well of butter in the middle of the mound. The colcannon was hot and the butter melted quickly. To retain the heat, my grandmother pounded the potatoes in the pot as it sat close to the fire on the hearth.

We ate the colcannon with a soup spoon, dipping each spoonful into the well of butter. We worked our way from the outside toward the center and the butter. A properly eaten plate of colcannon would have the bottom of the empty well of butter as the last spoonful.

On this day we observed the proper approach to the consumption of a mound of new potatoes, at least for the first plateful. It was considered by my grandmother a breach of good table manners if we busted (burst) the well of butter prematurely, or tried to tunnel under the colcannon to the well of butter as my two younger brothers, Frank and Niall (ages six and seven) tried to do. They were severely reprimanded for messing with their food. But that was only on their second plateful.

Colcannon was a very popular dish with all of us. We invariably had seconds, even though the first plateful was the equivalent of about five or six large Idaho potatoes. And I am not exaggerating. All of us, young and not so young, knew how to put away potatoes.

Refreshed from the break for dinner, we attacked the next step in our haymaking with enthusiasm. On returning to the meadow, we examined a few swaths to see if the hay was dry enough to gather into rows to be made into cocks. The sun and the wind had done their work. It was my uncle's judgment, and I concurred, that with the exception of a few spots where the crop was heaviest, we could prepare the hay to make haycocks. The not-so-dry spots, we shook out wherever we found them. We pulled these areas into rows at the very last.

We used the rakes to pull two swaths from each side onto a center swath. We proceeded around the meadow in this manner until the entire meadow consisted of rows of five swaths piled on top of each other. This was a slow process. In pulling the swaths together, we had to rake the hay clean so as to leave no straws of hay between the rows. Otherwise, we would have to rake the complete meadow at the end of the day.

When we finished this step, my uncle started to pile the rows of hay into stacks with his pitchfork. I raked into rows the hay that was scattered out to dry and then joined my uncle at piling the hay into stacks or cocks as we called them. He could make two stacks for every one of mine. I was a little too particular about the shape of my stacks of hay, which slowed me down. Piling the hay into stacks or haycocks was very strenuous work, and I could not lift as much with each pitchforkful as my uncle.

I was glad when I saw Shep scamper into the meadow wagging his tail at an accelerated pace. My two brothers and my grandmother were not far behind carrying the evening tea. This was a much-appreciated break. I was tiring fast. My uncle was a very hard worker and I took a lot of pride in keeping with him stride for stride. But there were occasions where I had to concede his superiority, and gathering hay into cocks was such an occasion.

Tay (tea) in the meadow was a special delight. You may have heard or even partaken of afternoon tea at the Gresham in Dublin, or Harrods in London, or at the St. Francis on Union Square in San Francisco, or at the Ritz Carlton in Chicago, Pasadena, or New York. But afternoon tay in the meadow on my grandmother's farm on the side of Gaigue Hill was streets ahead. I know, for I have partaken of both kinds on more than a few occasions. The fancy cups and saucers, the delicate triangular sandwiches with the crust cut off the bread, the little tea strainer to catch the tea leaves, the fancy cakes on the three-tiered trays were missing from the tay in the meadow. But for atmosphere, taste, and the feeling of being in tune with mother earth, the tay in the meadow was a much more satisfying experience.

We seated ourselves propped against a cock of hay. My grandmother spread out the buttered slices of brown skillet-baked bread on a double page of the *Longford Leader*. She poured each of us a mug of hot tay with milk and sugar, and my brothers passed the buttered bread. It all tasted so good. Each person had an allotment of slices including one slice each of raisin bread. I always wished there were more slices of raisin bread. Each person had a second mug of hot tay that he contentedly sipped to the last drop. Food always tasted better in the outdoors, be that in the meadow or on the bog.

We had a host of small company for tay. Tiny grasshoppers insisted on jumping all over the bread and into the tay. We fished them out of the tay with *thrawneens* (straws) of new hay, but others replaced them. My uncle, ever a patient man, let them be, blowing them to the far end of the mug before each swallow of tay.

Shep lay expectantly close by and enjoyed a bit of crust now and then when Granny was not looking. Granny did not appreciate having her baking thrown to the dog. But to us kids, Shep was family.

My brothers and Shep wandered playfully throughout the meadow, exploring as if for hidden treasures, and playing hide and seek among the cocks and rows of hay. But there was no successful hiding from Shep, no matter how much they buried themselves in the thick rows of new hay. Tiring quickly of hide and seek, my brothers examined the bees' nest, but wisely did not disturb them.

When they reported back to base, my grandmother asked them to count the haycocks. When they came back with two different counts, she asked for a recount. This time, whether by correct count or by collusion, they had the same count of seventeen.

With mission accomplished, they were off to play once more and to explore the meadow. But that did not last long. Granny had a more important assignment for them. They would help her make the ropes that tied down the cocks, so that the wind would not blow their tops off. Granny meted out the strands of hay which they took turns in twisting into ropes. They made the ropes by putting a few strands of hay around the head of a rake. Then one of my brothers twisted the rake while my grandmother fed hay to the rope in an unbroken line. Each rope that they twisted was about twelve feet long. For this meadow, they had to twist over eighty ropes. So it was a chore that would occupy most of the evening and wear out two subdued young men. It was my young brothers' reluctant contribution to saving the hay.

My uncle and I continued gathering the hay into cocks. But dark clouds began to appear in the evening sky. We wondered with some alarm if we could get the rest of the rows into cocks before the rains came. We doubled our efforts. Thunder rumbled in the distance. It would be a shame to have a downpour spoil a good day's work and a good crop of hay.

Three neighbors, who no doubt heard the mowing the previous morning and surmised that we might be facing a real problem, appeared with their pitchforks, and joined in throwing up haycocks at a rapid pace. The clouds looked more threatening. But the many hands quickly transformed the rows into cocks. As the first big drops came, my uncle, with a broad smile thanked our neighbors—Philip Brady, Jimmy Gorman and Frankie McQuade for their timely help. They disappeared as fast as they came. They did not want to get a drenching.

We continued working for the darkest clouds seemed to be shifting away from us. We got a few more heavy drops but that was all. We could finish up what we had started at 10 a.m.

Granny and my brothers continued to make ropes. The one whose turn it was not to twist, took two ropes to each cock. I set about pulling the butts of each cock. I got on my knees and pulled the loose hay closest to the ground all around each cock of hay. My uncle came after me, put the hay that I had pulled together with any loose hay that he had raked onto the cocks, and prepared each one for roping. When I had finished pulling the buts, I joined him in heading the haycocks and tying them down with two ropes placed strategically to best combat the winds. This trimming and heading process took a couple of hours—a few minutes to each stack.

Granny, Niall, Frank and Shep left for the house about 7:30 p.m. Their last chore before they left was to count all the cocks in the meadow. This time they had the same count of forty-one. My uncle said that was fairly close and, as if to fend off a recount, said that number was good enough for him. My brothers sighed with relief and took off with Shep in a race to be first at the house.

My uncle and I followed about an hour later. On our way out of the meadow, we filled in the gap my uncle had made to allow the horses and mowing machine to enter the meadow. We did not want any animals getting into the meadow and perhaps knock over some of the cocks of hay before they settled. The cocks would stay in the meadow about six weeks. They would be brought into the hay shed in mid to late August.

With a deep sense of satisfaction at a job well done, we trudged up the lane to the house. No words were spoken but none were needed. We knew we had done a good day's work.

After we had finished the milking and taken care of the farmyard chores, we had one last task to perform privately. It was rare when we did not carry with us back to the house some small creatures from the meadow. The most common of these stowaways were ticks. These tiny creatures sought out hard to get at places such as armpits, houghs (at the back of the knees) and the groin area, where they embedded themselves in the flesh to partake of some good fresh blood. They were so tiny that it was often difficult to find them, and once found it was difficult to get a hold of them to extract them. The secret was to push them in, which they resisted, in so doing loosened their hold, and were thereby easier to pull out. If I missed one, as sometimes happened, and left it there overnight, in the morning it would be bloated with my blood. It was then quite easy to remove this bulging sack of dark red blood.

This evening the milking and the farmyard chores were easy for my uncle helped. The cows, who had patiently waited longer than usual to give their evening contribution of milk, seemed to cooperate more, for the milk flowed more freely to the pressure of my squeezing fingers. The cats had also patiently waited for their evening meal, and licked contentedly the sprays of warm milk I sent their way. It was dark when I shut the hen house door, which usually was the last item I had to take care of. I patted Shep goodnight. My brothers were already asleep in the press bed.

Granny had to nudge me awake a few times during the rosary. She included a prayer of thanks for the three neighbors who helped. I had a pongerful of stirabout with fresh warm milk. It was another full day for all creatures on the farm.

As I climbed into bed, a corncrake was belting out his mating song. I appreciated the company. Questions arising from the day's activities surfaced in my sleepy head:

Did the corncrakes in the cut meadow move to an uncut meadow?

How were they received by the resident corncrakes?

Were the stowaway ticks missed by the other ticks left behind in the meadow?

How long would it take the crows to find the bees' nest?

These thoughts crowded my dwindling consciousness. I was asleep seconds after I stretched my legs to the bottom of my uncle's bed.

chapter 13

special occasions and feast days on the farm

As long as I have a want, I have a reason for living. Satisfaction is death.

—George Bernard Shaw (1856-1950)
Irish Playwright, Essayist, Lecturer and Philosopher

There was always something to look forward to at my grandmother's. There were special occasions and feast days on the farm that came around each year over which my grandmother presided, and which I did everything in my power not to miss, for she had a way of making these events quite special for us kids. I particularly looked forward to being at my grandmother's for the killing of the pig, for May Day on May 1, Easter Sunday, Halloween on October 31, threshing day, a moveable event that took place in November or December and the Wren Day on St. Stephen's Day, the day after Christmas.

Sundays, feast days, and special events were very important to me. They were very important to my grandmother. They made all the other days leading up to them worthwhile. A year of Mondays or Tuesdays with one day little different from the next would be unthinkable on my grandmother's farm. My grandmother made the calendar year a rosary of celebrations.

The Killing of the Pig

Granny loved to orchestrate the slaughtering of the pig, an event that took place at least once a year. On the night before the slaughter, she coached me, "First thing after the morning chores are done, I want you to clean out the stable and put an armful of fresh straw in the corner. Put another armful of fresh straw in the dairy, and I will need you, *a mhac,* to hold the basin for the blood."

"To hold the basin for the blood"! This assignment took me by surprise. I was both scared and proud of my expanded role. On previous occasions, I stayed in the house until the deed was done. This time, I was going to be right there in the middle of things, catching the pig's blood.

Granny handed me a tin basin and said, "Rinse it good and clean." She continued her instructions: "Also in the morning, put down an extra good fire. Fill the large pot full of water, and get it started, as it will take some time to boil. I will also want you, *a mhac*, later in the day to take some of the pig to the neighbors."

We shared some of the choice innards of the pig (the perishable parts) with the immediate neighbors, and they reciprocated when they slaughtered. But taking choice morsels of the slaughtered pig to the neighbors was the easy part. I had done that several times before and could do it in my sleep. Taking an active part in the actual slaughter of the pig was a new challenge, a new test of my emerging manhood. I was determined to fulfill my new responsibilities with at least an outward show of bravery. Not living up to my grandmother's confidence in me was unthinkable.

I sensed that Granny was watching me. I had not responded to her list of assignments. "Can you do all that?" she asked in a tone of voice that demanded a response.

I said, "Sure, you won't have to remind me again," and I ran out into the yard to examine the condition of the stable and what it would take to clean it out. The next morning I had the stable cleaned, placed a couple of armfuls of straw in the corner, placed another two armfuls of straw in the dairy, and had the big pot boiling well in advance of the happening.

"It's 9:30." Granny's voice came clear and distinct above the farmyard noises. Uncle Michael and I knew what it meant. My uncle drove one of the large pigs from the pigsty into the stable, tied his two hind legs together with a rope and, with little resistance, rolled the unsuspecting victim onto the fresh straw.

Granny sprinkled all four of us, including the prostrate pig, with holy water. She whispered to me, "Bless yourself, *a mhac*." In my nervousness, I had forgotten to cross myself, and I certainly needed all the help I could get.

She handed the long sharp knife to my uncle and mumbled what seemed to be a prayer. My uncle looked at me and with an assuring smile, asked, "Are you ready?" I simply nodded, not wanting to say anything lest the tremble in my voice reveal my fear and nervousness.

My uncle knelt and plunged the knife into the pig's throat. To my astonishment, the pig lay still. Blood gushed from the knife wound. I blinked when the blood started gushing out, but stood my ground when the pig gave a dying kick that almost knocked the basin out of my hands. But I held on to it. I got an approving smile from Granny.

When the last drop of blood dripped from the pig's neck, Granny ordered, "Take the basin into the kitchen, *a mhac*, and wash the blood from your hands." I had not noticed, but I indeed had blood all over my hands. Later that day, we made blood sausage from the blood mixed with oatmeal and spices, which we called black pudding. We stuffed the mixture into the pig's entrails that had been thoroughly washed. We made long sausages that we cut into 12-inch segments, tied the ends together making a circle, and boiled them. We had the blood sausage for breakfast, reheating them on the pan together with bacon and eggs. Some bed and breakfast places today include black pudding in their breakfast menus. It is a special treat.

When I returned to the stable, my uncle had the pig hanging from a hook in one of the beams of the stable's ceiling, and with Granny still acting as master of ceremonies, was cutting the animal apart. He had strung the end of the rope that had tied the pig's legs into a hook in the ceiling and pulled the pig up to where he could dress the body easily with the snout hovering a foot or two above the straw. I made several trips to the kitchen with various parts of the pig's insides.

With the inside cleaned out, my uncle then cut off the head, which I also took to the kitchen. By this time, I was getting used to handling and transporting bloodied parts, and the severed head in a bucket did not faze me. We washed down the outside of the pig with the big pot of boiling water, and shaved the hair or bristles off the pig's back and sides using a large homemade razor. My uncle then sawed the pig in two down the middle of its back.

We carried the two sides of the pig into the dairy, placed them on beds of straw on the dairy floor, and covered them with a two-inch layer of salt. After about three weeks, we brushed off the salt, and hung the sides of the pig over the fireplace in the kitchen where they got plenty of smoke from the open hearth. That was the curing process—healthy doses of salt and smoke.

To get bacon for breakfast or dinner, Granny stood on a stool and carved a few slices from the hanging sides of the pig, thin slices for breakfast, thick slices for dinner, and lean cuts from the pig's hams for special occasions. This was done until the sides were eaten. The process was then repeated with the slaughter of another pig.

While my uncle and I were giving the sides of the pig their temporary salty resting place in the dairy, Granny prepared packages of fresh pig meat that I took that afternoon to the neighbors. I delivered six packages that were warmly received, and I proudly retold at each house my role in making the package possible. That night at the rosary, Granny gave thanks to God for His bounty, and for enough bacon for several months to come.

May Day

May Day, the first day of summer, was a landmark day in the Irish farmer's calendar year. In years gone by, it was the day when the farmer's tenancy began with the payment of rent to the landlord or his tenancy ended with his eviction. The hiring of farm hands and the letting of land usually started from May 1. It was a day the farmers for centuries both celebrated and dreaded.

As kids, we welcomed the start of summer on May Day by throwing our boots under the stairs and going barefoot. May Day was the coming out of feet from hibernation and seclusion in dark heavy boots. After a long winter being shut in, soles were tender and sensitive to every twig and every piece of grit. May Day was also a re-acquaintance with toes and the realization that each toe had its own individuality.

Hidden within boots or shoes, toes were simply an extension of feet. But throw off the footwear, and toes emerged as distinct parts of the body with unique capabilities and means of coping with the outside world. This is particularly true of the little toes and the big toes. The little toe, the toe that was last to be tweaked by adults who played with babies' toes, was the toe most adept at lifting pebbles and throwing them at selected targets. It was also most adept at picking pencils off the floor in school, and making markings and writing names in the dirt or sand. The big toe lifted and threw larger stones, wrote with bold lettering; plucked daisies and dandelions and pulled the dog's tail. The booted foot did not have such nimbleness and dexterity. May Day resurrected and exposed to the light of day a whole new set of toe skills.

May Day was also the rediscovery of old sensations, feeling again the cool dampness of the earth under my bare feet and the sharp edges of gravel and stones, and having my soles and toes wallow in the mud of shallow puddles, old sensations being felt anew through bootless, liberated feet. Feet and toes were not meant to spend their days as shut-ins in boots and shoes, particularly young country feet and young country toes. May Day set them free to experience the earth and its many sensations. It was a part of communing with nature that for us lasted from May through September.

May Day was also the day when the cuckoo first announced its summer presence with its melodious two-note call. The cuckoo's unique call seemed to come from several directions at once, until my ear got used to it. William Wordsworth greeted the arrival of the cuckoo in verse. In his poem "To the Cuckoo," which I memorized as a school assignment, he penned:

> O Blithe New-comer! I have heard,
> I hear thee and rejoice:
> O Cuckoo! Shall I call thee Bird
> Or but a wandering Voice?
>
> While I am lying on the grass
> Thy twofold shout I hear;
> From hill to hill it seems to pass,
> At once far off and near.

Newly arrived from beyond the southern seas, this was the day when the cuckoo not only announced its arrival, but also laid its eggs in the ceremonial May bush. Granny had uncle Michael cut a furze bush covered with yellow blossoms, which she planted on the dunghill, and made a nest in its middle with wild daisies, primroses, cowslips, and buttercups gathered from the farm's young, lush meadows.

"That should do it," Granny said as she escorted me away from the bush, "Now the cuckoo, who never builds a nest of its own, and lays its eggs in other birds' nests, will have a nest of fresh flowers of its very own in which to lay its eggs."

My curiosity was aroused, so I asked, "What do the other birds do when they find the cuckoo's egg in their nest?" She went on to explain,

"They hatch it out with their other eggs thinking it is their own. But the young cuckoo is usually much larger than the other young birds, has the biggest beak, gets most of the food from the parent birds, grows faster than the others, and shoves them out of the nest."

"And the parent birds let this happen?" I asked, thinking that this was a pretty mean trick on the part of the cuckoo.

"In fact," Granny explained, "the parents probably think they have a very special baby and work from morning till night to satisfy its enormous appetite."

There was a long silence as I pondered this basic unfairness. The cuckoo dropped several notches in my estimation. The laying of its eggs in other bird's nests also explained to me the reason why the cuckoo was usually seen with a little bird pursuing her. The little bird had probably caught the cuckoo in the act of laying an egg in its nest and, incensed at the violation of its domestic rights, was giving the larger bird chase.

"Well," I said, "I hope the cuckoo uses the nest we made for her and does not lay its eggs uninvited in other bird's nests." Granny put her hand on my shoulder and nodded her agreement.

On the morning of May 1, I was awakened at dawn by Granny wondering aloud if the cuckoo had found its nest on the dunghill. I ran barefooted to the May bush and found there the cuckoo's blue egg, and then listened for the cuckoo's call. The cuckoo always obliged by laying its blue egg in the flower-decorated nest, but did not always announce its presence upon discovery of its egg, as I was led to believe. But I heard its call sometime that day, on my barefooted run to or from school.

As I grew older, I helped Granny prepare the May bush for my younger sisters and brothers. And in the days before May 1, I helped with selection of a small chicken egg. If I was lucky, I found the first egg of a young hen, which we called a pullet's egg, that was smaller than normal. It was about half the size of a regular hen's egg. I colored the egg with blue dye, which Granny used in washing clothes. I gathered wild flowers from the abundance of white daisies, yellow buttercups, pale primroses and pink cowslips that dotted the meadows and grassy ditches, where their breeze-tossed heads beckoned to be plucked. For it was an honor to be part of the cuckoo's nest.

I made a colorful, cozy nest of wild flowers that no cuckoo could pass up, and that Granny said was the prettiest nest that any cuckoo had ever seen. Then, late on the eve of May 1, I placed the blue egg in the nest just in case the cuckoo failed to do her part. If we had more than one young person to be surprised with a cuckoo's egg, I simply placed extra blue eggs in the nest, and prayed that no hungry crows were out too late that night. At the rosary, Granny forgot to pray that the cuckoo would find its own special nest on the dunghill. But she gave out the rosary, and I was not about to tell her what to do.

The discovery of the cuckoo's egg was always an early morning fun event with the cuckoo egg hunters jumping out of bed on awakening, and in PJs and bare feet, making a beeline for the dunghill. The blue eggs were taken upstairs to be shown to Granny, who feigned astonishment, and genuinely shared the joy of discovery of her grandchildren.

The blue eggs were shown to everybody. I told them that they could eat the cuckoo's eggs for breakfast, which was tantamount to heresy. What would the cuckoo think of such a thing? It might just stop singing. It might go back to Africa. What kind of summer would it be without its song? The blue eggs were taken to school to be shown to the teacher and classmates. They were at least that day's prize possessions.

Decorating the May bush was an ancient Celtic custom, pre-dating Christianity, associated with merrymaking, dancing and bonfires as a welcome to summer. The holding of May pole dances at crossroads were also part of the celebrations. In more recent years, May Day celebrations were mostly for children, and for the children the picking of May flowers was also in honor of the Virgin Mary, as May in the Christian calendar had become Her month. This was another example of the evolution of a pre-Christian festival into a Christian celebration.

My grandmother worked hard to make these special days memorable for us kids. This was particularly true of Easter Sunday and Halloween.

Easter Sunday

Easter Sunday was the day when the sun traditionally danced with joy at Christ's resurrection. Granny cautioned me, "Do not look at the sun directly to see it dancing, as it may damage your eyes." So she got a basin of sparkling water from the well in which I could see the sun's reflection dance and quiver.

When she took the basin into the kitchen, I saw the sun's rays coming through the window reflect off the water and dance on the walls and on the ceiling. With a little agitation of the water, the dancing was plain to see. Though death seemed very unreal to my young mind, resurrection and life seemed very real, and to me it was only natural that the sun would dance on Easter morning. On this Easter morning—

> I danced with the dancing sun,
> And the dancing sun danced with me.
> We danced together, the sun and I, and together,
> Basking in the glow of Easter morning,
> We danced the dance of life.

Easter Sunday was not only the day when I danced with the sun, it was also the day when I ate an inordinate amount of eggs. As many people abstained from eggs during the fasting of Holy Week, there was an abundance of eggs for the Easter Sunday breakfast table. Even my grandmother, who was quite tight with eggs during the other 364 days of the year, had no restrictions on the number of eggs I ate on this solemn feast day. To show the world how many eggs we actually consumed, we put the egg shells on top the flat clipped hedge outside the front of the house so that people passing by going to or from church could see the large number of eggs eaten.

The inevitable question on Sunday afternoon and on Monday morning was how many eggs did you eat? Everyone wanted to brag about the number of eggs personally consumed. Anything under a half-dozen eggs was not worth mentioning. I remember putting away a dozen or more on several occasions, and feeling none the worse for it. I felt good bragging about it.

Halloween

Halloween's roots were in Druidism rather than in Christianity. It has its origins in the ancient Celtic harvest festival of Samhain, which marked the beginning of the Celtic new year on November 1st. The Celts believed that on the last night of the old year, October 31st, the souls of those who died during the year journeyed to the other-world. So on the eve of Samhain, the ghosts of the dead were on the move and the people led by their priests, the Druids, put out food for their journey, lit bonfires to aid them on their travels, and at the same time dressed in ghoulish costumes to scare the traveling dead away from the living.

After Christianity came to Ireland in the 5th century, the festival of Samhain became in the Christian calendar the feast day of All Saints or All Hallows, and the day before became All Hallows' Eve or Halloween. Many of the ancient customs and beliefs surrounding the eve of Samhain have persisted down to the present time. Halloween is still a night when all kinds of creatures from the other-world are out and about, including ghosts of the dead, demons, witches and the Little People.

At my grandmother's, Halloween was both a magical evening of games and feasting, and a fearful evening when scary things could happen. We ducked for apples and coins in a bathtub of water with our hands behind our backs. The apples bobbed around on the top of the water and were very difficult to catch with my mouth no matter how big I opened it. The coins rested on the bottom of the bathtub and I had to pick them up with lips and teeth, which seemed fairly easy, if only I could keep my head under water a little longer. Ducking for apples and coins was why we often called Halloween "ducking night." Large apples were also hung by string from the ceiling, and I had to catch them with my mouth with my hands tied behind my back. These were not easy feats to accomplish but it was fun trying.

But I could never bring myself to try any of the scary dares, nor could anybody else. We were all cowards. Or perhaps we believed enough in the underlying reality of the dares not to take any chances. It was scary fun being presented with the challenges and envisioning what might happen.

One dare was to go out to the haggard alone that night, circle a stack of oats three times, pulling three straws from the stack on each go-around, and the devil would appear to me as I pulled the ninth straw. I could not imagine myself pulling that ninth straw. The very thought of what might happen sent icicles of fear up and down my spine. What would I say to the devil when I met him face to face? Would I be tongue-tied? Would I faint? Would I try to run and not be able to? What would the devil say to me? Would my life be forever changed? I was too scared even to venture into the haggard with others, let alone on my own, or even to go outside into the darkness of Halloween night.

Another dare was to walk backwards down the stairs holding a mirror, and the person that appeared in the mirror at the end of the stairs would be the person I would marry. The girls giggled about that one. We all wanted so much to find out who that person would be. But nobody put the dare to the test. We were afraid of what or whom we might see!

I doubt if Granny would have let us test these dares, for despite her strong Christian faith, she believed in many of the ancient Celtic ways. Halloween was a night when bad things could happen. There was both fear and excitement in the air. Granny warned us, "Abductions by the Little People occur mostly on this night. And Halloween is also the night when the devil is particularly active." No doubt some of the dead traveling to the other world that night were being reluctantly herded by the devil and his fallen angels to a place they would rather not go. Halloween was not a night for timid souls to be out and about.

Besides games and dares on Halloween, we had a feast of cakes, fruit, and nuts. The eating of the *bairin breac*, a special fruit-cake, was one of the evening's highlights. This cake was baked with three special items wrapped in paper and hidden within it. There was plenty of excitement as Granny cut the cake carefully so as not to reveal its hidden treasures. She explained, "There is a ring, a coin, and a religious medal hidden in this *bairin breac*. The person who gets the ring will be the first to marry, the finder of the coin will be rich, and the one who bites into the religious medal will be a priest or a nun." We fought over the thickest slices for they had the best chance of having a treasure. So Granny had to intervene, and she gave each person a slice beginning with the youngest.

Over the years I got all three treasures, so my destiny changed from year to year. I concluded that according to the *bairin breac*, my destiny was indefinite. I could hardly be all three!

Barn dances were also part of the harvest festival celebrations of Samhain. At my grandmother's, the barn dance usually took place in early November before the thresher came, for thereafter the barn floor would be stacked with grain. Neighbors from the townland of Gaigue and beyond gathered in the barn after they had completed their farmyard chores. With two or three lanterns providing light, and an accordion, a fiddle, a *bodhran* (pronounced "boughrawn," Gaelic for a drum made from goat hide) and a flute providing some lively music, neighbors, young and old, danced until the wee hours of the morning, refreshed between dances with a barrel of Guinness porter. Dancing was interspersed with songs by men and women, recitations from the old-timers, and step dancing from the young folk. I particularly liked old Jimmy Gorman (the father of young Jimmy, Paschal, and Vincent) giving a recitation, for he put his heart and soul in it as he stomped around the barn like an actor on a stage. My special assignment for the night, besides dancing a slip jig, was to keep the musicians supplied with porter.

The Wren Day

The Wren Day, another of my favorite days, was the day after Christmas. It was the feast day of St. Stephen, the first Christian martyr. It was known as Boxing Day in England because of the English tradition of giving gifts to service people in boxes on that day. On St. Stephen's Day in Ireland, we participated in the centuries-old custom of "hunting the wren," originally a primitive, inhumane custom as the phrase implies, but one that evolved into a day of harmless merry-making with song, music and dance with no hunting of wrens.

In years long gone by, it was the custom for teams of boys armed with sticks to hunt and kill wrens. This barbaric custom was based on the legend that the wren informed on St. Stephen, the first Christian martyr, who was hiding in bushes to escape his killers. The wren gave away Stephen's hiding place, and hence the annual hunt to even an old score with the informer's descendants. Happily, over the centuries, the actual hunting of the wren went out of vogue, and the Wren Day that I celebrated had nothing to do with hunting wrens, although we did sing the following anonymous jingle as an opening number going from house to house:

> The wren, the wren, the king of all birds;
> St. Stephen's Day, he was caught on the furze.
> Altho' he is little, his family is great;
> Put your hand in your pocket, and give us a treat.

In this jingle, we gave tribute to the "wren, the king of all birds." According to ancient legend, the birds had a contest to elect a king, and the birds agreed that the title of king would be bestowed on the bird that flew the highest. The eagle proudly soared above the clouds, and gloatingly looked down on all the other birds away beneath him. But when the eagle could fly no higher, the wren emerged from among the eagle's feathers and flew up above the eagle. To the great chagrin of the eagle and uproarious joy of all the other birds, the little wren was crowned king.

I planned for the Wren Day well in advance, selecting my outfit with Granny's help from discarded worn-out odds-and-ends. I dressed in the most raggedy old clothes that I could find, put a piece of old lace curtain under my cap so that it hid my face while allowing me to see, and joined the Gorman boys, Jimmy, Paschal, and Vincent, similarly dressed, in going from house to house to entertain and to earn some pennies and hopefully a few silver coins. Jimmy played the mouth organ, Paschal beat a *bodhran*, Vincent sang, and I danced a reel or double jig.

Our first challenge at each home was to get past the dog that saw in us a major threat to his guardianship. Where we knew the dog's name, we were usually able to calm him down by showing our faces combined with a little sweet-talk. Once we got past that first line of defense, the people, who were expecting several such groups as ours, invited us inside.

Depending on the audience and the reception we got, we performed one or more of our set pieces. Rebel ballads such as "The Rising of the Moon" and "Boulavogue" were invariably well received. Both ballads relate to the rebellion of 1798 of which the Battle of Ballinamuck was a part. "The Rising of the Moon" was written by J.K. Casey of County Westmeath, and "Boulavogue" was written by P.J. McCall, a native of county Dublin. We sang "The Rising of the Moon" to the air of "The Wearing of the Green," with the words:

> Oh then tell me Sean O' Farrell tell me why you hurry so,
> Hush a *bhuachaill* hush and listen, and his cheeks were all aglow,
> I bear orders from the captain: Get you ready quick and soon,
> For the pikes must be together at the rising of the moon.
> At the rising of the moon, at the rising of the moon,
> For the pikes must be together at the rising of the moon.

> Oh, then tell me Sean O' Farrell where the gathering is to be?
> In the old spot by the river, right well known to you and me.
> One word more for signal token, whistle up the marching tune,
> With your pike upon your shoulder at the rising of the moon.

> Chorus

> Out from many a mud-wall cabin eyes were watching through the night,
> Many a manly heart was throbbing for the blessed morning light.
> Murmurs passed along the valleys, like the banshee's lonely croon,
> And a thousand blades were flashing at the rising of the moon.

> Chorus

On a lighter note, we also sang songs like "Cockles and Mussels," "Courting in the Kitchen," and "Come Back Paddy Reilly," that most people knew and could join in the chorus. Sometimes we happened on a family gathering in a festive mood, who pleaded with us to stay a while, which we did, with the family joining in the singing and dancing. That was usually worth some silver coins. At the end of the day, we gathered at my grandmother's to give our last performance, to collect a little more money, to recount our exploits and to divide the day's "take" evenly among the four of us.

At my grandmother's, I lived in anticipation from celebration to celebration. But staying at my grandmother's farm was not all fun and games.

It always meant much work both before and after school. There was one particular chore on the farm that I would like to have avoided—the picking of the potatoes in late October when it was misty wet and freezing cold. My uncle would dig potatoes all day alone, row upon row with his favorite spade. It was my task after school to pick the potatoes in buckets, segregating the large potatoes from the small ones, and piling them in two separate heaps in the field. I would have a competition between my left and right hands to see which one would pick the most small potatoes. I could pick up to seven small potatoes in one hand and more if they were *poreens* (Gaelic for very small potatoes). Though I favored the left hand, steering it to the largest concentration of potatoes, the right hand was more adept in gathering the potatoes out of the dirt and almost always won. I am right-handed. But these little games did not last long. Within minutes my fingers would be numb with cold, my boots heavy as lead with several extra pounds of wet dirt clinging to them and my whole body would ache from the stooping. But the sooner the picking was done, the sooner we covered the heaps of potatoes with straw and clay, and got to the warmth of the kitchen fire. When I kept my mind on the vision of a roaring fire on the open hearth, both hands worked faster without much concern for which one was picking the most potatoes, and the finger-numbing cold seemed to be easier to bear.

I often wondered why my uncle Michael kept on digging despite the cold and the wet. But with winter approaching, he was under pressure to get the potatoes out of the ground. He simply kept on digging as long as he could. A stopping point was reached when it became too dark for him to dig anymore. I sighed with relief when he downed his spade, grabbed a bucket, and helped me finish the picking. Together we rapidly picked the last rows of the potatoes, covered the heaps of potatoes, and trudged over the lane to the welcoming warmth of the kitchen fire.

Gloves for potato picking on frosty, damp October evenings had not yet been invented. Gloves were what ladies wore to Mass on frosty Sunday mornings. That was the way it was. Some chores were punishing and there was no way around that fact.

But I cannot recall ever opting not to go to my grandmother's, even though I always had the choice of being at home. The farm offered what seemed to be limitless opportunities to be connected with the earth and its living creatures. Shep, a mixed breed collie, always welcomed me with an avalanche of licks that swept me off my feet. I would fall to the ground and cover my head with my arms and Shep would try to penetrate my defenses to lick my face. It was a delightful game of hide and lick that we played.

Shep epitomized the farm's welcoming embrace, though all other creatures of the farm, both human and animal, were far less demonstrative. The acceptance was felt deeply. I belonged and was needed. I was entrusted with many important daily farm chores, such as milking, separating the cream from the milk and feeding the animals. It was also my responsibility to clean the houses of all the farm animals. Among my charges there was no fear, them of me, nor I of them. I could reach out and touch them all, as I did often, particularly when I fed them. It was like living in a large open zoo where the animals were not caged, but roamed freely without fear, some staying close to the farmyard and others wandering several fields away.

Besides offering an abundance of opportunities to be connected with nature, my grandmother's farm also offered many occasions to be connected with the Cetlic past with its emphasis on the magical and on the hidden and intriguing world of the Little People. My village and my home, though very much part of rural Ireland, were a short step or two removed from these attractions of the farm.

chapter 14

the little people

Vision is the art of seeing things invisible.

—Jonathan Swift (1667-1745)
Anglo-Irish Satirist, Author and Clergyman

The Irish countryside is awash with stories of the Little People, also known as the Wee People and the Good People. Some conjecture there must have been a time when these wee folks outnumbered all other inhabitants of the island. There is a vast library of folk tales featuring the Little People and their more celebrated eccentric cousins: leprechauns and banshees. Irish writers such as William Butler Yeats (1923 Nobel Prize-winning poet), James Stephens, Liam O'Flaherty, Douglas Hyde (the first President of Ireland from 1938 to 1945), Lady Wilde, Gerald Griffin and Patrick Kennedy, to name but a few, researched and published a wealth of folk tales from the Irish countryside featuring the Little People. The Irish Folklore Commission has in its archives over two million pages of folk tales taken from storytellers around the country.

Who are the Little People? Yeats, in his book, *Fairy and Folk Tales of Ireland*, first published in 1888, contends that the Irish peasantry believed that they were "fallen angels who were not good enough to be saved, nor bad enough to be lost." Others contend that the Little People were the first people to occupy Ireland and are known to history and folklore as the Tuatha de Danan—a magical people who were driven to the hills and went underground with the coming of the larger more warlike peoples from Europe and Scandinavia over 2000 years ago.

Whatever their origins, the Little People have for centuries roamed the Irish countryside singing and dancing, feasting and inciting imaginations with their ravishing *ceol sidhe* (Gaelic for fairy music). It is believed by some that the more haunting old tunes of Ireland are in reality the music of the Little People. The last of the great bards of Ireland, Turlough O'Carolan, blind composer and harpist (1670-1738), was supposed to have fallen asleep on a fairy rath, and thereafter the music of the Little People ran through his fingers to his harp.

Like the cuckoos and the corncrakes, the Little People are found only in the countryside, and because of the encroachment of cities and civilization are a dwindling species who stay very much out of sight of the island's modern inhabitants. I may be the only member of my family to have seen a corncrake, a very shy and elusive creature of the Irish countryside. But none of us, when last I checked, has seen one of the Little People, who are also extremely shy and very selective in their association with modern human beings.

When I was growing up in the 1930s and 1940s, I shared in an unquestioning belief in the Little People. My belief was passed on to me primarily by my grandmother, who had a deep respect for all preternatural and supernatural beings. It never entered my mind to question my grandmother's belief in the Little People just as it never entered my mind to question her belief in God or in other supernatural beings like Guardian Angels. The Little People were simply part and parcel of my grandmother's belief system and the belief system of my youth.

This belief in the Little People I never discussed with my grandmother or with anybody else. In fact, despite the many folk tales featuring Little People, there was a vast conspiracy of silence about them. When I broached the topic with my grandmother on one occasion, she briskly silenced me with *"Whist, a mhac,"* which gave me to understand that it was best not to speak of them at all.

The Little People live principally in raths or forts: jungles of rock, bushes and briars, which dot the Irish landscape and are whispered to be the entrances to the other-world. These forts were simply not to be disturbed or messed with. When we hunted rabbits, if they scurried into forts, there they found sanctuary. We then called off the dogs and hunted elsewhere, which was just the right thing to do. The almost universal respect and fear of the Little People no doubt explains in part why forts have remained unmolested from generation to generation down the centuries. William Allingham, in his poem entitled "The Fairies," expressed the people's respectful fear of the Little People in these words:

Up the airy mountain,
Down the rushy glen,
We daren't go a-hunting
For fear of little men;
We folk, good folk,
Trooping all together;
Green jacket, red cap,
And white owl's feather!

By the craggy hill-side,
Through the mosses bare,
They have planted thorn-trees
For pleasure here and there.
Is any man so daring
As dig them up in spite,
He shall find their sharpest thorns
In his bed at night.

Unlike my belief in Santa Claus, my belief in the Little People was of a different dimension. It belonged to the preternatural if not the supernatural realm, or at least to the twilight zone that lingered somewhere between heaven and earth. Although I prayed to my Guardian Angel, reciting daily—

Angel of God, my guardian dear
To whom God's love commits me here
Ever this day be at my side
To light and guard, to rule and guide

—The Little People were in many respects more real than my Guardian Angel. At night I seldom thought of my Guardian Angel, but the Little People were seldom far removed from consciousness. My grandmother would not allow me to throw out after dusk the water in which I washed my dirty feet lest I douse the Little People and make them mad. I could only do it under her close supervision pouring out the water while holding the basin close to the ground and only after she had hushed them away with a shake of her bib. The Little People were very much part of the fabric of my youth, unseen but nonetheless, very real.

Strangely, I grew up with somewhat less faith in a more celebrated solitary member of the Little People—the leprechaun.

> Neath the old oak trees
> In the shadows of green
> Where moss covered rocks
> Line the babbling stream
> He sits 'mid the twining roots and sings;
> "Don't come too close
> You'd best be warned.
> For I am Larry the Leprechaun."

The name leprechaun comes from the Gaelic *Leith Brogan* (Gaelic for one-shoe maker), as leprechauns are usually seen making or mending one shoe. The leprechauns of Ireland are close cousins of the Brownies of Scotland, the Cluricauns of Southern Ireland, the Trolls and Gnomes of Scandinavia and the Pixies, Pookas, Knockers, Red Caps and Bogles of Great Britain. Leprechauns are considered the ugly ducklings of the Little People. They are somewhat smaller in stature, reaching up to one's knee, older with a face like a wizened apple, and more temperamental than their more flamboyant cousins.

Leprechauns are for the most part depicted as male, though I have read one story about a leprechaun named Lucy who was closer in nature to the Little People, for she loved to wear fine clothes, dance and play pranks. Male leprechauns are usually hard working, hard drinking, smart as a whip and wily little fellows who most of the time outwit their human captors, but have a soft spot for humans who treat them kindly.

Leprechauns are sometimes seen at sunset under a hedge, dressed in scarlet jacket with a leather apron, cocked hat and turned up toes singing and mending shoes. Leprechauns have been professional cobblers and bankers to the Little People for centuries, making shoes for them and protecting their treasures. As cobblers, Leprechauns are kept very busy for the Little People love to dance, often wearing their shoes threadbare in a single night of dusk to dawn dancing. There is a story told about a woman from Ballisadare, County Sligo, who lived among the Little People for years. When she returned home, she had no toes. She had worn them down to the stump dancing.

The Little People are also notoriously non-protective of their wealth, and are well served by the leprechauns who guard well the secrets of their hidden treasures as many an Irishman has found out. Every Irish person knows that the Little People's pots of gold are hidden at the end of rainbows. But what is not universally understood is that rainbows, by nature, seek out the locations of the hidden gold. This is much to the dismay and great frustration of leprechauns, whose task it is to keep the treasure from falling into the spendthrift hands of mortals.

The lucky person who happens upon a leprechaun in the Irish countryside must hold onto him tightly, keeping eyes fixed on him as he leads the way to where a pot of gold is buried. But if the eyes are taken off him, even for an instant, he is gone. He will use every trick in his repertoire (and he has many) to distract people into looking away. His shenanigans and tricks are the scourge of those who seek his pots of gold. The leprechaun's character and smarts are captured in Robert Dwyer Joyce's poem:

> In a shady nook one moonlight night,
> A leprechaun I spied
> In scarlet coat and cap of green,
> A *cruiskeen* by his side.
> 'Twas tick, tack, tick, his hammer went,
> Upon a weeny shoe,
> And I laughed to think of a purse of gold,
> But the fairy was laughing too.
>
> With tip-toe step and beating heart
> Quite softly I drew nigh.
> There was mischief in his merry face,
> A twinkle in his eye;
> He hammered and sang with tiny voice,
> And sipped the mountain dew;
> Oh! I laughed to think he was caught at last,
> But the fairy was laughing, too.
>
> As quick as thought I grasped the elf,
> "Your fairy purse," I cried,
> "My purse?" said he, "'tis in her hand,
> That lady by your side."
> I turned to look, the elf was off,
> And what was I to do?

Oh! I laughed to think what a fool I'd been,
And, the fairy was laughing too.

I must confess that I often listened for the tap, tap, tap of the little hammer, but was never lucky enough to come across one of the little fellows.

Another solitary figure of the Little People is the banshee. The word banshee is from the Gaelic *bean*, meaning woman, and *sidhe* meaning a fairy—hence a female fairy. The banshee follows certain families and is often heard wailing before a death. The *caoine* (*caoineadh* in Gaelic), or weeping of the country women at funerals, is said to be an imitation of the banshee's eerie cry.

When I was nine years old, I had an encounter with a banshee. I was at my grandmother's house. My great uncle Patrick, my grandmother's brother, was seriously ill. Uncle Michael had been up all night for a couple of nights helping my great uncle Patrick's family. There was also a challenging event of a different kind unfolding at my grandmother's. The sow was pigging. That evening she had given birth to fourteen little piglets. We brought the sow and her brood into the kitchen, where we'd strewn an armful of straw on the cement floor and turned two forums (wooden benches) on their sides to fence in the pig family in one section of the kitchen.

The twenty-four hours following birth were critical hours for the baby pigs as their mother often lay on them, crushing the fragile new life out of their tender bodies. These little squeakers needed round-the-clock vigilance. Uncle Michael had not gotten sleep for forty-eight hours, so I bravely volunteered to stay up with the sow's very young, large family. My uncle and grandmother retired for the night at 11:00 p.m., after assuring that I had plenty of turf for the fire, and tea and cake to take me through the night.

As they went up the stairs to bed, I felt proud that I was entrusted with the grown-up task of watching over this new farm family. The sow and her little ones were fast asleep. It was a happy scene, fourteen little bodies nestling in a heap against their mother's flabby belly. A cricket sang from a crack in the stones of the hob (the structure containing the fireplace).

I put a few more turf on the fire and relaxed in a low chair in the right corner of the hob. I watched the sparks chase each other up the chimney and wondered where they went when they died. I did not see them fall back into the fire.

I twiddled my thumbs as I often saw my grandmother do. It was relaxing and fear-abating. I found myself nodding off. I got up, rubbed the sleep from my eyes, and walked up and down the kitchen floor. Having knuckled back sleep, I settled again into the chair in the corner and continued to watch the sparks go up the chimney. They tried to catch each other as they flitted up and out into the night.

Shortly after midnight, I was jerked to a keen sense of awareness by noises outside in the farmyard that I could not identify. I listened with my whole being. The sow moved as if to get up, and I had to shove one piglet out of harm's way. He squeaked pitifully when I lifted him and did not stop till I rewarded him with his mother's tit. The commotion awakened his brothers and sisters, who scrambled to get their own tits. Within a short time they were all asleep again in one big heap.

My ears heard every little movement of the pigs and of the turf fire. I could even hear my own heart beating. I told myself that there was no reason to be afraid. After all, my grandmother and uncle Michael were only a few strides away upstairs. But fear was always near the surface of a nine-year-old's heart that was prone to misinterpret some of nature's peculiar sounds, particularly when alone after midnight with a heavy burden of responsibility for a large and potentially lucrative family on his mind.

It was nearing 2:00 a.m. when I heard the first cry. My body stiffened. I held my breath. I heard nothing but the crackling of the fire. I must have imagined it! Had I dozed off and was I dreaming? My tense body relaxed a little. After the lapse of a few minutes, I gingerly made another cup of tea and was sipping it quietly when an eerie wail pierced the night.

I froze. Eerie wail followed eerie wail. Was this the banshee announcing the imminent death of my great uncle Patrick? Through closed eyes I could see a crouched slender figure, robed in a white loose sheet-like garment, moving slowly from the turf-shed towards the house with arms half-raised as if pleading and her body swaying rhythmically from side to side. Her unearthly cries touched the core of my being. A cold shiver went straight to the marrow of my bones. I felt beads of cold sweat run down the hollow of my back. I was paralyzed with fear. What could I do? I was frozen in place. I expected a rap on the back door at any moment. How was I to respond?

Then the awful wails seemed to move away from the house. I could not bring myself to look at the curtained window. Yet, through tightly closed eyes, I clearly saw the white-robed, sloughed figure with bowed head, long hair almost trailing the ground, move out of the shadows of the back yard toward the sheugh and the more open space beyond. The moon was bright, but her departing figure cast no shadow.

Then, just as I gained a little composure, there was an unearthly howl that was repeated several times. I clung to my chair for what seemed like forever. Gradually, very gradually, I loosed my sweaty grip and looked at the clock. It was 3:00 a.m. I had the presence of mind to bless myself. I could raise my hand! I uttered a low sigh of relief. How could an hour seem so long? The sow and her piglets were not in the least bothered. Mother and family of fourteen were sound asleep, all of them. Why them and not me?

After 3:00 a.m., there were no more cries or howls. Morning came slowly, ever so slowly. As dawn pushed the darkness before it, mobility came back to my limbs. I had been crouched in a ball for so long my muscles ached all over. I felt aged. I moved, half stooped, to make a fresh pot of tea and brought a cup to my grandmother. It was 4:45 a.m. She was surprised that I had awakened her so early, and asked, "Och! What's up, *a mhac*?"

I did my best to hide my fear and my relief at seeing her awake. I must have succeeded for she did not repeat her question. I could not tell her of my experience, for that would be to admit my fear and confess to a lack of manliness. I did not tell anybody even when my great uncle died two days later. It was just best not to speak of these things. My experience bolstered my quiet, firm belief in the Little People.

It was several years later that I heard the same cries pierce the night. This time it was the human-like cries of cats. Some months after that, I heard Shep howl. I could not mistake those sounds. They were embossed in my soul. I felt both relieved and robbed of a unique experience.

chapter 15

ceíoleígheRs ano the long winter nights

Ireland is where strange tales begin
and happy endings are possible.

—Charles Haughty (1925-)
Irish Prime Minister,
1979-1981, 1982 and 1987

From November through February, it was dark by 5:00 p.m. By 4:30 p.m., the bats came swooping down over the barn, darting through the lengthening shadows of the departing day. I often watched their rapid movements as they crisscrossed the square patch of sky above the farmyard at rooftop level in pursuit of their evening meal. I did not see the smaller flying creatures that attracted the bats, but I knew that they were also there at rooftop level doing their mid-air twilight dance, some for the last time as day slipped into night.

At ground level, I also crisscrossed the farmyard at a somewhat slower pace as I carted armfuls of hay to the cows and the horses, and armfuls of turf into the kitchen for the long night ahead. I often stacked a small cartload of turf in the scullery by the back door—insurance against having to go out later in the night to keep the fire on the kitchen hearth burning strong. The Irish night was populated by ghosts and Little People and the last thing I wanted to do was to fetch more turf from the turf-shed in the dark of night. The night belonged to the Little People and I did everything I could to avoid trespassing on their dark domain.

When the chores were done, I had my stirabout and fresh warm milk from that evening's milking. We prayed the rosary kneeling against chairs with our bootless, socked feet to the fire and my thoughts everywhere but where they should be. I gave out my decade of the rosary with thoughtless repetition of one Our Father, ten Hail Marys, and one Glory Be. Granny and uncle Michael led two decades each. We each had our own peculiar, sleep-inducing praying mantra. Granny's mantra had the most conviction, pleading, monotonously pleading: "Holy Mary, Mother of God, pray for us sinners, now and at the hour of our death, amen."

I said the last "amen" with great finality and blessed myself, which somehow liberated me from the cobwebs of sleep. And with mounting expectation I awaited the *ceidleighers*—the nightly male visitors. Not every house in the area was a *ceidleighing* house, but my grandmother's house had that designation. How that came about, I do not know. All I know is that it was open to visitors almost every long night of the year with a few exceptions such as Christmas Eve, when there was a wake in the vicinity and when my grandmother was away, which was very seldom.

The origin of the *ceidleigh* is lost in antiquity. In the Parochial Survey of Ireland, published in 1814, it is told how storytellers, or *seanchai* (as storytellers were then known), since time immemorial sat around Irish hearths telling folk tales of battles, cattle raids, love tales, visions, encounters with the Little People, family sagas and the like.

The nightly gathering around my grandmother's hearth was a continuation of this centuries-old tradition. The stories told had evolved into local tales, sharing of local news and ghost stories that always left the hair on the back of my neck bristle with fear. But the love of gathering in groups to tell stories had not changed. As always, only men went *ceidleighing*. And usually, no food or refreshments were provided, only the warmth of the fire on the open hearth and good conversation. I felt that Granny regarded these nightly sessions as a sacred trust, and always welcomed the visitors night after night with a warm smile and a hearth glowing with a blazing fire.

One of my self-appointed positions for the nightly gathering of the storytellers was doorman, and like any good doorman, my guests never had to knock. My well-tuned ears picked up the approaching footsteps on the gravel that led to the front door. One by one the male neighbors from the townland of Gaigue dropped in, greeted my grandmother, acknowledged his neighbors already there, and settled in before the fire for a long warm chat.

By 6:30 p.m., I knew if I had to fetch more chairs from the room, as the half-circle around the kitchen fire widened. On cold nights, when the wind whined and whistled around the house, I had the added task, when I figured that everybody that was coming had arrived, of putting old rags at the base of the front and back doors to stop the cold drafts. But my primary task was to keep the fire burning strong, so that even the *ceidleighers* farthest away at the top of the half-circle by the stairs also felt the fire's glowing warmth.

On an average night, there would be four to six *ceidleighers*. On a good night, we would have a dozen or more. Regular *ceidleighers* included Jimmy Gorman and Sonny Cole from a few fields away; Jimmy Quinn from a half mile over the lane at the back of the house, who was almost always the first to arrive; Pakie Larkin and his dad, Joe Larkin, the Canada-man, who had spent some time in Canada, from a mile or so over the same lane; Johnny Hurson, who often helped my uncle Michael with the farmyard work for pay and his brother, Michael Hurson, who only helped occasionally; Philip Brady from the road by the school; Phil Brady, the fiddler from the side of the hill and his brother John; Frankie McWade from beside the Fort to which the Little People retreated during daylight hours; and Paddy Larkin from the shop beside the school, where my grandmother sold her eggs and butter, and purchased the *Longford Leader* and kerosene oil for the lamp.

Granny sat close to the fire on the left side of the hob from where she presided informally over the night's discourse. A kerosene lamp that competed with the fire in casting shadows around the kitchen, hung on the wall above my grandmother's head. I had my stool in the opposite corner close to the room where the extra chairs were and with easy access to the stack of turf in the scullery at the back door.

I knew we were in for a good night when the half-circle bulged back to the stairs and Jimmy Quinn, with some ceremony, loaded two pipes with sweet smelling tobacco, topped them off with a small red coal from the fire, and passed them around for each of the men to have a few puffs. Nobody seemed in any way concerned with the co-mingling of oral bacteria.

Spitting into the fire was an accepted exercise. Even the men on the bulge of the half-circle had no problem landing their spittle in the middle of the flames, though a few had to lean forward in their chairs to do so. When nobody was around, I tried to land a spit into the fire from the top of the circle with disastrous results. The spit did not even make it halfway. I concluded that to succeed I needed more spit, so I would have to grow bigger and stronger. It was just one more handicap of youth.

The night's chit-chat had no set agenda, but it followed a time-honored pattern. The conversation usually drifted from local gossip to the price of pigs and cattle at the local fairs; to what the Priest said at Sunday Mass, not in the sermon as that was never discussed, but in the announcements; to what some politician said in his speech outside the church after Sunday Mass. The *ceidleighers* shared the news of the surrounding area and swapped what they knew about fairs and the going prices for livestock, funerals, births (human and animal), foxes sighted, the state of crops, weddings, visits by doctors and veterinarians, visitors from England and America and every event worth noting within a five-mile radius. Their pooled information was the source of my grandmother's encyclopedic knowledge of what was happening in her own and neighboring townlands.

The men told stories of bygone days, the hardships endured, the near misses of being caught by the Black and Tans, the ghosts encountered and "other world" phenomena experience—all told in graphic detail in the first person singular as eyewitness accounts. The stories were told with such personal conviction that there was no room for doubting any of them as actual happenings, at least in my young mind.

The very personal tales of ghostly encounters were at once the most fascinating and the most frightening to me. The ghost stories usually started around 9:30 or 10:00 p.m., when it was nearing my bedtime. It seemed that the *ceidleighers* turned to ghost stories after they had exhausted all other topics of conversation. A round of ghost stories was a way of bringing the night to a close and me to trembling with fear, despite stoic attempts to hide my feelings.

The men told of seeing people long dead and buried, and how their ghosts followed them on more than one occasion as they walked past the dead person's former home around midnight. But they explained that the ghosts followed them in a non-threatening manner. After they had the priest say Mass for them, they saw them no more. And added that they must have needed that kind of help to attain eternal rest. And my grandmother blessed herself, and everyone did the same in domino fashion, including myself at the other end of the semicircle in the opposite corner of the hob.

I am still trying to figure out how a ghost can follow you in a non-threatening manner!

They told stories of how people they knew, who had died suddenly without a priest, and were seen regularly by them and others roaming around their fields at night as if in search of something, or had some unfinished business to be taken care of. And for some of these a Mass did not seem to help. That was not their need. So they can be seen still roaming their fields, and will continue to do so until the unfulfilled need is met. This partially explained to me "Flaherty's Light," which I had seen myself several times in the fields under Flaherty's house on Aughadowry Hill across from my grandmother's house. The light, about a mile away as the crow flies, was visible to the naked eye moving back and forth in the field after dusk. The light, which did not appear every night, was a more or less accepted phenomenon which some people called a "will-o-the-wisp."

With a shrug of his shoulders, Phil Brady, the fiddler with theological insight, explained: "These post-mortem wanderings were part of their purgatory, which could continue even to the end of time when purgatory would cease to be." This was the first time that I heard this. Such an explanation never came up in catechism class, and it got me thinking. Though death seemed to me to be a horrible event, this roaming about alone night after night, scaring the wits out of people, was an aspect of death that should be avoided at all costs. The prayer for eternal rest for the dead that was on everybody's lips when anybody died, took on a whole new depth of meaning for me. "Eternal rest grant unto her, O Lord, and let perpetual light shine upon her, and may she rest in peace," was indeed a powerful prayer of blessing for the restless soul. The ghost stories at least taught me how to pray with heartfelt fervor for eternal rest for the dead.

It was obvious to me that the *ceidleighers* strongly believed in what they were telling. And I believed it too with every hair that bristled on the back of my neck with sheer fright. The ghost stories scared the "be japers" out of me. I was glued to my stool with cold sweat despite the warm fire, afraid to look behind me, or up the chimney, or anywhere but into the fire.

Granny, sensing my uneasiness and blaming it on being sleepy, ordered me "off up to bed *a mhac.*" That was almost as bad as being asked to go out into the dark of night to the turf-shed for more turf. To get to bed, I had to climb a stairs that had no light at the top, take a step or two along a pitch black corridor to my room that I shared with my uncle Michael, and the room itself was pitch black. I huddled halfway up the stairs trying to muster enough courage to penetrate the darkness and the ghosts that surely lurked there. With my grandmother urging "Up, up to bed," I made a frantic dash to where I knew the bed to be, pulled the bed clothes over my fully clothed body, boots and all, and held my breadth until I fell asleep.

I marveled at the courage of the men, many of whom had to walk home alone passing Forts and other havens of the spirit world. And they did that close to the bewitching hour of midnight. I just could not do it, and live to tell about it. And I am telling you about it now, simply because I never did it. My greatest feat was to get to bed in the dark in the same house and that took a leap or two of superhuman effort.

In the morning, I got a mild scolding from my uncle Michael for taking my boots to bed. But he never told my grandmother of my cowardice. I thought that was very thoughtful and very considerate of my fragile psyche.

chapter 16

fishing and hunting

As I crossed the wooden bridge I wondered
As I looked into the drain
If ever a summer morning should find me
Shoveling up eels again.

—Patrick Kavanagh (1905-1967)
Irish Poet

Fishing and hunting at my grandmother's were mostly Sunday after-Mass sports. Ireland is blessed with an abundance of lakes, rivers and streams that have salmon, trout, pike, perch and sometimes eel. The island is a fisherman's paradise. Even the small streams can surprise a fisherman with the number and size of its trout.

One such small stream meandered at the foot of Gaigue Hill, separating my grandmother's farm from those of her neighbors. This stream, which we called a river, was about twenty feet at its widest, and trout and eel frolicked in its waters and muddy holes. When the water was high, I fished for trout with rod and line and worms dug from the vegetable garden. The best time to catch trout with rod and line was shortly after rain when the river had an influx of new muddy water from the ditches that fed into it. When the water was high and clear, I usually muddied the water up-stream to fool the fish into believing an influx of fresh worms were coming with the muddy water. Only these fresh worms had hooks in them. It worked almost every time.

During a dry spell, when the water in the river was low, we used a different fishing strategy that we called teeming, a strategy that required many hands to implement. If there was a law then forbidding teeming as a fishing technique, we were blissfully unaware of it. The only constraint on our fishing activities was the sensitivity of some farmers to what we did to the river. So

159

we had to be particularly careful to do nothing that would cause the river to alter its course in any way.

As soon as we got home from Mass, the Gorman boys (Jimmy, Paschal and Vincent) and I gathered up the appropriate equipment—a couple of spades, a few basins and buckets, a creel (usually used to carry turf)—and ran to the river. After a quick survey of the water flow and the larger water holes at the bends in the river, we selected the water hole that would give us the best catch of fish, and at the same time was a manageable hole for teeming. Our first task was to divert the flow of water from coming into the hole that we had selected. We built a dike of sod and tree branches that diverted the flow of water to the side of the river away from the deep hole in the river's elbow.

The dike ran from the upper end of the elbow to the lower end so that the water could neither flow into the hole from the upper end nor back up into it from the lower end. This operation usually took a couple of hours. We built a wall of sod using tree branches to strengthen and hold the sod together. Then, we posted one person to watch and maintain the dike, and the other three started teeming the water out of the hole with buckets and basins. Depending on the size of the hole, this took a couple of hours or more of constant teeming, ever careful not to throw fish down river with the buckets and basins of water. Twice we all had to rush to maintain and patch the dike as water began seeping through.

As the amount of water remaining in the elbow got low, Jimmy took the lead in dragging the creel, a deep basket made of sally rods, through the water. When the water drained, there were usually trout at the bottom of the creel. As the water got lower and the fish could no longer hide in the deep recesses of the river bank, we got more trout with each dragging of the creel. We continued to teem and soon we could see the trout splash hither and thither in the shallow muddy water of the hole.

We took turns dragging the creel through the muddy water and dumping the catch on the river bank before putting them into one of the buckets, lest they flip back into the river. Any fish less than six or seven inches, we threw back in downstream. When we were pretty satisfied that we had most of the trout, at least the larger ones, two of us dragged the creel through the twelve to eighteen inches of mud at the bottom of the hole to catch eel. A dozen or so draggings produced five eels. Additional attempts produced nothing. All four of us then searched the mud with our hands and bare feet. After crisscrossing the mud bed a few times and feeling nothing, we decided we had everything that we were going to get.

We dismantled the dike and returned the river as closely as possible to the way we found it, so that none of the farmers could complain that we contributed to the river changing course. We then sat down on the river bank and counted our catch, which came to forty-two trout and five eels. We divided the fish four ways with each one taking a selection working from the oldest to the youngest. I got the last two trout and the Gormans got the fifth eel. Dog-tired, but satisfied with the afternoon's catch, we trudged up the hill home.

The catch was welcomed enthusiastically by my grandmother, who had the frying pan ready on the open hearth. Together, we cleaned the fish and she cooked them in butter. The eel curled up and flipped on the pan, as if in a final effort to escape being cooked and eaten. But it did not succeed. The eel tasted a little oily to me, so I passed my portion of it to uncle Michael, who seemed to relish the extra helping. I ate three yummy trout as I proudly recounted for my grandmother and uncle each step of the afternoon's fishing.

When we did not go fishing after Sunday Mass, we went hunting. Rabbits were our principal game. And how the local rabbit population must have dreaded Sundays after Mass! We did not see rabbits as romantically as Padraic Pearse, the Irish educator, patriot, and poet who wrote:

Sometimes my heart hath shaken with great joy
To see a leaping squirrel in a tree,
Or a red lady-bird upon a stalk,
Or little rabbits in a field at evening,
Lit by a slanting sun.

Like trout and eel, we saw rabbits as food. We did not have guns so the hunting of birds such as partridge, grouse, quail, and pheasant was something we did not indulge in. We seldom saw wild duck or wild geese. Evidently, we were not on any of the flyways for these birds. Occasionally in the fall, we saw flocks of geese flying in formation high in the sky, but I do not recall seeing wild duck.

On rare occasions, we hunted fox when we saw one in the area or some of the local farmers complained of losing chickens. Fox hunting was lucrative as the government paid seven shillings (about one dollar at that time) for each fox tongue. If we happened on a den of young fox cubs, which the Gormans did on one occasion when I was not along, then we were really in the money. Each tongue, young or old, brought seven shillings. An entire fox family usually meant six or seven tongues.

On our way to the rabbit hunt across the fields, we sometimes stirred up a hare and the dogs gave chase. But it was usually a wasted effort as the hare, a much faster animal than rabbits, quickly left the dogs behind. But it was hard not to get excited and not to try to catch the hare. The hare invariably headed for the nearest hill, where its short front legs gave it a real advantage in the chase with the dogs. We made every effort to deny the hare that advantage and tried to divert the chase away from a hill, not an easy task, as we were surrounded by hills. When we failed, as sooner or later we did, we watched as the hare separated itself from the dogs up and over a hill. Eventually the dogs gave up and returned to us and the more promising task of hunting the much slower rabbits.

Rabbit hunting was our specialty. I usually went hunting with the three Gorman boys: Jimmy, Paschal, and Vincent. Jimmy was a year or two older than I, Paschal was my age and Vincent was a year or two younger. Jimmy, being the eldest and the wisest, usually selected the location or locations of the hunt. Our hunting tools consisted of three dogs, a ferret, a couple of spades, a few small nets and a burlap sack. Rabbits were fairly plentiful and Jimmy selected the areas that would give us the best return on our efforts. He knew the haunts of rabbits like he was one of them.

When we got to the first location, and the dogs' sniffing and yelping indicated the presence of rabbits, we reconnoitered the area to locate the rabbit burrows. We had to clear away briars and undergrowth to get a good view of the burrow openings. Usually rabbit burrows have two or more exits. We put nets over the openings, securing them to roots of nearby bushes, and posted a person with a dog at each burrow exit. Jimmy was in charge of the ferret and he put the ferret in the exit without a net. We waited and prayed that the ferret would scare the rabbits into our waiting nets. It was important that the rabbits had another way out of their burrows other than the one the ferret entered. For if the ferret caught a rabbit inside the burrow, it would suck the rabbit's blood and then fall asleep. We would then have a major problem locating the ferret perhaps deep in the burrow and digging it out. That could take all afternoon.

We waited. No rabbits emerged. Usually they come out pretty quickly. They don't wait around with a ferret on their tails. Finally the ferret appeared at one of the exits. This was an empty burrow, at least on this afternoon, or the occupants escaped through an exit we had not spotted.

We moved quickly to the next rabbit haven hoping that we would find somebody home. We located the burrow exits, set our nets, posted our sentries and sent in the ferret on his mission of scare the rascals out. He did just that with lightning speed. Two rabbits hit my net almost at the same time. My dog jumped on them at the same time that I did. In the confusion, one rabbit got loose and scurried through the bushes with the dog in hot pursuit. One of the other nets also had a rabbit entangled in it, which Vincent caught and deposited in the burlap sack. We now had two rabbits. The dogs were yelping and scurrying hither and thither as they picked up the scent of the rabbits. But where was the ferret? He finally showed up at one of the exits. We picked him up, gathered our equipment, and moved smartly to the next rabbit haven, which was a few fields away or about half a mile.

Along the way, I was given some tips on how to secure two rabbits in one net. This time I was determined not to let the side down. I would fall on the rabbits and lie on them until help came. But I was denied the opportunity to test my strategy.

We hunted six locations that afternoon and netted seven rabbits. At two of the locations, the ferret must have taken a grand tour of all the burrows before showing up, which made us all a little nervous. We did not want to be digging burrows into the night. And the farmers would not like to see their ditches leveled.

I took home two rabbits and the Gormans took the rest. uncle Michael skinned them, and Granny roasted them in a skillet with whole onions, potatoes and carrots. She put live coals both underneath and on the lid of the cast-iron skillet as it rested on the open hearth alongside the fire. Rabbit was always a tasty treat and made an appetizing Sunday evening meal.

chapter 17

threshing day

This was where the haggard was,
Where stacks were thrashed and winnowed
Till axels deep in chaff grew muffled
And straw ricks grew and billowed
For bed and thatch and fodder,
And oats that spilled were bagged
And milled for skillets
And a breakfast table.

—Philip Brady (1942-)
Irish Family Physician and Poet

The thresher came each year in November or December with the regularity of a moveable feast. I heard the thresher's distinctive rhythmic whining several days in advance of its arrival as it moved from farm to farm on its way to my grandmother's. I looked forward to Threshing Day with at least as much anticipation as I did Christmas. I prayed that the thresher would come on a Saturday rather than on a school day. Granny even more fervently prayed for no rain. Only once were my prayers answered. When the thresher came on a school day, I ran non-stop from school to the haggard at the back of the house where the threshing was in progress. I wanted to be a part of as much of the threshing operation as possible. Above all, I wanted to be part of, if not lead, the rat elimination task force.

The haggard was an enclosed open-air area of about a quarter acre close to the farmhouse where the stacked sheaves of grain awaited the thresher. When we brought the sheaves of oats (and some years a small amount of wheat and rye) in from the fields in late August or early September, we stored them in oblong or circular stacks with the grain at the center and the stalks at the outer edges. We placed the sheaves on beds of tree branches and stacked them eight to ten feet high. We thatched the top of each stack with rushes to protect the grain from rain and the crows.

To wish an Irish farmer "May the crows never pick your stacks" was a blessing on a par with "May you be in heaven three days before the devil knows that you are dead." If the crows got half a chance, they scratched open the stacks of grain to the wind and the rain, which meant grain damage and loss. As further protection against the crows, we capped the thatched stacks with a mesh of thorny blackberry briar. But sometimes even the blackberry briar mesh did not deter the thieving, grain-hungry crows.

The haggard was prepared for threshing several days in advance. Uncle Michael selected and marked the best spot for the thresher. The thresher had to be on firm, even ground, otherwise one or more wheels would sink with the threshing motion and cause lengthy delays. We also prepared the bed or foundation for the rick of straw, which consisted of limbs and branches of trees that surrounded the haggard. This bed of branches kept the straw off the wet ground.

The thresher that I knew in the 1940s was a large lumbering machine shaped like a long, oversized double-decker coffin on four wheels. It whined and groaned as its innards beat the sheaves of ripened grain to separate the grain from the straw. This sheave-devouring and straw-belching noisy annual visitor captured my soul and demanded and got the full attention of the townland for the week or two that it was in the area. Threshing was an extended festival of hard work.

The thresher came to the farm the evening or night before Threshing Day, when it had finished threshing at the neighbor's. The thresher was pulled from farm to farm by two horses. A mule pulled the engine that turned the large belts that provided the machine with the threshing power. The thresher was pulled and pushed to its appointed position. The big belts were put in place. The engine was test started. The stage was set for an early morning threshing start.

Threshing was very labor intensive. It took a *meitheal* (Gaelic for a group of workers) of about fourteen pairs of hands and feet to support the threshing operation. The two men who traveled with the thresher from townland to townland and from farm to farm either owned the thresher or worked directly for the owner. Their primary task was to ensure the proper mechanical operation of the thresher. Each townland provided the other dozen men needed to feed the sheaves of grain to the thresher; attend to the burlap sacks that collected the threshed grain, which came out of two chutes in the side of the machine; carry the bulging sacks of grain on their backs to the barn; and gather the grain-less straw and build it into one large rick on the prepared foundation of tree branches. The straw was used as bedding for all the farm animals, particularly during the winter months. This straw was not used to thatch cottages. That straw got special handling. It was not fed to the thresher. The grain was extracted by hand-flailing, which protected the straw stalk from being beaten and broken.

This is the Garvey Thresher, the type of machine that came to the Townland of Gaigue Upper and to my grandmother's farm each winter to thresh the oats. (Photograph courtesy of the Ballinamuck Bicentenary Committee.)

Threshing was a non-stop operation that started at dawn, which in November was around 8:00 a.m., and ended when all the stacks of sheaves in the haggard were translated into a barn full of sacks of grain and a large rick of straw. All hands worked all the time. Meals were served in shifts. Neighbor women helped with the cooking and the serving. The men changed chores regularly as some chores were more demanding and more strenuous than others. Only men with strong backs opted to carry the 100-plus-pound burlap sacks of grain to the barn.

The man and job that I envied the most fed the sheaves of grain to the thresher. He stood in a box that was at the feeding end of the thresher, not unlike the priest in the pulpit or the captain on the bridge—in command of the entire goings on. He took possession of the sheaves that were thrown up to him, cut the binding that held the sheaves together with a knife, loosened the sheaves and fed them to the thresher grain first in a constant stream. The thresher sucked in the sheaves with such vigor that it could easily suck in a hand or an arm. Only the older men were entrusted with this exacting and somewhat hazardous pivotal task.

My main task was to maintain communication between the kitchen and the haggard, and to ensure that all got fed, including the horses and the mule. I particularly enjoyed helping to tramp down and build the rick of straw. As the rick got higher, we needed a ladder to get up on it. I enjoyed sneaking a slide down the side away from the thresher where nobody could see me.

My most challenging and exciting task was marshalling the help of the Gorman boys armed with sticks and dogs to rid the haggard of its most nasty pests. As the last sheaves were being removed from each stack, we positioned ourselves encircling the stack to ensure that no rat escaped. There were also mice, but the rats were the big prize. The stacks provided these critters with a home where they had an abundance of food and warm shelter.

When the rats broke their cover, there were shouts of "get them" from all sides. The rats scurried in all directions. So did the mice. The dogs yelped and pounced on moving straw. Sticks also beat on anything that moved. After a few moments of pandemonium, with everyone shouting orders and dogs dashing hither and thither, there was a lull in the excitement and a quick assessment of the toll in dead and injured. It was impossible to control the dogs and get them to ignore the mice and go after the rats. Even the humans found it difficult to ignore the mice. We got four rats and twice that many mice. Others escaped to the other stacks, but that was ok for we would have another chance at them when we got to the last sheaves on those stacks. At the end of the day, the score was thirteen dead rats and five escapees that we knew of. We lost count and track of the mice.

When the thresher belched out the last sheaf of straw, everyone was dog-tired, even the dogs. The men quickly scattered to take care of their farmyard chores. The thresher owners moved the thresher to the next farm. I buried the rats in the haggard where they died.

I milked the cows and tucked all the animals in for the night, very much aware that there were at least five additional animals of the unwanted variety lurking in the shadows that I would somehow have to deal with in the days ahead.

I had my porringer of stirabout and fresh milk. After I led my decade of the rosary, I slept on and off through the rest, despite my grandmother's nudging and prodding. The next morning I did not remember going to bed.

part 3

church

chapter 18

the surround presence of the church

Question 138: What is the Church?
The Church is the visible society founded by Christ Himself, to continue on earth his work of teaching, sanctifying and ruling mankind, for their eternal salvation.

—Irish Catechism of Catholic Doctrine

The village church bells rang out each morning at ten to eight summoning the villagers to 8:00 a.m. Mass. The bells pealed the Angelus (prayer said to commemorate the Annunciation) at noon and again at 6:00 p.m., and people stopped what they were doing in the shops, on the street, and in the fields to pray the Angelus. Men doffed their hats going by the church, women and children blessed themselves or genuflected, and policemen saluted. Men also tipped their caps or hats to the priest and all greeted him as Father.

I memorized in primary school the catechism answer to the question: What is the Church? But my experience of the Church did not match very well with the catechism answer given above, or so it seemed. Church was where I went to Mass every Sunday. It was where I was baptized, received my first Holy Communion, went to confession, got confirmed by the bishop, where I would someday be married, and one day, far off, be buried. Church was an integral part of my life. It was something more than a house or a building. Like family, the Church seemed to be all around me and ever-present.

Everybody in my village went to church. Perhaps not everybody went to church every Sunday, as they were supposed to, but it seemed that way to me for the two Sunday Masses were almost always crowded. I went to church two to three times most Sundays. I served as an altar boy at the 8:00 a.m. Mass, then returned to the 11:00 a.m. Mass as a member of the congregation. I returned again as an altar boy at 6:00 p.m. for Benediction and rosary, which we called evening devotions. In my family this was a Sunday routine.

My mother was the quiet motivator behind this church attendance. She firmly believed that we should go to the two scheduled Masses on Sunday, unless we had something more important going on. But very little was more important than Mass. A fever of 103 or 104 maybe, but that was it. Many people in the village went to church twice on Sundays, once to morning Mass and again to evening devotions. The people who lived out of town seldom returned for evening devotions. Getting the horse and sidecar or the pony and trap ready for a second Sunday trip to town simply for Benediction was just not done. They said the rosary in their homes.

When I was eight, I became an altar boy and assisted the priest at baptisms, weddings and funerals, as well as at Sunday and daily Mass. I mastered the Latin responses to the priest at Mass and rattled them off as if Latin was my second nature. Later, when I studied Latin in secondary school and learned something about what I was saying serving Mass, it still did not make much sense:

"De profundis clamavi ad te Domine: Domine exaudi vocem meam. Fiant aures tuae intendentes in vocem deprecationis meae."("Out of the depths I cry to Thee, O Lord: Lord hear my voice. Let your ears be attentive to the voice of my supplications." Psalm 130, verses 1 and 2.) The psalms as prayers were lost on me in those years.

But I enjoyed the exposure in black cassock and white surplus, hand-washed and ironed by my mother, and of being on the altar before a packed church. I particularly enjoyed holding the paten under chins during the distribution of Holy Communion, and getting a close-up look at tongues and the odd gold filling in teeth.

I enjoyed ringing the bells at the elevation of the Host and Chalice, and draining on my head the last drops of wine from the cruets in the sacristy after Mass when the priest's back was turned. Just as well that Mrs. Flanagan from the post office across the street did not know of these little swigs or I would not have overheard her say to my mother after Mass one morning, "Wouldn't he make a lovely priest some day, God bless him."

Being an altar boy gave me something to do during church besides praying, which I wasn't very good at. Besides ringing bells and assisting at communion, I changed the big missal from one side of the altar to the other and back again at the appropriate times. I brought the water and wine to the priest, and the water and towel to wash and dry his fingers. I raised the priest's alb from off his shoes as he ascended the altar steps, and again when he descended so that he would not trip on his vestments. For special occasions such as at funeral Masses and at Benediction, I vied with other altar boys to be thurifer (censer-bearer) and to swing the thurible (censer) with its lighted charcoal, smoking with sweet-smelling incense.

Being a good altar boy meant knowing each priest's preferences and oddities and responding appropriately. In short, being an altar boy meant being always on your toes with plenty of action, including a long list of Latin responses given at appropriate times and signals. As an altar boy, time flew in church as I was almost as busy as the priest himself. No wonder that when I was in the congregation and not serving, Mass seemed to drag a lot. I thought that one way of taking care of that would be to become a priest. But that would hardly be a proper motive!

Being an altar boy had a lucrative season. Drumlish families gave a goodly number of their sons to the church, who devoted their lives to working in England, Scotland, Africa and America. After World War II was over, two Burbage brothers, Thomas and Edward, brothers to Michael and Molly Burbage of the Burbage hardware/grocery/pub, who were priests in Birmingham, England, came home each summer for a couple of weeks. Father Patrick Whitney, a white-haired man who had an easy way with him and stayed with the Rogers of the mill, also came every year for two or more weeks. He was a founding member of St. Patrick's Missionary Society in 1932, and worked in West Africa. Father Lawrence Brady, a jovial man who was a parish priest in Glasgow, Scotland, was a regular summer visitor to his brother across the street from us. And two Kane brothers, Monsignors Stephen and Bart (brothers to John, Hughey, and Michael Kane of the shoe shop), who were priests in Des Moines, Iowa, U.S.A., the same diocese as Monsignor John Reynolds, my mother's brother. They came home for a couple of months during the summer every three or four years.

Monsignor Stephen Kane was a chaplain with the U.S. Armed forces in World War II. He was taken prisoner by the Germans and spent a couple of years in a German prison camp. Dad loved to listen to him tell of his experiences. I wanted to listen too but Dad always ordered me out to play, as adult conversation was not for young ears.

These visiting priests, every day that they were at home, came to the church to say Mass usually after the scheduled 8:00 a.m. Mass. They were happy to have us altar boys assist them. We usually received a tanner to a shilling from each of the English priests and two bob to a half crown from the Yankee priests, who seemed to have much more money in their pockets.

The Yankee priests wore black suits of shiny light fabric, smoked cigars, were always upbeat and cheerful, and talked to us about our parents, brothers, and sisters. The English priests wore black suits of heavy fabric, smoked cigarettes, were serious and businesslike, and seldom talked to us.

A good week of extra Mass serving at the height of the season could add up to eight to ten shillings—a small bonanza. With the visiting members of the cloth, there was also a better than normal opportunity for us to imbibe a little wine.

Weddings and funerals were also occasions for altar boy tips. Weddings usually occurred on Saturdays, and after the ceremony, the best man came to the sacristy with an envelope for the priest and a shilling each for the altar boys. Weddings were joyful happenings, so happy that the mother of the bride and the bride often cried. Everybody flung confetti at the newly married couple on the church steps after the ceremony, which made the sexton mad, for he had to clean up afterwards.

Funerals took place on any day except Sunday. The doleful single pealing of the church bell, ten seconds apart, welcomed the mourners to the removal of the remains to the church the day before burial. And the same doleful pealing of the church bell welcomed the people to the funeral Mass at 10:00 a.m. on the day of burial.

As there were no funeral homes, the dead person, usually referred to as "the remains" or what was left when the soul departed, was laid out in his or her bed. Family, neighbors and friends came by to pay their last respects and to comfort the family of the deceased. Usually the wake was an all-night affair with food, Guinness and clay pipes filled with tobacco being served to everybody who came.

In years gone by, when people were less able to determine when death had taken place, the wake had a very practical purpose. The custom of an all-night vigil with the corpse had its origin in the desire to make sure that the person was really dead. Irish folklore abounds with stories of people waking up after being left for dead, or they pounded on their coffin as they were being taken to the church or to the cemetery. So families would lay them out in their beds and neighbors would gather around and eat and drink and wait and see if they would wake up, which is how the custom of holding a "wake" came about.

It was customary for each visitor to first visit with the remains for a while in the bedroom, say a prayer or two for his or her soul's eternal rest, and then visit with the living in the kitchen while lighting up the clay pipe with a red hot coal from the open hearth, and sharing in the food, drink and the conversation. Not everybody stayed all night, but it was a mark of ultimate respect to do so.

The Irish wake is immortalized by novels, stage plays and films, where the wake is often characterized as a drunken brawl. But that was more the rare exception than the rule. Almost all wakes, in my experience, had a barrel or at least a half-barrel of Guinness porter for mourners. Those who opted to stay all night might be feeling no pain by the wee hours of the morning. But drunken brawls at wakes were very rare occurrences, celebrated mostly in fiction and in jokes that poked fun at Irish social life asking: "What is the difference between an Irish wake and an Irish wedding? Give up? Well, there is one less drunk at the wake!"

The remains were brought to the church in a coffin the day following the wake in the home and stayed in the church overnight. On the day of the removal of the remains from the home to the church, mourners accompanied the coffin from the home in a long procession of horse-drawn sidecars and traps that followed the horse-drawn hearse to the church. If you met a funeral procession on the road, it was considered respectful to stop and tag on at the end of the procession for a little ways, as still is done in some rural parts of the U.S., and then go about your business. The deceased person's popularity and influence was usually gauged by the size of the procession from home to church.

When the remains got to the church, the priest met the casket at the door, sprinkled it with holy water, and led it to the altar, reciting some of the psalms in Latin. Following a few short prayers, the priest, flanked by two members of the family, stood at a small table beside the altar, and each mourner filed by the table and gave an offering. Family members and close relatives gave more than others. Apart from the immediate family, which usually gave paper money from a ten-shilling note to a twenty-pound note, the amount of the offering by the average mourner was dictated by what was given by the family of the deceased at a funeral of the mourner's family. If I went to a funeral of my friend's father and gave an offering of five shillings, my friend would be obliged to give an offering of five shillings at the funeral of my father.

The family members at the table with the priest recorded in their memories what each mourner gave. Nothing was ever written down, yet they remembered who gave what for years. I remember my grandmother saying that this funeral was a two-shilling funeral and that another funeral was a five-shilling funeral, meaning that she was obliged to give two or five shillings or whatever the amount that was given by that family at a funeral of one of her family.

The funeral offerings, as these donations were called, went to support the priests of the parish. My reaction was, wow! What is Father going to do with all this money? But I never had the gumption to ask. It seemed like bagfuls of money to me then, but in reality it was only a portion of what was needed to support a rectory, a housekeeper, and all other expenses of the parish.

After the funeral Mass on the following day, the day of burial, we had the prayers for the dead and the blessing of the closed casket with incense and holy water. Then the altar boys, dressed in cassocks and surplices and carrying the processional cross and holy water, accompanied the priest in the procession to the cemetery about a half-mile to the other end of the village. We fought with each other to see who would carry the processional cross, for that altar boy led the procession.

At the graveside, the cross-bearer stood at the end of the grave opposite the priest. The other altar boy with the holy water stood alongside the priest. As altar boys, we had the best graveside positions. We were at the center of the burial drama. We saw the color of the clay change on the interior sides of the grave as it got deeper. We counted the teeth in the skulls of the more recently buried. We heard the whisperings of consolation and encouragement among family members. We saw women mourners cry uncontrollably, some to the point of having to be restrained from throwing themselves into the grave on top of the coffin. We saw the stoicism of the men, who looked stiff and solemn but seldom shed a tear. Happily, we were usually the only children at the graveside ceremony.

On rainy days, which happened often, the graveside was a slippery, muddy mess. The bottom of the grave usually had a half-foot of water. The dirt from the grave was piled on one side with the skulls and bones of those previously buried in the grave placed on top the pile. Each family had a plot of at least two graves in the cemetery, which the family owned for generations. Burial of family members alternated between the two graves. If the family was expecting deaths to follow soon after one another, as in the case of an elderly couple, the first to die was buried deeper than normal so that the second casket could be buried in the same grave on top of the first casket without disturbing it too much.

With each burial, the family saw the skulls and bones of some of their ancestors. Old-timers, in the fashion of the gravedigger in Shakespeare's play, *Hamlet*, conjectured on the identity of the skulls and bones, and

176

whispered among themselves to whom they might belong. The men of the family of the deceased placed the skulls and bones alongside the new casket before they filled in the grave with dirt.

Like it or not, Irish families were united in the same grave with their ancestors. This burial custom gave a wealth of meaning to the old Irish proposal for marriage: "How would you like to be buried with my people?" Marriage was more than a commitment for life. For the bride, it was also a commitment to burial with the in-laws in the family grave.

The immediate family usually stayed at the graveside until the last shovel of dirt was placed on top of the remains. The family of the deceased was responsible for digging the grave, maintaining the graveside, and keeping the weeds and grass cut—a practice that gave the cemetery a very uneven and often un-kept look. But Irish village burials, without artificial grass blankets to hide the dirt and without flowers, provided a fitting backdrop to the priest's words: "From ashes to ashes and dust to dust...." reminding all of our final fate. The lineup of the welcoming committee of ancestral skulls and bones sitting atop the dirt weeping drops of rain, underlined the all too clear message of the mortality of our lives. "Dust to dust...."

No wonder I was afraid to walk past the cemetery after dark. When I had to pass it, which was seldom, I ran. I had visions of the ghosts of the dead, packed together in their four feet by six feet cramped quarters, crawling out to stretch their bones once darkness fell. I had heard of whistling past the cemetery but when I tried, nothing came out. My tongue stayed flat and dry in my mouth. I was too scared to whistle. But running was something I did well. I always ran past the cemetery, even in the daytime, blessing myself for protection as I ran.

Rain or shine, I usually got a shilling for my graveside presence, and for that reason seldom missed an opportunity to assist in what the catechism called "one of the corporal works of mercy," burying the dead.

Not all altar-boy chores resulted in tips. Serving the regularly scheduled Masses on Sundays, weekdays and Holy Week ceremonies, some of which lasted for several hours, brought no financial rewards. Similarly, churchings, which took place after Sunday Mass, meant no financial gain. Churching was a short ceremony that took place fairly regularly. A woman of the parish would approach the altar rails after Mass, and the priest, assisted by an altar boy with a small bucket of holy water, would pray over her in Latin. And would then sprinkle her generously with the holy water as she made the sign of the cross on herself. I paid no attention to the significance of this ceremony until one Sunday my mother presented herself at the altar rails to be churched. I held the holy water for the priest, and as the priest read the Latin prayers, I kept wondering, *why is my mother getting this done? Did she do something wrong?* Not my mother. If anyone in the village was a saint, she was one. I would not be so bold as to ask her or ask the priest. It was something between my mother, the priest and God. It was their business alone.

It was years later that I learned the meaning of what took place at churchings. It was a ritual cleansing after the birth of a baby. The birth of a baby somehow made the mother unclean, and she had to submit to the cleansing rite of churching before she could receive the sacraments again. This relic from a less enlightened age did not survive the candid questioning of church ceremonies that came with the Second Vatican Council and churching quietly disappeared from church rituals.

Being an altar boy also meant some sacrifices. Serving Mass or Benediction came before all else, even before Gaelic football, as sometimes happened on Sunday evenings. But it was much better being active on the altar than being quiet and trying to look prayerful in the pew. Because of my experience as an altar boy, I was as much at home in church as I was in my own house.

My parish priest, during my years growing up, was Canon Meehan, an even-tempered practical man with a dry wit and a limp, who was as won't to say "boo" in confession as "God bless you." I do not remember him ever getting mad at us altar boys, although we often gave him plenty of reason to get mad. His practical, down-to-earth approach can best be illustrated by his advice to a young man of our village, who upon completion of his high school sought the advice of the Canon on whether he should enter the seminary to become a priest. The Canon told him that since he was an only child he would be better off giving grandchildren to his parents. He did not take the Canon's advice, at least not right away. He became a priest and fifteen years later left the priesthood, married, and presented his parents with two grandchildren.

I had two curates while growing up: Father O'Farrell and Father Peter O'Flynn who drilled the boys of the village into altar boys. I got my altar boy training from Father O'Farrell. He was a tall, serious man who liked to walk down the middle of the street. I did not know his first name. Father Peter O'Flynn was an enthusiastic advocate of the Gaelic language and spoke to us in Gaelic whenever he could. He liked to chat with people wherever he found them. He attended our Gaelic games and visited people in their shops and homes. I never saw him walk the middle of the street and we all knew his first name.

Besides serving Mass as an altar boy, I came in regular contact with Canon Meehan at school where he was a weekly visitor. And as I mentioned previously, he was always a welcome sight to us students. Irish schools follow the British denominational education system rather than the American system of church-state separation. The practice of supporting denominational schools with public money was established simultaneously in England and Ireland. In 1831, when the British government set up an educational system for Ireland, then a British possession, it tried to bring Protestant and Catholic children together in the same schools. But the clergy of both religions would not hear of it. The clergy succeeded in having the school system established their way. And strictly denominational schools has been the norm ever since.

As in the British system of denominational education, the Irish government, which adopted the system following independence for the twenty-six counties of the south in 1921, pays the salaries of teachers and almost all school running expenses. The schools have to meet government-imposed standards. But the Protestant or Catholic pastors are the school administrators and select the teachers. However, the clerical administrators do not draw government salaries, but if ministers, nuns, or priests are assigned as teachers, other than teachers of religion, they are paid by the government like all other teachers.

This system gave the local pastor near total control over the secular and religious education of the youth in his parish. In my parish of Drumlish, where everybody was Catholic, there were no churches and no schools other than those run by the Catholic Church. Some Irish writers like James Joyce and George Bernard Shaw have found fault with the Irish education system as priest-ridden, but I was not conscious of that in any degree while growing up. Nor did I ever hear the matter being discussed by my elders. Such considerations were happily outside my experience.

The first time I became aware of the existence of a functioning Protestant church, I did not know what to make of it. The Protestant church in my village was never used, and I regarded it like any other ancient ruins and never asked questions about it. It was just part of the landscape. But a Protestant church that people attended raised all kind of questions in my mind.

I was visiting my aunt and uncle, Maggie and Pakie Brady, in Edgeworthstown. It was a Sunday morning and I was waiting outside the house for my aunt and uncle to go to Mass, when I heard the church bell ring. I ran inside to tell them that the bell was ringing and to hurry or we would be late for Mass. They told me not to worry that we had plenty of time. When I insisted that the bell had rung, giving us but 10 minutes to the start of Mass, they explained that the bell I heard was from the Protestant church six fields away at the edge of town. This was something totally new to me. What was a Protestant church? Did people go to Mass there?

On the way to Mass I kept asking questions. If they don't have Mass at this church, then why do people go? Why would they want to worship God in a different way? Could we go to that church next Sunday? Why would that be wrong? Their answers to my questions only gave rise to further questions. Finally, my aunt Maggie said that it was a little complicated and that I would understand some day. That put a stop to my questions but not to my questioning.

During Mass that Sunday I kept asking myself, why would there be a different way of worshiping God? If it was right for people who went to the Protestant church to worship God in a different way, why was it wrong for us? It was a puzzlement. I never heard of a Protestant church in catechism class. How was it different from a Catholic church?

That afternoon, I walked up the six fields to the edge of town, and sure enough there was a church there, a different church from where we went to Mass. My understanding of church was shattered. It would take some time to put the pieces back together, but not all the pieces and not in the same simple configuration.

From that morning on, doubts about the church and its teachings would pop into my mind from time to time, and I had to treat them as bad thoughts, like thoughts about girls, and put them out of my head as quickly as I could. We had learned in catechism that dallying with doubts about our faith was an occasion of sin and had to be avoided.

We did not have church picnics, bazaars, bake sales, or carnivals, but we did have annual church missions. These were designed to build and fortify the religious rather than social aspects of human character. For one week in the year, usually after the crops were harvested, a robed, religious order priest, usually a Redemptorist with his toes protruding through his sandals, came to our church and took over the pulpit. Starting on Sunday, he told the people what he expected of them for the next week. Children would have their mission on Saturday afternoon, but the rest of the week was reserved for the grown-ups. Monday, Wednesday, and Friday were for the men of the parish, and

Tuesday, Thursday, and Saturday were for the women.

Each night the mission would start with a sermon and end with Benediction. Confessions would commence at 6:00 p.m. and continue after Benediction for as long as necessary. Children were to come to confession only on Saturday. The mission Father urged everybody to go to confession during the mission and to reconcile their lives with God.

Since I was an altar boy for three of the six nights, I got to listen to what the mission Father had reserved for the grown-ups. I could not tell what was special, if anything, in his talks, at least on the nights that I was present. The big difference was that he hollered more and pounded the pulpit more at them, and seemed to indicate that many of them were in danger of losing their immortal souls. It was one time that I was sure glad that I was not a grown-up.

The mission had a stall sponsored by the Women's Sodality where parishioners could buy prayer books, rosary beads, scapulars, medals, holy cards, candles, bibles, crucifixes and pamphlets on various religious topics. The stall did a brisk business on the women's nights, but was fairly quiet on the men's nights.

A tradition in my parish, which has its roots in the Penal Laws of the eighteenth century, was having Mass in parishioners' homes. Throughout most of the eighteenth century, the British Government, in an attempt to deprive the Catholics of Ireland of all civil, social and religious life, enacted a series of laws—known in Irish history as the Penal Laws—that forbad Catholics the exercise of their religion, forbad them to receive education, to engage in trade or commerce, to live in a town or within five miles thereof, to purchase land, to enter a profession, to hold public office, etc., etc. Typical of the exclusion and repression of Catholics was the town of Bandon's inscription on the town's gates which read:

> Enter here, Turk, Jew, or atheist,
> Any man except a Papist.

Underneath this legend, a witty papist wrote in chalk a rhyming couplet of his own:

> The man who wrote this wrote it well;
> For the same is writ on the gates of Hell.

We had learned in history class that in the Penal Laws, the priest and schoolmaster were banned from the island, were hunted with bloodhounds, and when caught were killed or banished from the country. In this environment, where the priest and schoolmaster were constantly in hiding and on the run, they conducted their priestly and teaching functions mostly behind hedges, for if it was discovered that priest or schoolmaster used a home for forbidden purposes, it was burned to the ground and the homeowner's land was confiscated. In memory of those trying times, and as a tribute to the people who held on to their faith despite loss of land and property and being reduced to utter destitution, the priest continues to go to their homes to celebrate Mass.

We referred to this tradition simply as the "Station." Each home in the townland took its turn hosting a Mass to which all the adults of the townland were invited. I do not recall having a Station in our home in Drumlish, but I served as the altar boy for such a Mass in my grandmother's house. It was a big event. We cleaned the house inside and out. My grandmother cut flowers from her flower garden and put them on the table in the sitting room that was to serve as an altar. Uncle Michael whitewashed the outside walls of the house. The house sparkled.

The priest arrived about 9:00 a.m. and used the sitting room as a confessional. When the confessions were over, he then celebrated Mass and everybody went to communion. When Mass was over, the priest and the first sitting had breakfast in the dining room. The breakfast consisted of boiled eggs, brown bread, jam, butter, and tea. My grandmother decided who sat with the priest at the first breakfast served, which seemingly was a big deal. I got to eat at the last sitting and like everybody else had two eggs, which for me was a big deal.

The only other time that I got more than one egg or the tops of two eggs for breakfast was Easter Sunday when I got as many eggs as I could eat. Nothing else in my experience—neither weddings, funerals, threshing, stations, First Holy Communions, nor Confirmations—merited unlimited eggs.

chapter 19

first holy communion and first confession

The Irish developed a form of confession that was exclusively private... In the ancient church, confession of one's sins...had always been public... The Irish innovation was to make all confession a completely private affair between penitent and priest and to make it as repeatable as necessary.

—Thomas Cahill (1942-), *How the Irish Saved Civilization*, page 176. Author of the Series, "The Hinges of History." Born in New York of Irish-American parents.

First Holy Communion was a major milestone in my spiritual upbringing. I could now go to Communion at Mass with the grown-ups. I no longer had to stay behind in the pew and wonder what Holy Communion tasted like. But this big step forward came with a price. Like the grown-ups, I now had to go to confession and tell the priest my sins. My difficulty with this was that I felt I had to tell sins in confession whether I had any sins to tell or not.

I believed that I was a sinner, otherwise why would Jesus have died for me. I was a child of Adam and Eve, who were thrown out of the Garden of Eden for their sins, and I inherited their evil ways somehow. But despite my conviction that I was a sinner, I had a real hard time coming up with some good believable sins—sins that any young man would in a sense be proud to confess; sins that were worthwhile going to confession over and that I felt good about getting off my chest; sins that would not be wasting the priest's and God's time. The search for real sins became a weekly unwanted burden.

Attaining to the use of reason was the primary condition for eligibility for Holy Communion. The average person was supposed to reach the use of reason by the age of seven when we were able to distinguish right from wrong, and be capable of committing sin as well as understanding what Holy Communion was all about. It never did seem right that I had to be capable of committing sin, and actually commit some, before I could go to Holy Communion. At least it seemed that way for we had to go to confession first.

Anyway, toward the end of first class in primary school was the usual time for receiving First Confession and First Holy Communion. We spent several months preparing for these two sacraments. At school, we were drilled in the "short catechism," a condensed version of the complete catechism, which we called the "long catechism." We had to memorize the short catechism from cover to cover. The short catechism had questions and answers dealing with such topics as God and His Goodness; the Creation of the World; the Ten Commandments; Jesus and His Life, Death, and Resurrection; the Seven Sacraments with special emphasis on Confession and Holy Communion; Sin: Original, Mortal and Venial; and Heaven, Purgatory and Hell.

We also had to know by heart the Our Father, the Hail Mary, the Glory Be to the Father, the Apostles' Creed, the Confiteor, the Act of Contrition, the Ten Commandments, the Angelus and the Prayer to our Guardian Angel. This was a fairly tall order for seven-year-olds, but we seemed to take it in stride. The prize was worth the effort.

When our teacher believed that we were as ready as she could make us, the priest came to the school to examine us. He asked the entire class of about forty: "Boys and girls, whom do we receive in Holy Communion?"

We answered as with a single voice, "Jesus."

"And who is Jesus?" he asked, and we bellowed out, "God."

"And why is God coming to us in this special way?"

"Because He loves us," we shouted.

As a group we were doing fine. Our teacher was smiling broadly. The priest then asked individual members of the class to stand up and he asked them questions from the catechism. Of one he asked, "What is the Fourth Commandment of God?"

She answered without hesitation, "The Fourth Commandment of God is: Honor thy father and thy mother."

Of another, he asked, "What is the Seventh Commandment?"

"The Seventh Commandment is: Thou shalt not steal," came the quick response.

"And what is forbidden by the Seventh Commandment?" he asked a third person.

"The Seventh Commandment forbids us to take, to keep, or to damage unjustly what belongs to another," was the almost instant reply.

We knew the catechism answers backwards and forwards. He only asked questions of about a dozen and he helped those who were shy or hesitant in answering. Then he said that we all did very fine and talked about how great a day our First Holy Communion would be with Jesus coming to us as food for our souls. He said that we would remember this day for the rest of our lives.

In addition to learning our catechism and our prayers, we were drilled in the proper way to go to confession and receive Holy Communion. Confession came first, as we first had to get rid of our sins. Of course we first had to have committed some, not a problem to most grown-ups, but a very real problem to some of us kids. The presumption was that we had indeed committed sin. It was only a matter of identifying what they were. And we were helped in that process. I think that some of us ended up confessing the examples of sins that the teacher gave, for we had no real sins of our own. We were drilled in the proper examination of our conscience to find out what sins we had committed and how many times we had committed them.

This was not an easy task, particularly for one's First Confession. I was disobedient to my parents, a violation of the Fourth Commandment. But how often was I disobedient? Once a day? No. Perhaps twice or three times a week, but I was not sure. Did I steal? Yes. I stole buttons from my brother's stash of buttons because he cheated me out of buttons in a game of pitch and toss. I fought with my brothers and sisters. Daily? Yes. But how often each day, I had no way of telling. I lied. But how often? Sometimes a lot when I lied myself into a corner and had to lie more to get out, and at other times not at all. So I had to guess how many times I committed each type of sin.

Some of my class in practice sessions for confession listed as sins: "I picked my nose many, many times. I pulled the cat's tail ten times. I sucked my thumb daily." Parents had said that these were bad things to do. Were they sins? Did these things offend God? They certainly offended parents. So they fell into the category of smaller sins or imperfections and we confessed them. What did the priest think? Well, he had the patience and understanding of God.

But deep down, I recoiled from confessing such nothing sins. Confession seemed to be for honest to goodness sins like stealing money or a bicycle, or stealing turf or a calf or a pig, or kicking somebody when he was down, or wishing that The Master would fall off his bike and not be able to teach school or at least not be able to use the cane.

But absent these real sins, I rattled off the same list of near sins time after time in confession. I felt that if God was in the confession box, He would throw me out for wasting His eternal time. But His deputy, the priest, accepted what I presented without question and rattled off time after time the same penance of one three Our Fathers or one Our Father and one Hail Mary.

But my most difficult task in my examination of conscience was knowing when a venial sin became a mortal sin. I knew what the catechism said about mortal and venial sins: "Mortal sin is a grievous offence against God, kills the soul, makes us an enemy of God, and places us in danger of eternal damnation in hell.—Venial sin is a less grievous offense, displeases God, weakens our power to resist temptation, and disposes us to commit bigger sins, even mortal sin." But when did the less grievous offense become a grievous offense? My teacher said never, but I could not figure that out. Despite the teacher's assurance that we did not have to worry about mortal sin, as all our sins were venial, there lingered the doubt that some might have slipped over the line. What if I had wished that The Master fall off his bike and hurt himself seriously? It was a troubling thought that I might have crossed the line and committed a mortal sin and not known it. It was little consolation that my teacher said that that was not possible, for in order for a sin to be mortal it had to be committed with clear knowledge of the gravity of the sin and full consent of the mind to commit the sin.

We went to First Confession on Saturday, the day before our First Holy Communion. We all knelt in the pews outside the confessional and for one more time I examined my conscience. I went over the list of my sins, or near sins, that I was to tell the priest. Before the priest started confessions, he asked us to pray together the Confiteor, so that we would not have to say it individually in confession.

When my turn came, I went into the confession box, knelt down, and waited for the priest to open the shutter on my side of the confessional. It was fairly dark inside, but I was not afraid for I could peep out and see the others outside. When the priest opened the shutter, I could see his head outlined through the screen.

I began: "Bless me, Father, for I have sinned. This is my first confession, and these are my sins. I lied, sometimes many times a day and other days not at all. I disobeyed my parents about twice a week, but I am not sure exactly how many times. I fought with my brothers and sisters every day, but how often I do not know. I stole some buttons from my brother's button jar and did not give them back. For these and all the other sins that I cannot remember, I am sorry."

To my surprise the priest did not ask any questions, not even about stealing my brother's buttons and not giving them back. The priest put his hand to his mouth as if to stifle a yawn and said, "For your penance say one Our Father and one Hail Mary. Now tell God you are sorry for your sins in your Act of Contrition."

I said the Act of Contrition and before I was finished, the priest had finished his Latin prayer and said, "God bless you," and closed the shutter.

That was much easier than I was led to believe. I got through with a light penance and a yawn. I got up, stepped out of the confessional, proudly walked to the altar rails, knelt, and said my penance of one Our Father and one Hail Mary. I felt good about being forgiven for all the sins, particularly for those that I could not remember. Now I really had a clean soul like a clean slate!

We were also drilled in the proper way to receive Holy Communion. We had to fast from all food and drink from midnight the night before, and we had to be free from all mortal sins. On our First Holy Communion Sunday the girls all wore white dresses, delicate white veils, and white shoes and socks, and occupied the first pews on the left side of the center aisle of the church. They looked like angels.

We were dressed in navy blue short pants, white shirts and blue ties, navy blue jackets, and black shoes and white socks, and occupied the front pews on the right side of the center aisle. We looked like penguins. We all carried rosary beads and small prayer books in our hands.

The priest preached a sermon on the meaning of First Holy Communion and congratulated us, our parents and our teacher. When time came for Communion, which seemed to take forever, we were the first to receive. We approached the altar rails with hands joined, eyes cast down, and knelt at the railing. When the priest came to me, the altar boy assisting the priest put the paten under my chin, I opened my mouth, extended my tongue, and closed my eyes as I was instructed to do.

When I felt the priest place the Host on my tongue, I closed my mouth slowly so as not to snap the priest's fingers, swallowed the host, returned to the pew with hands joined and eyes cast down, knelt, and quietly gave thanks to Jesus and God for coming to me. I also asked Jesus to bless my parents, brothers and sisters, grandmother, aunts and uncles, and the teacher as I was instructed to do.

We were told not to use our teeth on the Host, which we translated as: we were not to bite Jesus. We were to swallow Him whole. If the Host stuck to the roof of our mouths, as it sometimes did, we were to loosen it with our tongue, never with a finger, and to swallow it immediately. I wondered what happened to Jesus when he went into my tummy. Where did he go from there? Would I drown Him if I drank water? But nobody seemed very much concerned about such matters, so these questions were never asked, and were never answered.

Outside the church after Mass, I was mobbed by parents, aunts and uncles, grandmother, and friends of the family. All wanted their picture taken with me. Everybody gave me a gift, mostly money, a two-shilling piece or a half crown. I felt special and wealthy. We went home where a big breakfast of bacon, eggs, sausages, toast and tea awaited us. After breakfast, we had more picture-taking. With that over, I took off my navy blue suit and went out to play.

chapter 20

confirmation day

Question 346: What is Confirmation?
Confirmation is the sacrament through which the Holy Ghost is
given to us, with his graces and his seven gifts, to make us strong
and perfect Christians and soldiers of Jesus Christ.

—Irish Catechism of Catholic Doctrine

Confirmation Day will not likely be forgotten by my brother Eamonn or
myself. The reason is not that on that day we became soldiers of Christ. On
that day we were caught smoking cigarettes.

Shortly after being confirmed by Bishop Joseph McNamee in his tall
mitered hat, crozier and gold-embroidered cape, and with the holy oil of
chrism still fresh on our foreheads, we sneaked out of the post-Confirmation
family celebration, opened a new twenty-pack of Player's cigarettes, casually
lit up in the turf-shed and got caught in the act. We are still experiencing the
consequences.

Like our preparation for First Holy Communion, we spent several months
being drilled in the catechism on the road to becoming a soldier of Christ.
This time we had not only to memorize the entire long catechism, we also
had to understand the explanations of the catechism contained in a companion
volume called the *Catechism Notes*. Confirmation was a Sacrament that
conferred maturation in the Christian way of living. Now it was no longer
good enough to memorize catechism answers. We were reminded that parrots
could do that with a little training. We now had to understand the answers, be
able to explain their meaning, and have the conviction and capacity to defend
the doctrines contained in them.

The Sacrament of Confirmation empowered us not only to live our Catholic
faith, but to actively participate in spreading it, and to defend it even to the

point of dying for it. Confirmation made us soldiers in Christ's army of believers, which was what the catechism and the *Catechism Notes* taught.

As with our First Holy Communion, the school again had the task of getting us intellectually and spiritually ready for the Sacrament. There was little or no distinction drawn between the two states of readiness. The emphasis of the school was, as might be expected, on intellectual readiness, which was enforced when needed by the power of the cane.

In school, catechism was one of those subjects when the cane was very apt to make its appearance. And down the stretch towards Confirmation, the cane was almost constantly visible and frequently used. Despite the threat of the cane, which soured the relationship between student and teacher—and, in this instance, between student, teacher and religion—many of us took a keen interest in our catechism, particularly in the *Catechism Notes*. This compact little book challenged us to think of religion on a higher level, above the battle of the classroom, and seemed to appeal to higher instincts and personal values of commitment and sacrifice. But these occasions were all too fleeting. The all-prevailing thrust was intellectual understanding, for that was what was going to be evaluated by the parish priest and the bishop. In this environment, spiritual readiness seemed to take a back seat.

My brother, Eamonn, and I were among the best students in our catechism class. We seldom missed a question from either the catechism or the *Catechism Notes*. But we never saw our newly acquired habit of smoking as being in any way incompatible with our preparation for Confirmation. Stopping smoking never crossed our minds. Evidently we were simply not challenged to give up this bad habit. We knew that our parents would hit the roof if they found out. My mom never smoked. My dad was a life-long chain smoker, but was adamantly opposed to any of his kids smoking, particularly at the immature ages of ten and eleven years, the ages of my brother and I as we approached our Confirmation Day.

We were confirmed on Sunday afternoon. We formed a processional into the church led by three acolytes carrying a cross and two candles. Then came our adult sponsors, visiting clergy, and finally the bishop in a flowing gold cape, miter (tall hat) and crozier with our pastor and curate at his left and right. All eyes were on the bishop. As my grandmother would say, "He cut a fine figure."

The bishop did not look the least bit nervous. We were the nervous ones. The bishop went up to the top altar step, knelt for a moment in prayer, turned around to face us and the congregation, and beckoned to us to be seated.

190

Standing on the top altar step, he began to talk to us about the Sacrament we were about to receive. He said that Confirmation conferred on us the Holy Spirit, empowering us to fearlessly profess and defend our faith. For our part we had to know our faith. He said that our pastor assured him that we had been working hard at this, and that he was going to give us the opportunity to demonstrate our knowledge and understanding.

The bishop then proceeded to talk about the scripture account of the coming of the Holy Spirit on the Apostles gathered in an upper room in Jerusalem and asked us how the Apostles felt both before and after the coming of the Holy Spirit. All our hands shot up. He smiled at our enthusiastic response. For the next half-hour he asked many questions and got as many answers. We demonstrated to the assembled parish that we knew our stuff. The bishop said we did well, that he was proud of us, and he knew our parents, teachers and priests were proud too. He then sat down and invited the first row to come forward.

Confirmation was in many respects a passive Sacrament. We did not have to do or say anything in the actual liturgy of the Sacrament. All the actions and words were performed by others, mostly by the bishop. The drills for the actual conferring of the Sacrament were surprisingly simple. We marched one by one, the girls going first, to the altar steps where the bishop sat, flanked by our parish priest and our curate.

We knelt before the bishop. Our adult sponsor stood directly behind us and placed a right hand on our right shoulder. The bishop dipped his thumb into a small container of chrism packed with cotton to prevent the holy oil from spilling, and made the sign of the cross on our foreheads with his oily thumb. He said the words of the Sacrament in Latin, made the sign of the cross over us, and gave us a pat on the cheek, which was meant to be a reminder that we could be called upon to suffer for our faith. We then moved to one side where a priest from a neighboring parish rubbed off the oil from our foreheads with a cotton ball. We returned with our sponsor to our pew.

The Sacrament of Confirmation was also passive in other respects. There were no lasting visible signs of its reception beyond the day itself. With First Holy Communion, I could go to Communion each Sunday or at least once a month on the young people's Communion Sunday. There was no such lasting reminder of the Sacrament of Confirmation. There was much talk of becoming an adult Christian, of becoming a soldier of Christ, but nothing in real life took cognizance of those truths. The gentle pat on the cheek was a let-down after all the talk of becoming a soldier in Christ's army. Soldiers are not tested with a pat on the cheek. After Confirmation, we simply carried on as before. There were no visible or external changes at home, at school, or at church to remind us of what had taken place. Hence, there were no lasting internal changes either.

Was this an opportunity lost? Not entirely. There was one positive commitment that directly effected our lives for the good. After Confirmation was conferred and we were all back in our pews, the bishop stood before us, asked us to stand and make with him our commitment not to take alcoholic beverages of any kind until we had completed our twenty-first birthday. This was referred to as the "Confirmation Pledge" or simply "The Pledge." At school and at home, we were often reminded of the dangers of alcohol to both our physical and spiritual well-being. We willingly and gladly took this pledge. The only immediate impact it had on my life was that as an altar boy, I could no longer turn the wine cruet on my head after serving Mass and drain what was left in it. As a result, I did not drink alcohol until I was twenty-nine.

The Confirmation pledge against using alcohol had its roots a century earlier when the abuse of alcohol among the population generally was pandemic. The problem was so serious that a young priest by the name of Father Matthew mounted a successful national campaign to get Ireland's youth to take a pledge never to use alcohol in order to atone for those who abused it. This was known as the "pioneer pledge." This would be something analogous to young people today being asked to take a pledge against using tobacco or drugs.

In the absence of any pledge against smoking, my brother and I thought it fitting to celebrate our Confirmation with a smoke. That turned out to be a fateful celebration. As we lit up in the turf-shed, we looked up and saw our Aunt Nellie staring at us in disbelief. She said nothing. She just turned on her heel and went into the house. Would she tell our parents? We had no way of knowing. We could not take any chances. We went down the garden and dumped the new pack of cigarettes in the ditch. We also dumped the box of matches that came with them. We examined our fingers to see if there were any telltale cigarette stains on them. There were none. Maybe she would not tell!

In the months before Confirmation, we had got into a routine of smoking four or five cigarettes a day each. At first we stole an odd cigarette from Dad's packages, but that was very risky. We saved our pennies and bought packs of Will's Woodbines for thrupence, five in a pack. That lasted for a few months until we graduated to the cigarettes that Dad smoked—Player's cigarettes. I had a half-crown that I had received from my grandmother, and we decided to buy a 20-pack of Player's cigarettes at McQuade's Hardware and Grocery shop. We presented our half-crown to one of the shop owners, who was particularly friendly to us whenever we came into the shop. He asked us if the cigarettes were for our dad or for ourselves. We hesitated to answer, so he gave us a pack of twenty Player's, rang us up in the till, and with a wink gave us back the half-crown, saying, "Your change, boys." We instantly knew we had a good thing going. We treasured that half-crown and used it repeatedly with the same owner to "purchase" a twenty-pack of Player's every few days. The same half-crown was returned to us as change on each occasion.

We now asked ourselves should we also get rid of the half-crown? Maybe Aunt Nellie would not tell! We lived in fear of what would happen if she did tell. We waited. For six days we did not smoke. The half-crown weighed heavily in my pocket. She must not have told. Should we venture back to McQuade's shop for a pack of Player's? As we pondered this step on Saturday following Confirmation, we were called into the house. Both our parents took us into the sitting room and closed the door. We looked around for the stick. There was no stick in sight. What was coming down?

Without anger, but with deep disappointment and sadness in their voices, our parents told us that they knew of our smoking on Confirmation Day. They did not demand to know how long this was going on, or where we got the cigarettes. They simply told us that young people our age should not smoke, that it was not good for our young, growing bodies. If we decided to smoke when we were grown up, then that was another matter. But now we should not smoke. Amid tears, my mother wondered out loud what she had done or failed to do to have caused us to smoke. Their approach to our transgressions was totally unexpected and totally out of character, particularly for our father, who on other occasions for much less took the stick to us.

We left the room not knowing what to think. We had deserved a beating, but none materialized. The way our parents handled the situation profoundly influenced us. We never went back to McQuade's shop to purchase cigarettes, even for Dad. To this day neither of us has smoked. We owe a debt of gratitude to our Aunt Nellie and to our parents, for taking our smoking at the ages of ten and eleven as the serious matter that it was. It was much more serious than we or they then understood.

chapter 21

boarding school – st. mel's

What we truly and earnestly aspire to be,
that in some sense we are. The mere aspiration,
by changing the frame of the mind, for the
moment realizes itself.

—Anna Jameson (1774-1860)
Irish Author and Art Critic

At the age of thirteen, on a damp day in September, 1946, following completion of my eighth class in primary school earlier that summer, I followed my brother Eamonn to St. Mel's secondary school, a boarding school for boys. Eamonn had completed his first year at the school and knew his way around, so I simply tagged along behind my brother. We said good-bye to our mother in the shadow of the statue of Bishop Kilduff in front of the school, gathered up our few belongings, climbed the three flights of stairs two at a time to the third floor, and checked into a large, long dormitory that was known as "Spike."

There were twenty-four beds in this long room with a row of beds on each long wall, separated by double rows of twelve washbasins and twelve lockers (that had no locks) that ran down the middle of the room between the rows of beds. Eamonn selected two beds beside each other in the left corner near the door and told me to put my stuff in the second locker on the right side. He took the first locker on the right.

For the first time in my life I had my own bed, my own wash basin with running water, and my own locker. There was much more. I would not have to go to the pump or well for water to wash my face. Nor would I have to go down to the bottom of the garden to the outhouse. There were toilets everywhere with small boxes of white squares of paper instead of cut up pages of the *Longford Leader*. These toilets had small water tanks on the wall five feet or so above the toilet. We pulled the chain that hung from the tanks to flush the toilet and a cavalcade of water gushed into the bowl, some of which carried the appropriate trade name of "The Deluge."

The vast majority of Irish teens who went to secondary school when I was growing up went to a boarding school. Girls, including my three sisters, Mary, Eileen and Teresa, went to convents to be taught exclusively by nuns. Boys went to boarding schools taught almost exclusively by priests and Christian Brothers. The government paid the teachers' salaries. Student tuition paid for room and board and other school expenses.

Four of my five brothers—Eamonn, Frank, Niall, Colm—and I went to St. Mel's College, a secondary school campus on the north side of Longford town, staffed and run by diocesan priests. My youngest brother, Seamus, went to St. Nathy's secondary school in Ballaghaderreen, County Roscommon. St. Mel's offered boys from Longford and surrounding counties the normal five-year secondary school education. The priests at the school had the reputation of being strict, using the cane to enforce discipline and promote learning. But that did not bother me much, for surely priests would be fair and even-tempered and not use the cane excessively like The Master sometimes did.

The school, built in 1862 to 1865 on a ten-acre site (later expanded to twenty-four acres), bears the name of the first Bishop of the Diocese of Ardagh, Saint Mel. According to tradition, he was appointed to that post by St. Patrick in the fifth century. A life-size statue of Bishop John Kilduff, who built St. Mel's in tough economic times following the Great Famine, graces a clearing of lawn, shrubs and flower beds at the end of an avenue of large copper beech trees, leading to an imposing three story building. The school was built from the same granite stone that went into the building of the adjacent St. Mel's Cathedral, completed by Bishop Kilduff some nine years earlier in 1856. The school opened on September 29, 1865, with forty-eight boarders and twenty-five day pupils, and a staff of three priests and one lay teacher.

In the late 1940s and early 1950s, when I attended St. Mel's, the school accommodated 120 boarding students from the counties of Longford, Leitrim, Offaly, Westmeath and Cavan, and about twenty day-students from Longford town and vicinity. It had a teaching staff of eleven priests and one part-time lay teacher, Herr Nierman, a native of Germany, who taught music and served as organist in the cathedral.

The curriculum was liberal arts where, besides mathematics, English, and Gaelic, the emphasis was on the classics of Latin and Greek. But more important in my hierarchy of values, St. Mel's had the reputation of fielding winning football teams in the Leinster college championships. On visits to my brother the previous year, I had walked through the college gates and down the impressive tree-lined avenue and had seen the college's three football fields with their white goalposts. There were separate football fields for fourth and fifth year students, for students in the intermediate years, and for preps or first year students. I was impressed and could hardly wait to make my debut on the prep football field.

St Mel's College, Longford, where I attended boarding school for five years from September 1946 to May 1951. (Photograph taken by the author in the summer of 2000.)

In the days ahead, I would discover even more conveniences than those mentioned earlier. I would get my own locker on the first floor off the large common shower room, where I would keep my shower togs, towels, footwear and football gear. I would be assigned my own desk in the prep study hall, where I would keep all my books and class material. There were three study halls, just as there were three football fields, one for fourth and fifth year students, one for intermediate students, and one for the preps or first year students. The dormitories were similarly divided, except that fifth year students had rooms, two to a room.

In the chapel, I was assigned a position in the second pew, which I retained for that first year. Each year thereafter, I moved back a couple of pews. The position in the classroom that I happened to find myself in for the first class in each subject, that position I had to retain for the year. Within a couple of days, I knew my way around and I was on my own. Eamonn was now a second year student, and moved almost exclusively among his classmates. We would be together only at meals and when we retired to the dorm for the night. But then, with the rule of silence, we were not supposed to talk.

I would move almost exclusively for the next five years among my classmates, all thirty of them, twenty-six boarders and four day-students from around the diocese of Ardagh and Clonmacnoise, which consisted of the counties of Longford, Leitrim, and parts of Offaly, Westmeath and Cavan. I knew two students in my class, Berks Murphy, who was also a student from Gaigue National School, and Mickey Rogers from the village of Drumlish. Besides my brother, I knew three upper-class students. All three were from the village of Drumlish, Sean McWade, Joe Black and T.P. Cullen, but other than a cursory hello when we ran into each other, we had no communication.

Special friendships between students of different years were discouraged. We called such relationships "sucks." Any upper class student caught showing friendship of any kind to a junior class student was given a bad time by the student body. This kept fraternization between students of different classes to a minimum. The student body also registered its disapproval of priests showing partiality or favoritism to students in the classes they taught. When any such behavior was observed, students would make a sucking sound with their lips to the embarrassment of priest and student. Only a couple of priests were prone to this kind of behavior. These priests had the annoying habit of pulling ears in class, but when it came to favorite students, the ear-pulling was more like an ear massage. It was not a popular thing to be a "suck" of any student, and it was worse still to be identified as a "suck" of any priest.

I quickly learned that the second floor of the main school building where the priests had their rooms was off limits to students. We were also forbidden to visit other dorms unless we had permission of the dean, the disciplinarian, who loomed large in the everyday life of students.

The school grounds had a large black-topped oval walkway between the three football fields, where the students walked for exercise and recreation when they were doing nothing else. It looked a little silly to me at first,

197

walking in circles going nowhere. But within a week, I was circling the walk like everybody else.

Smoking was prohibited, though some students smoked using the back handball alleys, running the risk of getting caught and being expelled. Newspapers and magazines were also prohibited, though day students brought in newspaper clippings of football matches, particularly those involving St. Mel's. The safest way to read clandestine newspapers was under the bed clothes at night with a flashlight. In-coming and out-going student mail was censored. We had to leave our letters for mailing unsealed. The result was that in my five years at the school, I did not write a single letter. We had no radios and, other than weekly visits by parents, we had little or no contact with the outside world.

Going to town was permissible only for dental and special doctor appointments, which were rare. We did not leave the school grounds, except for Christmas, Easter and summer vacations, school walks, going to the cathedral in a group for confession or to sing in the choir at noon Sunday High Mass, and going to football matches at Pearse Park, Longford town's Gaelic football pitch, or going out of town for a game. We half jokingly and half in earnest referred to the school as our prison without walls.

My first full day at St. Mel's had no scheduled classes and was supposed to be devoted to getting acquainted with my new surroundings. To my surprise, I spent most of my time at pitch and toss on the Long Alley, a stretch of unpaved ground beside the handball alleys that was often used for impromptu soccer games, but was ideally suited to this gambling game played with large copper pennies. I knew this game well, as I played it most Sunday evenings at the crossroads in my home village of Drumlish. Most students, including myself, had a little money in our pockets, and the opportunity to add to our little stash of spending money was too much to resist. Unfortunately, my little stash did not last that first full day. I was penniless. But I quickly learned that I had no real need for pocket money. There was no place to spend money, at least legitimately. The game of pitch and toss did not last beyond the second day. It was against school rules that, by tradition, were not strictly enforced for the first couple of days of the new school year. Also, during these couple of days most students finished whatever cigarettes they brought back with them. The risk of getting caught smoking and possible expulsion increased dramatically thereafter.

I quickly got into the daily routine, which remained substantially the same for my five years at the school. We arose at 6:30 a.m. to the loud clanging of a hand-bell in the corridor outside our dorm. We were to jump out of bed the instant we heard the bell, wash our faces in the washbasin's cold water and get dressed for the day. Each dorm had a prefect, a fifth year student, whose task it was to enforce the rules and to ensure that we got out of bed promptly at the bell, and that we made our beds when we returned to the dorm after breakfast. After we made our beds, we could not go back to the dorm until bedtime without the dean's permission.

Morning prayer in the chapel was at 6:50 a.m. followed by Mass, when most of the student body went to communion. We then had an hour's study followed by breakfast at 8:30 a.m., which consisted of oatmeal porridge, and a couple of slices of buttered bread and tea. On feast days and on special occasions, we got scrambled eggs and sausage.

In the spring of 1949, following an outbreak of TB (tuberculosis) at the school when two students died and many were hospitalized, the morning rising bell rang an hour later at 7:30 a.m. The hour of study before breakfast was eliminated. Dr. Dick Stokes was in charge of controlling the TB outbreak. The entire student body was tested for the virus. We got an injection in the arm, and if we had a reaction with the arm swelling and the spot injected turning red, we were considered to be okay. That was not explained to us at the time, and when my arm and my brother Eamonn's arm turned red I thought we were infected. To my surprise nothing else happened to us.

The outbreak presented a serious problem to the school. Should the students be sent home and possibly contaminate their families, or should the matter be handled at the school? The decision was made to keep us at school, but now we got up an hour later, which to us students seemed then like a big benefit. We were kept largely in the dark as regards the gravity of the situation. We never knew how many students were infected, or how many were hospitalized or went home. The outbreak was controlled and the school continued with its normal routine with the one adjustment—the time of rising.

After breakfast at about 9:15 a.m. we went to our lockers beside the shower room to exchange our house slippers for shoes or boots, and to polish our footwear for the day. We then had a break before the school bell rang for class at 9:45 a.m. We had three class periods of forty-five minutes each before lunch at noon. We had another three class periods after lunch from 12:45 to 3:15 with a short fifteen-minute break from 2:15 to 2:30. That was the daily class schedule, Monday through Saturday, except for Wednesdays, when we had a half day's class with four forty-five minute classes beginning at 9:30 a.m and ending at 12:30. p.m. We had no class on Sundays.

Sunday afternoon was reserved for our weekly community showers, which were mandatory whether we needed them or not. Each class as a group, dressed in bathing suits, received a hot shower in the large shower room, administered usually by the president. A strict rule of silence was enforced during shower time, even when occasionally the water got too hot, and when we got a couple of minutes of ice cold water at the end of the shower. Each shower was as much an exercise in self-control as in self-cleansing. As mentioned above, showering was normally a weekly happening, except following football matches when the football pitch was wet and mucky. We then had a quick five-minute shower.

We had dinner at 3:15 p.m., our principal meal of the day. It consisted of meat, mostly sliced beef, with potatoes, vegetables, milk, and a dessert. Sometimes instead of sliced beef, we had what we called "mush," a meat casserole, which most of us refused to eat because it usually had a strong unpleasant odor. At times in frustration, and to protest the too frequent appearance of "mush," we had "mush" fights when the dean's back was turned. We would lob large spoonfuls of "mush" at other tables, which would trigger reciprocation in kind. If the dean made the mistake to leave the refectory, then it was usually a free for all with "mush" flying in all directions. To this day, my stomach revolts against any dish resembling "mush."

After dinner, we had our longest period of recreation of the day, when most students played football and some played handball on the school's four handball alleys. This was the period of the day when we played the intramural football leagues at the prep, intermediate and senior levels, with three football matches going on simultaneously. Senior students, who were not playing that day, refereed the prep and intermediate level matches, and one of the priest-faculty refereed the senior match. The games ended at 4:35. It was a scramble to change and get ready for study period.

At 4:45 p.m., the school bell rang for study hall, where silence was strictly imposed. We had a break of fifteen minutes at 6:00 p.m. followed by more study, and then evening tea at 7:30.p.m. This consisted of buttered bread and tea, supplemented by goodies from our parents. Then we had a short recreation break before the last study session of the day from 8:15 p.m. to 9:30 p.m., followed by a change to house slippers, rosary and night prayer in the chapel, and bed. We had to maintain silence from night prayers to after Mass the next morning.

There were few exceptions to this routine. One exception was the big snow of March, 1947, when several feet of snow fell overnight. We awoke to no electricity with everywhere blanketed in drifts of up to six feet of soft, wet snow. This necessitated many changes to our day, the most memorable one being that we went to bed at 6.30 p.m. when it got dark, for there was no light to study. This lasted for two weeks and the novelty of such a big snowfall, the disruption it caused, and the many snowfights quickly wore thin, for it meant that there was no football.

At the beginning of each school year in the second or third week, we had a three-day spiritual retreat. This was a totally new experience for me. The retreat consisted of three days of silence at all times, even at meals, talking to nobody but God. We had no class, no study, no football, only a retreat master. He was usually a Franciscan or a Dominican priest giving us four or five spiritual talks a day on which we were to think and meditate.

So for three days we listened to talks on prayer, the importance of regular confession, coping with temptation, God's sanctifying grace, the awfulness of sin (particularly mortal sin), eternal damnation of hell's fire, the importance of prayer and the school rule as God's will. Like everybody else, I walked the grounds alone trying to think about these things. Not talking was the difficult part. And talking only to God was even more difficult still. How could you talk to someone who knew what you were going to say even before you opened your mouth?

This was the first time in thirteen years that I was forbidden to talk or express myself audibly to other human beings for three whole days. They seemed to go by so slowly. It felt unnatural, like going for three whole days without seeing. I felt like an animal tied in its stall in the farmhouse for three long days. I recall envying the prefect, who read the morning and night prayers in the chapel. I wanted to be able to say something out loud. Answering the rosary during these three days felt good, as I exercised my vocal chords.

Silence had its weird results. I was certainly more appreciative of the regular daily routine that permitted talking most of the time. I was supposed to be holier at the end of the retreat, but I had no way of measuring that. I was certainly happier when the exercise came to an end, and could not imagine myself taking an oath of silence for life like some of the cloistered Irish monks and nuns.

With each passing year, I began to appreciate the retreat little by little. Toward the end of the five years, I even began to look forward to these days of quiet, which now seemed to get shorter and shorter. On my fifth retreat, I recall sitting under a tree between spiritual talks, examining the tree's leaves and discovering that the veins in no two leaves were alike, listening to the birds chirping and watching them scratch for grubs among the bushes, and being in awe of the richness and diversity of God's creation. I felt at one with the earth and its maker, and wanted to somehow preserve that feeling.

As might be expected, the school's food was a constant source of complaints by students, but we never went hungry. We were allowed to supplement what the school provided with care packages from parents, which they dutifully brought during visiting hours on Saturdays. Mom came almost every Saturday, since we had the car running again now that World War II and petrol rationing was over. She always brought butter, jams, cheeses and a cake with raisins she had baked.

We all shared the goodies that our parents brought with those seated at our table of twelve, or more precisely among those seated at half the table. My half of the table had Liam Moore from Granard, Eddie Rowley and Brian Bohan from Mohill in County Leitrim, Paddy Hagan from Killoe, my brother Eamonn and myself. Brian Bohan's parents brought the best goodies. They owned a store in Mohill, and part of the excitement of Saturday's evening tea was looking forward to and feasting on what came from Bohan's store: jellies, sardines, cheeses, tarts, fruitcakes, etc. The Bohan goodies were unpredictable, which made them all the more appreciated. The other half of the table shared with the six at their end. We reserved the goodies for evening tea, as that was the lightest meal served by the school. With a little planning and discipline, we were usually able to spread the Saturday goodies from home over the entire week.

During the two daily study sessions, we had to do all our homework: math assignments in algebra, geometry and arithmetic; write essays in English and Gaelic; memorize assigned English and Gaelic poems, and read assigned readings in both languages; memorize Latin and Greek grammar; and work on translating Caesar's *Gallic Wars* and Homer's *Odyssey*.

Each study hall had a fifth year student as the prefect in charge, whose task it was to maintain strict silence. The dean looked in once in a while, and if he heard talking, he would ask the prefect for a list of the students who were breaking the rule of silence. The dean called out the names, took the offenders outside the door, gave them eight to ten strokes of a cane on each hand, and sent them back to continue their studies. This happened a few times a week. The list of names we called a "prog," and I got listed on my share of "progs." I seldom got any study done after the slogging, as I was preoccupied with nursing my hands and sitting on them to ease the pain.

This often put me in double jeopardy, for if I did not have my homework done, I was liable to get a slogging in class the next day for failure to memorize a poem, or to complete an essay, or complete my math, or to know the assigned grammar lesson in any of the four languages.

Like most schools of the time, corporal punishment was an accepted practice. Some priests carried a cane with them to class regularly, hidden under their cassocks. The cane was not only a discipline enforcer but a homework and learning enforcer, and was used by some priests more liberally and more menacingly than others. Most priests were fair and even-tempered in their caning of students with a few even giving the distinct impression that it hurt them as much to give the punishment as it hurt you to receive it. A few priests at times seemingly lost control and were impassioned in their use of the cane.

The prefect we had in our study hall for the first year, Miles Gray, was understanding and helpful. On Mondays, when a new dean was starting his week, he would tell us what to expect and how we should behave so as to avoid getting slogged. We did not always follow his advice but whenever we did, we escaped being slogged that week. I thought that all prefects would be like Miles, but I would learn otherwise.

We had an incident one night the first year that caused a lot of commotion in our study hall. Midway in the second study period, somebody screamed that he saw a rat in the room. Most of the students jumped up on their desks. Paddy Hagan, who was sitting beside me, shouted, "I got him, I got him." He was clutching his leg above his knee. We did not know what he meant until he explained, rather calmly, that he had the rat in his grasp. The rat had run up his pant leg in an effort to get away from screaming students. The prefect urged him to hold on to it, and half-ushered, half-carried him out into the corridor, where he let go of it, and the rat fell to the floor half-dazed. The prefect stomped on it, picked it up by the tail, and threw it out in the yard. He then calmed us down, warning that the dean would be along any minute, for no doubt he heard the commotion.

The prefect met the dean at the door and explained what had happened. The dean took Paddy Hagan to see Sister Thecla, the infirmarian, to ensure that he had not been bitten. When Paddy returned to the study hall, he got a round of applause led by the prefect. Paddy, or Art to his buddies, a quiet but determined lad who became one of my close friends, was our hero. Paddy went on to become the Vicar-General of the Kiltegan Fathers in Africa. The college must have done something to prevent the reoccurrence of such an event, for we saw no more rats.

Learning was for the most part motivated by the cane or the threat of it. Despite this, the college produced many students who went on to have highly successful careers in business and in the priesthood. Yet for my part, I have to say that not a single teacher in my five-year experience challenged me to learn for its own sake or even tried to instill in me a love of learning. Not a single teacher even attempted to share with us an appreciation for Ireland's literary tradition that produced four Nobel Prize winners. Some Irish writers like James Joyce, Bernard Shaw, and Sean O'Casey were unabashedly anti-clerical and their writings were banned by the church. Perhaps, because of this, our teachers had a mistrust of all Irish writers. Anyway, the works of Irish writers were conspicuously absent from my secondary school curriculum.

I do not recall a single instance when a student was ever permitted, let alone encouraged, by a teacher to challenge or question a stated position. Thinking for ourselves was what was done on the back alley or behind blocked doors, if at all. It was never done in class. Whatever education I got was beaten into me with a cane or with the threat of it, with the result that I did just enough to get by and avoid the cane and no more.

Our teachers were all diocesan priests, ordained to minister to the spiritual needs of people in parishes, but were assigned to teach. They did this out of obedience to their bishop and not out of any desire for, or commitment to teaching. As students, we got the impression that they would rather be doing something else. It seemed to me that they approached teaching, not as a calling, but as a chore. At times they took out their frustrations on us, slogging us beyond reason. Some had mean streaks and would wallop us across the face in class with the back of their hands or fists when we least expected it, and could not defend ourselves. Like generations who went before us, we did not take well to unjustified severity or meanness on the part of authority, be that authority religious or secular.

Whenever our teachers seriously crossed the line of common decency and fair play, we would shove a desk against the door when they left the classroom, and boo them as loud as we could, so as to embarrass them before the other priests who were leaving their classrooms at the same time. This never happened when we got slogged, however severely, for not doing homework or for misbehaving or breaking the rules. That punishment was expected and accepted. But when a priest in frustration or in anger mistreated a student and our sense of justice and decency was violated, we fought back in the only ways we knew how. By rebelling and venting our anger at injustices, we were unconsciously following a centuries-old tradition of not accepting injustice passively.

These rebellions against perceived injustices were not confined to individual classrooms. They sometimes involved the majority of the student body. Each priest, other than the president, vice president, and spiritual director of the school, took turns acting as dean for a week at a time. As I have mentioned, the dean was the school disciplinarian, whose task it was to see that the rules were kept in the dorms, study halls, playgrounds and refectory. He monitored all student activity and meted out punishment to those he caught breaking school rules. He used the cane to enforce discipline in the dorms and in the refectory, as well as in the study halls. If there was talking in the dorm, as in the case of the study hall, the dean would ask the prefect for a list of names. Offenders would stand in their pajamas beside their beds to get their punishment. The rest of us pulled the bedclothes over our heads and counted the strokes of the cane. Whenever I made the list, sleep came slowly as I nursed my aching hands between my legs.

Another punishment besides slogging that the dean meted out to rule breakers was to walk the oval walkway alone, anti-clockwise, during all recreation periods, meeting all the students going the other way. This punishment, which we called "The Pack," could be for a day, even up to a week with no recreational activities of any kind being permitted. This form of punishment we abhorred. We much preferred to take a slogging and get it over with.

Some priests were much stricter in enforcing the rules than others. After our first year, we knew what to expect from each priest when his week as dean came around, and we made the appropriate adjustments. But sometimes, antagonisms developed between the students and the dean when the students felt that they were being treated unjustly, or that the dean had crossed the line of common fairness and decency with respect to the punishment of some students.

Since there were no mechanisms for redress of grievances in such situations, the students resorted to silence and/or to stomping their feet in the refectory, to booing, and with some going so far as to shower stones on the long open shed, where the dean walked after dark. Happily these antagonisms came to an end when the dean went off duty on Sunday night at the end of his week. Then students and priest returned to being civil to one another. By the time his turn as dean came around again, the old wounds had healed and past excesses were not held against him, unless, of course, he repeated those excesses. Unfortunately, sometimes this happened.

The priests were *in loco parentis* and had all the authority of parents over us. Perhaps we rebelled against them rather than against our parents. But the relationship between priest and student at St. Mel's could be more accurately characterized as that of autocrat and subject, rather than that of parent and child or teacher and pupil. We had eleven priests who were our teachers and three nuns who took care of the sick and supervised the kitchen. We had nicknames for each priest. When talking among ourselves, we always referred to the priests by their nicknames. We had no nicknames for the good nuns, who mothered us when we were sick.

The president of the college, Father Michael Kearney, known to students as "The Far" (the Gaelic word *Fear*, pronounced Far, means "man"), was a sometimes jolly, sometimes stern, round, half-barrel of a man who spoke with a slight lisp. As president, he was always on duty and was like a second dean. Sometimes he would barge into the study hall and ask the prefect for a "prog." He would take those on the list outside into the corridor, and stand on the second step of the stairs to give himself more leverage in his strokes of the cane, for he was smaller than most students. At night, we could hear him coming a mile away, for he wore a pair of house slippers that sounded like he was dragging a ball and chain. He certainly was not trying to sneak up on anybody.

Most evenings before the last study period at 7:00 p.m., we would find him standing on the second step of the stairs hearing the requests of students for permission to take a sleep because of a cold or other ailment, which meant going to bed there and then and getting up for breakfast, or permission to leave campus to go to the dentist or to go home for a funeral. That was also the occasion when students would report back in.

My brother Frank tells the story of when he, my brother Niall and our first cousin, Sean Donnelly, got permission to attend our grandmother's funeral. When they reported back in, "The Far" singled out Sean and said, "Come'er you. Who gave you permission to leave the college?" Sean was stunned, for he had gotten permission with the other two.

Before he could say anything, "The Far" told him, "You may no longer consider yourself a student of this establishment," and turned and went up the stairs, leaving Sean with his mouth open wondering what he was to do now. Frank told Sean to go to his study hall (for he was a couple of years his senior) and to stay out of "The Far's" sight until his mother could talk to the little fat man and clear up the misunderstanding, which she did.

My parents regarded Father Kearney as a good president, as I suspect did most parents. Father Kearney became a teacher of Gaelic at St. Mel's in 1921, and in the late 1920s and early 1930s, in addition to his teaching duties, he served as trainer and coach of the college's football teams. He is credited with establishing a winning football tradition at the school, leading the team to Leinster titles in 1928, 1934, and 1935. He served as president of the school from 1944 to 1956. He then became Canon Kearney and pastor of the parish of Carrick-on-Shannon in County Leitrim. As Canon, he was an advisor to the bishop, an honorary title for the most part, as most Irish bishops had the reputation of not asking, and not accepting, advice from others.

The vice president, Father James Cosgrove, or "The Whack" to us students, taught commerce and drawing. He had the reputation of being a holy terror, often losing his temper with students, slogging them until his red face turned a blue purple. Fortunately for us, he had mellowed somewhat in his later years, and spent most of his spare time in the college's garden and greenhouses attending to his plants and vegetables, instead of hunting down and slogging rule-breaking students.

In my fourth year, along with two other students, I experienced firsthand the more mellow "Whack." Paddy Hagan, Liam Moore and I were bringing up the rear of a school walk, with Father Dan Kelly, the dean that week, walking solo behind us. As we were walking through Longford town on our way back from a three-mile walk, "The Dawn," our nickname for Father Kelly, felt that the students up the line were going into shops, which was contrary to school rules. On these walks through town, students often dashed into sweet shops to get the best bargain of the day, a slab of Cleeve's toffee for a shilling. This toffee was as hard as a rock. The slab had twenty-four squares of toffee, with each square having up to twenty minutes lasting power in the normal mouth. A square was much sought after by students, and the owner of a slab could become an instant celebrity.

"The Dawn" ran ahead of us to catch students in the act of coming out of shops, which he failed to do. That left us 200 yards or so behind him. He waited for us at the school gate and accused us of going into shops, which we had not done. He told us he wanted to see us at the foot of the stairs outside the big study hall, the usual slogging location.

We made up our minds that since we had done no wrong, we would not accept any punishment. "The Dawn" showed up with a cane and demanded that we hold out our hands. When each of us refused in turn, he flew into a rage and ran up the stairs shouting that he would take care of us. He went looking for the president, and not finding him, he sought out the vice president.

We waited around for a half-hour wondering what was going to happen. Finally, one of the prefects informed us that "The Whack" wanted us to wait for him in the middle study hall. An hour passed, giving all sides time to cool it, and giving us much too much time to envision and sweat all kinds of punishments, including expulsion.

Just before study time, "The Whack" showed up. Our eyes searched for the cane, but we didn't see one. In a calm voice he said, "I want you boys to apologize to Father Kelly. Will you do that?" We all said yes, hardly believing our ears. Without another word, he left the room.

That evening after tea, we went to the "The Dawn" and, in subdued tones, apologized for refusing to be slogged. He smiled with satisfaction and asked, "Will you, will you give me the pleasure of caning–of caning you then?" We all nodded a little sheepishly. He dismissed us saying, "I will see you later, later when I get my–my cane."

"The Dawn" had a slight stutter when he was excited. We waited the rest of the evening expecting to be called out of study, but nothing happened. It was Sunday, the last day of "The Dawn's" week as dean. We heard nothing more about it.

How the priests got their nicknames and why they got them was not part of the school's lore that was handed down from class to class. Nicknames like The Far, The Whack, The Ram, The Rabbit, Hookey, Miko, Wonky, Bakey, The Dawn and The War, we learned the first week at school. No one asked for an explanation of the meaning and origin of the nicknames, and none was ever given. A priest who left my second year to a parish appointment, we called Tom the Horse. Why, I will never know.

Most students had nicknames too. My brother, Eamonn was called "Boco," supposedly because of his big nose. When I came along, I inherited his nickname and was called "Young Boco," and Eamonn was then called "Ould Boco." Some students resented being called by their nicknames and, as a result, their nicknames were used more often. But most of us could care less what we were called and, as a result, our nicknames were used less often.

The confrontations between priests and students do not mean that priests and students were constantly at war. There were stretches of relative peace and tranquility. There were even short periods of what one would expect in good teacher/student relationships, particularly approaching exams and vacations. The last classes before exams were almost always free classes, when the teacher read to us a story or essay of an entertaining nature. Our Gaelic language teacher, Father J.J. Lennon, known to us as "Hookey," always read the exploits of "Curly Wee and Gussie Goose" from the cartoon strip of that name featured in *The Irish Independent*, one of the country's daily newspapers. The exploits and opinions of these characters, a pig and a goose, were presented in rhyming couplets. They were a social commentary on Irish life, and were totally lost on us. Being denied access to newspapers and radio, we were ignorant of current events. We feigned understanding and laughed when the reader laughed.

We had house exams twice a year before Christmas and summer vacations, and national exams administered by the Irish Government at the end of three years and at the end of five years. At the end of three years, we had the government-administered Intermediate Certificate, which all high school students across Ireland had to pass before they could proceed to the Leaving Certificate. This was given at the end of the five years of high school. Passing the Leaving Certificate was a requirement for university and was a prerequisite for certain kinds of employment.

One of the essential pieces of equipment for a student entering St. Mel's was a pair of football boots. I bought mine at Heaton's in Longford town well in advance of the start of school. I rubbed them well with goose grease to make the leather soft and pliable, as well as waterproof. I also got football socks, football shorts and a royal blue football jersey, the school colors. I was set. To me books, clothes, pajamas, bed sheets, house slippers, towels and other incidentals were less important. In my mind, St. Mel's was synonymous with football. Where else could one play football almost every day of the year? I was determined to excel in the sport.

My first year, I did not miss a single opportunity to play football. I was always one of the first out on the prep playing field. And after we choose sides, I played with total commitment to winning. I was not by any means the tallest or the strongest or the most skilled player. But I was one of the most committed and for that was usually selected one of the first in choosing sides. The prep field had its own league with several teams competing. In that first semester, I was on the winning team. In the second semester, I captained the winning team. That set the pattern for my involvement in football.

In my second year, the school won the All-Ireland Championship. We beat St. Patrick's College, Cavan, four goals and seven points to three goals and three points. St Patrick's College was the Ulster Champions and was the favorite by sportswriters to win the Hogan Cup, the All-Ireland trophy. For that game the entire St. Mel's school went to Croke Park in Dublin, where all football and hurling national finals were played.

It was my first time in the big city and, although we did not see much other than the inside of Croke Park, it was a memorable day. We were all hoarse from yelling and cheering, but that did not stop us from cheering all the fifty miles back to the school. The bus driver slowed down going through the towns along the way to permit us to vent our jubilation upon the local populations. He slowed the bus to a crawl going by St. Fenian's College outside the town of Mullingar to allow us to wave our school colors out the windows, holler and cheer, and taunt our perennial rivals in the Leinster championship.

To our big surprise, Longford town residents had organized a welcome for the All-Ireland champions and met us at the outskirts of the town with a brass band and thousands of people waving St. Mel's colors. A rousing victory parade through town was an exciting finale to a great day.

In my third year at St. Mel's, I had a setback in my aspirations to make the college football team. While playing ball without my football boots, I pulled on a football against Colm Smith, one of the better football players at the school, who was twice my size. The ball did not move, but my ankle gave way. When I put my foot to the ground, my foot was at right angles to my leg. I was standing on the leg's shank. I was rushed to hospital.

Several people advised my parents to take me to a bone-setter rather than to a medical doctor. My parents had the good sense to put their faith in Doctor O'Shea at the County Hospital. He told them that I would never play football again. But that he would get me walking again, although in all probability it would be with a limp. He reset the bones after the swelling went down and gave me a heavy plaster of paris cast that went up to my knee. Within five days, I was back in school on crutches getting a lot of sympathy from teachers and students, including Colm Smith. That was in early May, and since football was out for me for the rest of the year at least, I was able to give more attention to my studies. I surprised my teachers and myself by getting honors in the Intermediate Certificate that June.

I spent the entire summer on crutches. I got the cast off before returning to St. Mel's in September. But Dr. O'Shea and my parents warned me not to play football. By the end of the year, I had no visible limp. In January, when I returned to school after the Christmas holidays, I tried kicking a ball again. The ankle felt strong and I played in the senior league. The following September, my senior year, I was elected captain of the senior team. We went on to win the Leinster Cup. My thanks to Dr. O'Shea for a job well done. The ankle has never been a problem.

When it came to my turn to play on the school football team, I felt that I had a lot to live up to. The tradition of winning had to be upheld. Some of the priests held themselves aloof from football and did not come to the games. But to the players and to the student body, the games were major events. They were what we lived for.

On the day of a game, the players got two boiled eggs each for breakfast. That made them the envy of all the other students. If the match was at Pearse Park in Longford, the entire school marched the couple of miles to the game. If the school won, the students marched triumphantly back through town. For away-games, we usually traveled in cars. We stopped halfway to allow the team to walk a mile or so to limber muscles and to prevent leg cramps during the game itself.

A victory, whether at home or away, usually meant an extra free half-day the following week. The two top prefects would go to the president, armed with the appropriate rationale to request a half-day free from class. Sometimes it was a challenge to find him and when they did, the request was not always granted. When they were successful, a cheer would signal the happy event and, of course, I played football, as did most of the school.

In my last year, I captioned St. Mel's team to victory in the Leinster championship at Croke Park. The photo below was taken outside the dressing room at the back of the Hogan Stand immediately after the game. My white headgear was occasioned by a misjudgment on my part. My timing was off in jumping up for the ball at centerfield. When I was going up my opponent was coming down and his teeth embedded themselves on the top of my head. It looked worse than it was, but the paramedics assigned to the game quickly stopped the blood and bandaged my head so that I continued playing.

Also, I was one of six players from St. Mel's including Jimmie McKeon, Eddie Rowley, Wally Cahill, Mike Dillon and Tony Hayden selected to the Leinster provincial team. This was big stuff for us students. But our bishop, Doctor James Joseph McNamee, in his 75th year and 24th year as our bishop, was having second thoughts about his school playing football on Sundays and forbade us to play. We did not know of his decision until the Sunday we were to play Connaught. We felt betrayed, and so did the coaches and players of the other teams in Leinster who had to scramble to field a full team. Wally Cahill, our goalie, who was a day student and to whom the ban did not apply, captained the Leinster side. But they did not win. I did not pray for my bishop that day, nor for many a day thereafter.

211

St. Mel's College Leinster Champions, 1951. Standing: Jim Harold, Ciaran Ryan, Jimmy Ryan, Eddie Duffy, Ciaran Murray, Paddy Hagan, Jimmie McKeon, Padraig Gearty, Mel Murtagh, Liam Moore and kneeling: Colm Heeran, Eamonn Meagher (my brother), Eddie Rowley, myself with the cup, Mike Dillon, Tony Hayden, Matt Moran and Wally Cahill. With the flag in the back is Colm Smith, St Mel's football star and member of St. Mel's 1948 All-Ireland winning team. (Photograph provided by a Meagher family album.)

For me football was the mortar that held St. Mel's together and made life at the school tolerable at the worst of times, enjoyable most of the time, and exciting when the school was winning championships.

To the disappointment of my parents, football was more important to me than studies. They were not against football, but they would like to see the studies get more attention. They were right. I failed by a narrow margin to get honors in the Leaving Certificate. I too was disappointed. I knew I would have to give more time to the books, if I went on to higher studies.

epilogue

Thanks for journeying with me through my boyhood years in an Irish rural village. Having gone through the rewarding exercise of writing these stories, retelling and reliving many aspects of my youth, I have to confess that I struggled with how to tie the stories together. With no juicy scandals to relate and with no darker side lurking in the shadows to grip the reader's attention, I was left with celebrating the everyday joys and fears in the life of a young lad learning to appreciate and cope with his world and in so doing capture something of the magic and charm of rural Ireland.

I grew out of most of the fears of my boyhood, though remnants linger with me still. But the joys have not diminished over time. Distance, not only in time but in geography, has served to deepen my appreciation of village, family, farm, school and church. I do not know if I would recall my growing up so fondly and so vividly, if I had remained in Ireland.

As is everybody's experience, my boyhood years have affected my adult life in countless little ways. Here are a few that come immediately to mind. The repeated blessing of my world with holy water and the respect of my grandmother and uncle Michael for their farm and everything on it bestowed on me a lasting respect and reverence for the soil and all its inhabitants.

I still get cold shivers up and down my spine when I pass by a cemetery at night. Intellectually I can argue convincingly that that is an irrational response. But years of ghost stories and believing in ghosts engender a response that is automatic and ignores or bypasses intellectual conviction.

When I misspell a word, I still feel I should put a finger up over my head.

Though I no longer search for a pot of gold at the end of rainbows, I play lotto with similar lack of success. As my grandmother would say, "As the twig is bent, so shall the tree grow."

I have stirabout for breakfast almost every morning. When I am on the road, if the hotel does not have oatmeal porridge on the breakfast menu, I make my own. All I need is access to a microwave. But I still miss the fresh milk, warm from the cow's udder. Whenever I have a boiled egg or two for breakfast, I give myself generous helpings of the egg yoke in the tops of the eggs in remembrance of breakfast at my grandmother's.

Though it is nigh on sixty years since I picked potatoes on cold damp October evenings, on November evenings after a storm when there are lots of pecans on the ground from the pecan trees around my house in Eufaula, Alabama, my hands fall into competition with each other to pick the most pecans. I still favor the underdog left hand. But if I lose concentration, the right hand invariably out-picks the left. When concentration returns, the right hand hands over its pecans to the left hand to put them in the bucket in an attempt to make up for its errant behavior.

I still have a keen eye for the nesting activity of birds and enjoy tracking the comings and goings of bluebirds, mockingbirds, woodpeckers, blue jays, finches, cardinals, chickadees, sparrows, wrens, brown thrasher, titmouse, cowbirds and hummingbirds that inhabit my front and back yards. A short time ago, I witnessed a wren in my vegetable garden feeding a young bird learning to fly that was three times the wren's size. I subsequently learned that the young bird the wren was so solicitously feeding was a cowbird, and was surprised to find out that the cowbird in America, like the cuckoo in Ireland, is a brood parasite that lays its eggs in another bird's nest and lets other birds like the poor little wren work overtime feeding and raising its chicks. What a carefree method of absentee parenting that nature has somehow allowed to evolve!

But the most enduring consequence of my boyhood experiences is that I have not smoked since my confirmation day when I was caught smoking in the turf-shed. My lungs and my whole being thank Aunt Nellie and my parents.

You might be interested in knowing how, after wandering around the U.S., I came to settle in a small southern town in southeast Alabama. It was more by happenstance than by careful planning. My partner, with whom I have worked for over a dozen years, hails from this corner of the world. When he and his wife, who is also a native of these parts, decided, for family reasons, to move back here, my family packed our bags and followed. Eufaula is largely open country, and the friendliness of neighbors reminds me of Ireland's heartland, and I get to dig and grow things in my own acre of earth, as on my grandmother's farm.

You might also be interested in knowing what has happened to the Meagher family and what we are doing today, fifty years later. My parents went to their eternal reward in 1975 and 1978, but their nine children are still kicking up a little dust on two continents. As regards myself, after St. Mel's secondary school, I attended All Hallows College in Dublin, where I got a better understanding of how to study, and was ordained a priest. I emigrated to the United States and the Sacramento Valley of California in 1957 and for 15 years served in the diocese of Sacramento as assistant pastor in the parishes of Immaculate Conception, Sacramento City; Saint Isadore, Yuba City; and Holy Rosary, Woodland. I attended graduate school at the University of California, Davis Campus, where I met my wife, Jackie Devlin, then a graduate student in economics. She coached me in statistics, a subject I was having difficulty with, and enlightened my mind and won my heart. I left the priesthood, got a dispensation from the church to get married, and got a Ph.D. in Latin American History.

For a brief period, I taught Latin American history at the University of Houston, Clear Lake campus, while my wife worked as an economist for Exxon, and taught courses in economics at Rice University. Over the years, I have had my share of career changes. I owned and operated a small writing company in Houston, served as manager of communications for a Houston engineering firm, and was the proprietor of Irish retail shops in Houston and Chicago. For the past 15 years I have been earning a living assisting commercial companies write proposals to win large government projects. Jackie has retired to gardening in Eufaula, where she writes a gardening column for the *Eufaula Tribune*, the local newspaper, and my son, Brian, attends Georgia Tech University in Atlanta, where he is majoring in computer science.

As for the rest of the family, I have mentioned that three of the nine children emigrated and settled in the U.S., three are in Ireland, and three emigrated to England. Besides myself, my sister Eileen came to the U.S. in 1955, entered the Sisters of Humility at Ottumwa Heights, Iowa, taught school at the elementary, high school and college levels, left the community after 21 years, got a Ph. D. in English from Rensselaer Polytechnic Institute, Troy, NY, and currently is a Professor of English and Coordinator of the MA Track in Rhetoric and Writing at the University of Tennessee, Chattanooga. My brother Niall followed me to All Hallows College and to the Sacramento valley in 1963, served as a priest in the Sacramento diocese for eight years, left the ministry, got married, has three children, and has recently retired after serving 31 years as a Probation Officer and Supervising Probation Officer for the Sacramento County Probation Department.

As for the three siblings in Ireland, my older brother Eamonn is a retired bank manager and lives and enjoys a little golf in Galway together with children and grandchildren. He lost his wife to a tragic car accident in 1996.

Frank has his own accounting firm in Dublin and his wife, Loretto, owns and operates the Leinster Gallery, featuring the works of modern Irish artists. They have two children. And Mary, my oldest sister, came to the U.S in 1956, got married, but returned to Ireland with her two daughters following her husband's death in 1966 from a heart attack at the early age of 38. She lives in Dublin, retired from the banking industry.

The three youngest of the family live in London, England. Colm is a retired accountant with a wife and two children, and in his retirement, taking after his father, has become the governor (proprietor) of a quaint London neighborhood pub, the "Famous Royal Oak." Teresa, whose husband died of cancer in 2001, besides the demands of four children and two grandchildren, is building a new career in interior decorating. Seamus, the youngest, is married with three children and manages the demolition arm of a London construction firm. We all get together every four or five years for a family reunion. That about wraps it up.

> May the road rise to meet you.
> May the wind be always at your back,
> The sun shine warm upon your face,
> The rain fall soft upon your fields,
> And until we meet again
> May God hold you in the hollow of His hand—
> But not too tightly!
>
> —An Irish Leave Taking

glossary

A mhac: a Gaelic phrase meaning "my son," usually used by parents or elders in addressing a small boy

Bairin breac: a Gaelic phrase meaning a fruitcake

Bhuachaill: Gaelic for boy

Bodhran: a Gaelic word for a drum made out of goat hide

Ceidleigh: a Gaelic word meaning a visit. Can also mean a music festival

Ceidleighers: Gaelic for visitors

Ceidleighing: Gaelic for visiting

Ceol sidhe: Gaelic phrase meaning" fairy music" or the music of the Little People

Cruiskeen: Gaelic for a small jug

Gossun: Gaelic for "young lad"

Griosach: Gaelic for "red hot coals and ashes," used to put under and on top of cooking skillets on the open hearth

Feis: Gaelic word, pronounced "fesh," meaning Irish step-dancing competition

Garda Siochana: Gaelic for civic guard or member of Ireland's national police force

Guban: Gaelic word for a tin mug put over a baby calf's mouth to keep it from sucking objects that might be harmful

Meitheal: Gaelic for a group of workers assigned to a single task

Poreen: Gaelic for a very small potato

Samhain: Celtic harvest festival that marked the beginning of the New Year on Nov. 1

Seanchai: Gaelic for "old storyteller"

Sheugh: Scottish for a small pond or ditch

Sleaghan: Gaelic for the long-handled tool used to cut turf on the bog. See photograph in Chapter 17

Smidereens: Gaelic for "tiny pieces"

Stirabout: colloquialism, meaning "oatmeal porridge"

Taoiseach: Gaelic for Prime Minister

Tay: colloquialism, meaning "tea"

Thrawneen: Gaelic for a "straw" of hay